CONTENTS

Introduction

The 'FCE Use of English 1' is a practice book intended mainly for intermediate and post-intermediate students, but it is also useful for more advanced students for revision and consolidation.

The aim of the book is to help students to understand and use English grammar through structurally graded material and full-colour pictures. In addition the book offers preparation for the Cambridge ESOL Examination or any other similar examinations.

Oral Development sections
These appear throughout the book and help students practise the grammar structures presented.

Consolidation sections
Each unit is followed by exercises which provide general practice for the FCE Examination or any other similar examinations. **Phrasal Verbs** are listed in alphabetical order and the use of **Prepositions** is explained in Appendix 1 at the back of the book. There are also open cloze texts, multiple choice cloze texts, word formation and 'key' word transformation exercises, collocations and tense revision exercises.

Practice test sections
After every second unit there is a section which trains students to cope with the Cambridge FCE Examination Paper 3 - Use of English or any other similar examinations.

Revision sections
After every four units there is a section which familiarises the students with the format and level of difficulty of the actual tests. These appear in the Teacher's Book and revise all structures taught up to this point.

Further Practice Sections
There are five practice sections, each including exercises on words often confused, open close texts, 'key' word transformations and multiple-choice cloze texts, providing general practice for the FCE examination – Paper 3 – Use of English – or any other similar examinations.

A Teacher's Book accompanies the Student's Book. This contains the answers to the exercises in the Student's Book and presents useful grammar tips as well as three tests in two separate versions.

The modal verbs are: **can, could, may, might, must, ought to, will, would, shall, should**. They take **no -s** in the third person singular. *She **can** sing well.* They come before the subject in questions and are followed by "not" in negations. *"**May** I use your phone?" "I'm afraid you **can't**".* The modal verbs, except for "ought", are followed by an infinitive without to. *You **ought to** be there on time.* Certain verbs and expressions have virtually the same meaning as some modals. These are: **need** (= must), **had better** (= should), **have to/have got to** (= must), **be able to** (= can), **used to** (= would) etc. *You'd **better** go.*

Modal verbs are used to express: **ability, advice, criticism, logical assumptions, necessity, offers, obligation/duty, permission, possibility, prohibition, requests** or **suggestions**.

1 Identify the use of the verbs in bold, then write a synonymous expression.

1	She **can't** have left yet. Her coat's still here.	*...logical assumption...*	*...I don't think...*
2	I **have got to** meet my boss for lunch.		
3	**May** I have a glass of water?		
4	**Shall** we go and see Andrea tonight?		
5	We **should** be home before midnight.		
6	She **can** speak four languages fluently.		
7	**Can** I leave early today?		
8	You **should** stop spending so much money.		
9	They **must have** got married recently.		
10	You **needn't** buy a present.		
11	Peter **might** be able to come tonight.		
12	He **could have** at least phoned me last night.		
13	**Would you like** me to make the arrangements?		
14	You **can't** leave your bags here, sir.		
15	All employees **had to** work overtime.		
16	You **don't need** to book in advance.		
17	**Can** you give Cathy a message?		
18	She **should** phone to confirm her appointment.		
19	**Shall** we go shopping at the weekend?		

2 Fill in the blanks as in the example.

	MODAL	USE	SYNONYMOUS EXPRESSION
1	She could swim before she could walk.	*... ability ...*	*...She was able to swim before she was able to walk. ...*
2	He .... an actor.		I'm sure he's an actor.
3	Shall we have a barbecue tonight?	suggestion	
4	He .... busy.		Perhaps he's busy.
5	.... finishing the report before you leave?	polite request	
6	.... I show you the way?		Would you like me to show you the way?
7	You .... exercise regularly.		It's a good idea to exercise regularly.
8	Children mustn't play on the grass.		
9	You .... told him the truth.		It would have been better if you had told him the truth.
10	You .... wear a school uniform.	obligation	You are expected to wear a school uniform.
11	He .... tonight.	logical assumption	I don't think he's coming tonight.
12	You may board the plane now.	permission (formal)	
13	.... borrow your book, please?	polite request	
14	I .... send the letter today.		It's urgent that I send the letter today.
15	She .... lost it.		I'm sure she hasn't lost it.

 **Modals**

	Summary of Functions of Modal Verbs	
USE	**PRESENT / FUTURE**	**PAST**
ability	He **can** speak Japanese. She**'s able** to make people laugh.	He **could/was able to** speak Japanese. (repeated action – ability in the past) We **were able to** go on a three-month tour of Australia. (single action)
possibility	He **can** still be at work. (90% certain) She **could** be angry. (50% certain; it's possible she is angry) Sally **may** be teaching. (50% certain; it's possible that she is teaching) You **might** need to come tomorrow. (40% certain; perhaps you need to come tomorrow) **It is likely that** Sue will give up working. **Sue is likely to** give up working.	— We **could have** had an accident. (luckily we didn't) John **may have** broken that vase. (perhaps he did it) Jane **might have** lost our telephone number. (perhaps she has lost it) **It was likely that** she had taken the last train. **She was likely to** have taken the last train.
probability	They **will** be in Spain tomorrow. (100% certain; prediction) We **should** see him there. (90% certain; future only; it's probable) She **ought to** be in Canada by now. (90% certain; she will probably be in Canada)	— He **should have** finished by now. (He has probably finished.) They **ought to have** started the course by now. (They have probably started the course.)
logical assumptions	He **must** be exhausted. (90% certain – positive; I'm sure he's exhausted) She **can't** be serious. (negative; I'm sure she's not serious) They **couldn't** be on holiday. (negative; I don't think they are on holiday)	He **must have** won the pools. (positive; I'm sure he has won the pools) She **can't have** married Ted. (negative; I'm sure she didn't marry Ted) They **couldn't have** been friends. (negative; I don't think they were friends)
permission	You **can/can't** have a party. (giving or refusing permission; informal) **Could** I be excused? (more polite; asking for permission) You **may** be excused. (formal; giving permission) **Might** I bring a friend to the wedding? (more formal; asking for permission) I'm afraid you **can't/mustn't** have visitors. (informal; refusing permission) Guests **may not** smoke in their rooms. (formal; refusing permission – written notice)	He **wasn't allowed to/couldn't** board the plane. He **was allowed to** see the patient. (NOT: ~~could~~) — — — —
necessity	I **must** return these books soon. (I say so) She **has to** find a new job. (necessity coming from outside the speaker) They**'ve got to** sell their caravan. (informal) The plants **need** watering. *or* The plants **need to be** watered. (it's necessary) She **doesn't have to/doesn't need to/ needn't** leave when they do. (it isn't necessary – absence of necessity) We **ought to** reply to the invitation. (it's necessary)	I **had to** return the books to the library. (I was obliged to) She **had to** find a new job after she was dismissed. They **had to** sell their caravan. The plants **needed** watering. *or* The plants **needed to be** watered. (it was necessary) She **didn't have to/didn't need to** work as hard as me. (it wasn't necessary for her to work as hard as me and she didn't – absence of necessity) She **needn't have** got a taxi. (it wasn't necessary for her to get a taxi but she did)

Summary of Functions of Modal Verbs

USE	PRESENT / FUTURE	PAST
advice	You **should** try to make more of an effort. (general advice; I advise you) You **ought to** keep to the speed limit. (I advise you; most people believe this) You **had better** not keep her waiting. (It's not a good idea; advice on a specific situation) **Shall** I apply for the job? (asking for advice)	You **should have** paid more attention. (but you didn't) She **ought to have** reserved a table. (but she didn't) It **would have been better** if you hadn't kept her waiting. (but you did) —
criticism	She **could** at least wait until 5 o'clock. They **should** warn us. You **ought to** be more polite to her.	She **could** at least **have** waited until 5 o'clock. They **should have** warned us. (but they didn't) You **ought to have** been more polite to her. (It was the right thing to do, but you didn't do it.)
obligation	I **must** get more exercise. (I need to; I say so) I **have to** get more exercise. (I'm obliged to; the doctor says so) We **ought to** give more money to charity. (It's the right thing to do, but we don't always do it.)	I **had to** get more exercise because I was unfit. I **had to** get more exercise because I was unfit. We **ought to have** given more money to charity. (It was the right thing to do but we didn't do it.)
requests	**Can I** use your phone? (informal) **Could I** use your phone? (polite) **May I** make a phone call, please? (formal) **Might I** borrow your pen? (very formal) **Will you** give me a hand? (very friendly) **Would you mind** helping me? (polite)	— — — — — —
offers	**Can I/we** do anything to help? (informal) **Shall I/we** help you tidy up? (informal) **Would you like me** to do it for you?	— — —
suggestions	**Shall we** stop for a drink? **I/we can** always leave early. We **could** eat out tonight if you want.	— — He **could have** asked for advice.
prohibition	You **can't** wear jeans at work. (you aren't allowed to) You **mustn't** walk on the grass. (it's forbidden) You **may not** talk during the test. (formal)	They **couldn't** wear jeans at work. (they weren't allowed to) — —
duty	All members **must** follow the rules. People **ought to** live in peace. (It's the right thing to do, but people don't do it.)	All members **had to** follow the rules. She **ought to have** treated us more fairly. (It was the right thing to do but she didn't always do it.)

3   Rephrase the following in as many ways as possible.

1 She might have misunderstood you. **2** I'm sure they are tired. **3** They ought to pay more attention.
4 I don't think she's sold her house. **5** It's likely that he'll object. **6** We may have to wait for them.
7 I'm sure she isn't Australian. **8** I'm sure he is terrified. **9** We ought to offer to help. **10** They'll probably want something to eat. **11** You can't park here. **12** He should have warned us about the dog.

Mustn't – Needn't

- **mustn't** (it's forbidden) *You **mustn't** cross the street when the light is red.*
- **needn't / don't have to** (it isn't necessary) *You **needn't** worry about it. I'll do it in a minute.*

4 Complete the sentences using the words in bold. Use two to five words.

1 Soldiers are forbidden to leave the camp unless they get special permission.
   not   Soldiers ...*must not leave the camp*... unless they get special permission.
2 Unauthorised personnel are not allowed to go beyond this point.
   must   Unauthorised personnel .... this point.
3 It isn't necessary for Jim to get up early tomorrow as it is a holiday.
   have   Jim .... up early tomorrow as it is a holiday.
4 Readers are not allowed to take books out of the library without first filling in a form.
   not   Readers .... out of the library without first filling in a form.
5 It isn't necessary for Julie to work today; she can have the day off.
   have   Julie .... today; she can have the day off.

5 Fill the gaps with must, mustn't or needn't.

"Welcome to "Finest Foods" factory

We are happy that you have come to work for us. Before you start work, I want to familiarise you with some rules and regulations.
First of all, you 1) ...*must*... wear the uniforms which are supplied, and you 2) .... keep your hair covered at all times. You 3) .... wear gloves unless you choose to, except in a few special areas. You 4) .... smoke anywhere in the factory apart from the canteen, and you 5) .... forget to wash your hands after breaks. You 6) .... stay in the factory during your breaks, but you 7) .... clock in and out if you do leave the premises. You 8) .... work overtime, but we do encourage our workers to do so if they wish to. Last but not least, if you have any problems, you 9) .... go to your supervisor who will help you to sort them out

Needn't – Didn't need to – Needn't have

- **don't have to/don't need to/needn't + present infinitive** (It is not necessary in the present or future) *You **don't have to/don't need to/needn't** wear an evening dress. It's an informal party. (It is not necessary to wear ...)*
- **didn't need to/didn't have to** (It was not necessary in the past and we may not know if the action happened or not.) *She **didn't need to/didn't have to** wear an evening dress as it was an informal party. (It wasn't necessary for her to wear an evening dress, and we don't know if she did or not.)*
- **needn't + bare perfect infinitive** (We know that something happened in the past although it was not necessary.) *You **needn't have** cooked as much food as you did last night. (You did, although it was not necessary.)*

6 Complete the sentences using the words in bold. Use two to five words.

1 It wasn't necessary for him to write to his mum because she rang him.
   need   He ...*didn't need to write*... to his mum because she rang him.
2 We took more luggage than was necessary on our holiday.
   taken   We .... much luggage on our holiday.
3 There's no need for you to water the plants this morning.
   have   You .... the plants this morning.
4 It wasn't necessary for Arthur to get the train because his brother offered to give him a lift.
   need   Arthur .... the train because his brother offered to give him a lift.
5 She came early last night, which wasn't necessary because the party didn't start till ten.
   come   She .... early last night because the party didn't start till ten.

	Must (affirmative logical assumption) – May/Might (possibility) – Can't/Couldn't (negative logical assumption)	
Present Infinitive	*I'm sure he* **studies** *a lot.* *Perhaps he* **will study** *a lot.*	*He must* **study** *a lot.* *He may/might* **study** *a lot.*
Present Cont. Infinitive	*I'm sure he* **is studying.** *Perhaps he* **will be studying.**	*He must* **be studying.** *He may/might* **be studying.**
Perfect Infinitive	*I'm sure he* **didn't study.** *I'm sure he* **hasn't studied.** *I'm sure he* **hadn't studied.**	*He can't* **have studied.** *He can't* **have studied.** *He can't* **have studied.**
Perfect Cont. Infinitive	*Perhaps he* **was studying.** *Perhaps he* **has been studying.**	*He may/might* **have been studying.** *He may/might* **have been studying.**

7 Complete the sentences using the words in bold. Use two to five words.

1 I'm sure she has given up smoking.
have She ...*must have given up*... smoking.

2 I'm sure she isn't feeling sick now.
be She .... now.

3 Perhaps they were working for the enemy.
have They .... for the enemy.

4 Perhaps he will be on time.
be He .... time.

5 Perhaps he was too ill to take part in the race.
been He .... to take part in the race.

6 I'm sure they informed the police about the robbery.
have They .... about the robbery.

7 Perhaps Harry will be sunbathing this time tomorrow.
be Harry .... tomorrow.

8 I'm sure he had warned the soldiers about the coming danger.
have He .... about the coming danger.

9 I'm sure Jenny hasn't been working there that long.
have Jenny .... there that long.

10 Perhaps she was telling you the truth.
been She .... the truth.

11 Perhaps she's been working hard.
been She .... hard.

12 Perhaps she'll come with us.
may She .... us.

13 I'm sure she hadn't prepared her speech.
have She .... her speech.

14 Perhaps he was asleep when we rang.
been He .... when we rang.

15 Perhaps he'll be waiting when we get there.
may He .... when we get there.

16 I'm sure she didn't know about it.
known She .... about it.

17 I'm certain it has stopped raining now.
have It .... raining now.

18 It's possible that Jane has left already.
have Jane .... already.

1 Modals

Expressions similar to Modal Verbs

- **Be supposed to + infinitive** means "should" but it expresses the idea that someone else expects something to be done. *You're supposed to wear a suit to work. (Your employer expects you to.) You should wear a suit. (It is a good idea because it makes a better impression.)*
- **Be to + infinitive** means "must" but it expresses the idea that someone else demands something. *I am to report for military training. (It's the law so I must obey.) I must report for military training. (If I don't, the army will look for me.)* **Be supposed to** and **be to** are used to express what someone expects about a previously arranged event. *Recruits are supposed to/are to have a haircut when they arrive. (It is scheduled.)*
- **Be likely to** means "may" (possibility). To express possibility in questions we don't use "may", we use: Is he likely to ...?, Is it likely that he ...?, Can he ...?, Could he ...?, Might he ...?. *Is he likely to understand my feelings? Is it likely that he will understand my feelings? Could he understand my feelings?*
- **Would you mind** is used to express polite, formal requests. *Would you mind holding this for a moment?*
- **Let's.../How about...?/Why don't we...?/What about...?** are used to make suggestions. *Let's stay in tonight. How about staying in tonight? Why don't we stay in tonight? What about staying in tonight?*
- **Would you like to/Would you like me to...?** (= Shall I...?) are used when we offer to do something. *Would you like me to read you a story? (Shall I read you a story?)*
- **Be allowed to** is used to express permission, to say what the rule is. *He was allowed to visit the prisoner. (NOT: Could he visit) Was he allowed to visit the prisoner?*

8 How else can we say the following?

1 It is likely that she has got lost. ...*She is likely to have got lost....*
2 Shall I book a ticket for you as well? ....
3 How about inviting Paul and Helen? ....
4 I am to welcome the guests and show them to their rooms. ....
....
5 Might he have forgotten all about it? ....
6 You have to wait until dark before you leave. ....

9 Fill in a modal or a synonymous expression and the appropriate form of the verb in brackets.

1 There's no reply when I ring him. He ...*must have left*... **(leave)** the office already.
2 Don't give up so easily. You .... **(do)** it if you tried a little harder.
3 That's no excuse! You know you .... **(finish)** this report by today.
4 He .... **(mention)** his plans on the phone last night but I really can't remember.
5 Since she crashed the car, she .... **(walk)** to work every day.
6 If you find something valuable, you .... **(take)** it to the nearest police station.
7 Passengers .... **(not/walk)** across the lines. They should use the footbridge.
8 You .... **(know)** better than to tell her all your secrets.
9 You .... **(destroy)** the letter as soon as you receive it.
10 You .... **(enter)** the building if you have a special pass.
11 Can you help me? .... **(find out)** what time the London train arrives.
12 He looks very annoyed. He .... **(wait)** for ages.
13 I .... **(take)** the library books back yesterday but I forgot and now I'll have to pay a fine.
14 Increased sales mean that all employees .... **(be given)** an extra Christmas bonus.
15 .... **(you/take)** grandma to the cinema tonight as I have to go out?
16 When I was at school we .... **(not/wear)** jewellery.
17 You .... **(bring)** the map with you so we wouldn't have to ask people the way.
18 Those bags look heavy. .... **(I/carry)** some of them for you?
19 Don't pretend you don't know that you .... **(have)** a valid ticket on the bus.
20 You .... **(ring)** me to let me know you'd be late. I was worried.

In Other Words

- Perhaps he is working now.
  He may be working now.
- I'm sure he hasn't got the letter yet.
  He can't have got the letter yet.
- I'm sure she understood.
  She must have understood.
- Shall I help you do your homework?
  Would you like me to help you do your homework?
- Was it necessary for you to help her?
  Did you need to help her?
- It's forbidden to smoke in here.
  You mustn't smoke in here.
  You aren't allowed to smoke in here.

- He is likely to buy a sports car.
  It is likely that he will buy a sports car.
  He'll probably buy a sports car.
- It isn't necessary for him to work today.
  He doesn't have to/doesn't need to/needn't work today.
- It wasn't necessary for them to buy so much food.
  They needn't have bought so much food.
- It would be a good idea to avoid eating sweets.
  You should avoid eating sweets.
- Let's try doing this exercise.
  Shall we try doing this exercise?
- Would you mind if I used your pen?
  May/Might I use your pen?

10 Complete the sentences using the words in bold. Use two to five words.

1 Perhaps the bridge collapsed because of the storm.
   have The bridge ...*may/might have collapsed*... because of the storm.

2 He'll probably come to the party.
   likely He .... the party.

3 You mustn't photograph any of the paintings.
   allowed You .... any of the paintings.

4 It's forbidden to touch the statues in the museum.
   touch You .... in the museum.

5 I'm sure he didn't cheat in the exam.
   cheated He .... in the exam.

6 Was it necessary for you to call a doctor?
   need Did .... a doctor?

7 Shall I carry your shopping for you?
   me Would .... your shopping for you?

8 I'm sure Ann didn't do it on purpose.
   have Ann .... on purpose.

9 Might I take some photos?
   if Would .... some photos?

10 Let's go and see "The Blob" tonight.
   we Shall .... "The Blob" tonight?

11 It isn't necessary for you to do that exercise.
   need You .... that exercise.

12 It would be a good idea to eat less high-cholesterol food.
   should You .... high-cholesterol food.

13 It wasn't necessary for him to take a coat but he did.
   taken He .... a coat.

14 I'm sure Ann spends all her money on clothes.
   spend Ann .... on clothes.

15 Was it necessary for you to say that?
   have Did .... that?

16 I'm sure he knew what he was doing.
   known He .... he was doing.

11 Use the words in capitals to form a word that fits in the space in the same line.

CELEBRITY CHEF

Becoming (0) ...*successful*... in your career is often a
(1) .... of hard work, the right background and luck.
Top chef, Jamie Oliver, is a good example.

His parents were restaurant (2) ...., so from an early age
Oliver had the chance to develop his (3) .... skills in the
kitchen. He attended colleges in London and France, and gained
several years' (4) .... experience in London restaurants.
In the famous River Café, in particular, Oliver made his TV debut
when a (5) .... about the restaurant was being filmed
there. From there, he has never looked back. His own
(6) .... programme, *The Naked Chef*, became a
(7) .... favourite. He has also published many
(8) .... popular cook books.

Two things have made Oliver stand out as a chef. The first is his
chain of restaurants, *Fifteen*, that (9) .... in training
young people from poor backgrounds in the catering business. The
second is his campaign to ban (10) .... junk food from being
served in British schools, replacing it with more nutritional meals.

SUCCESS
COMBINE

OWN
CREATE

PRACTISE

DOCUMENT

COOK
NATION
HIGH

SPECIAL

HEALTH

Oral Development 1

Make speculations for the following pictures as in the example.

He is a disabled man. He can't walk.
He may have had a car accident.
The lady may be his wife. etc

Phrasal Verbs

be about to: be on the point of
be after: go after; chase
be against: be opposed to
be away: be absent
be back: return; come back
be in: be at home/in one's office etc
be in for: be about to experience (usu bad)
be on: be shown in cinemas, theatres etc
be over: be finished
be up to: 1) be equal to, 2) depend on

....

break down: 1) (of machinery) stop working,
2) (of a person) lose control of feelings
break in: 1) (intr) enter by force, 2) **(on)** interrupt,
3) (horses etc) train
break into: 1) (tr) enter by force, 2) burst into
(song, laughter etc)
break off: 1) stop temporarily, 2) (tr) end a
relationship
break out: 1) begin suddenly (war, disease,
fire etc), 2) (of) escape from a place
break up: 1) (intr) separate; split up, 2) stop for
holidays (schools etc)

12 Fill in the correct particle(s).

1 After months of preparation, the director is ...*about to*... start shooting his new film.
2 It's .... you to decide what to do.
3 I thought the match would be .... by now.
4 I'm afraid we're .... a bumpy flight.
5 Your work isn't .... your normal standard.
6 My washing machine is being repaired as it broke .... yesterday.
7 The waiter broke .... our conversation to take our order.
8 She broke .... their engagement because she realised she didn't love him.
9 School breaks .... for the Christmas holidays on 23rd December.
10 He broke .... after hearing the news of his wife's death.
11 Robbers broke .... the bank yesterday.
12 Two dangerous criminals have broken .... jail.
13 Their marriage broke .... after five years.
14 Mr Jones broke .... the interview to answer the phone.
15 The horse must be broken .... before anyone can ride it.

13 Look at Appendix 1, then fill in the correct preposition.

1 Catherine was absent ...*from*... school yesterday.
2 Mr King received fifty letters in answer .... his advertisement.
3 She was amazed .... the fantastic view.
4 He is very attached .... his parents.
5 She isn't accustomed .... drinking champagne.
6 She decided to apply .... Jones Ltd .... the job advertised in the local paper.
7 She accused her son .... taking some money from her purse.
8 My doctor doesn't approve .... smoking.
9 He argues .... his wife .... everything.
10 Do you believe .... ghosts?
11 He was angry .... Ann .... her behaviour.
12 The antique dealer took advantage .... the customer's ignorance and sold him a fake.
13 She was very anxious .... him to arrive.
14 She was so anxious .... her exams that she couldn't sleep.
15 He agreed .... his boss that the office needed reorganising and agreed .... do it himself.
16 Her latest novel is based .... the life of Joan Collins.
17 I can see no basis .... changing our plans now.
18 He enjoys betting .... the horses.

14 Complete the sentences using the words in bold. Use two to five words.

1 I advise you to check the details before you sign the contract.
   had   You ...*had better check the details*... before you sign the contract.
2 It isn't necessary for you to drive me to the station.
   have   You .... me to the station.
3 There's no milk left.
   run   We .... milk.
4 Don't blame me if there's no food in the house.
   fault   It .... there's no food in the house.

5 Diana moved to London after finishing her degree.
since Diana .... she finished her degree.

6 Our house is an hour's walk from the village.
takes It .... to our house from the village.

7 She should be told the truth.
better It .... her the truth.

8 I should wash the curtains.
need The curtains .... washed.

9 I'm sure he read about it in the newspaper.
have He .... in the newspaper.

How to treat Open Cloze Texts

- Read the whole passage at least once to become acquainted with the general meaning.
- Try to find out what kind of word is missing (noun, adjective, adverb, modal, article, preposition etc). Look at the words which are close to each blank or in the same sentence but consider other words as well.
  a) *They were tired .... they decided to have a rest for a couple of hours. (The second clause is a result of the first clause, therefore we need "so".)*
  b) *He has got .... fastest car I've ever seen. (The adjective is a superlative – it needs "the".)*
  c) *......... awful weather! (The exclamation mark shows that this sentence is an exclamatory one, so we need either "what" or "how" – in this case "what" because there is an uncountable noun after the gap.)*
  d) *He was .... absorbed in the book that he didn't notice that someone had entered the room. (There is a "that" in the sentence, therefore we need to use either "so" or "such" – in this case "so" because there is an adjective but no noun after the blank.)*
  e) *He didn't have .... money to go on holiday. (The infinitive construction shows that we need either "too" or "enough" to fill the gap. The word "money" determines that the appropriate word is "enough" because "too" can only be used with adjectives or adverbs.)*
- One area that needs particular care is constructions with modal verbs.
  You needn't .... left so early. (the missing word is "have" – needn't + have + past participle)
- Another area which needs particular care is constructions with relative pronouns/adverbs.
  Claire, ... has been in the USA for three years, has come back. (correct answer: who – that cannot be used after a comma.)
  The man .... house belongs to is in Paris. (correct answer: the/this/that)
- When you have completed the cloze text, read the passage carefully to see if it makes sense and is grammatically correct.

---

15 **Choose the correct item.**

1 She has got ...C... loudest voice I've ever heard.
  A this   **B** a   **C** the

2 There were not .... chairs for everyone.
  A enough   **B** quite   **C** so

3 I was .... interested in what the teacher was saying that I didn't notice the time.
  A too   **B** as   **C** so

4 These cars are not as big .... some I've seen in America.
  A than   **B** as   **C** to

5 If cars weren't so expensive, we .... buy a new one.
  A shall   **B** did   **C** would

6 Jane, ... has just passed her driving test, is having a party to celebrate.
  A which   **B** who   **C** that

7 I had .... little time to go to the shops.
  A too   **B** such   **C** enough

8 The woman .... cat belongs to has gone away for a week.
  A this   **B** which   **C** of

9 This is the beach .... we go every weekend.
  A which   **B** where   **C** that

10 .... tasty food!
  A What   **B** So   **C** How

11 It was .... cold to go for a swim in the sea.
    A as   **B** enough   **C** too

12 You shouldn't .... drunk all the milk.
    A have   **B** had   **C** has

13 After you had given me the money, I put .... in the bank.
    A they   **B** them   **C** it

14 He is .... a good athlete that he is certain to make the team.
    A so   **B** such   **C** too

15 .... lovely you look in that dress!
    A Such   **B** How   **C** What

16 They were late .... they decided to take a taxi.
    A so   **B** as   **C** that

17 She was much .... after she had changed her job.
    A happiest **B** happy   **C** happier

18 I was .... tired to watch television, so I went straight to bed.
    A quite   **B** so   **C** too

19 If only we .... left earlier, we would have been there by now.
    A did   **B** had   **C** were

20 The weather in Greece is hotter .... in England.
    A as   **B** than   **C** like

16 Think of the word which best fits each gap. Write only one word in each one.

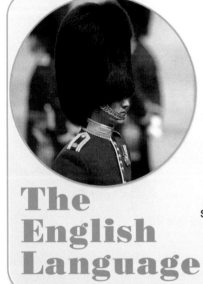

The English Language

Today English is, without doubt, the world's **(0)** ...*most*... important language. One **(1)** .... ten people speak it as their mother tongue and it has a larger vocabulary **(2)** .... any other language. English belongs to the Indo-European family of languages, **(3)** .... developed from a parent language first spoken about five thousand years ago in central-northern Europe. From there, it spread to the **(4)** .... of Europe and the Middle East, and over time it developed into a series of new language groups. One of **(5)** .... was Germanic, which later split into old English, Dutch, German and the Scandinavian languages. Old English was later heavily influenced by French following the Norman invasion in the eleventh century. Then, in the sixteenth century, due **(6)** .... the invention of printing, the increase **(7)** .... opportunities for education and the growth of international trade and communication, this form of English, which is known **(8)** .... Middle English, changed into the language spoken nowadays, Modern English. Language change continues **(9)** .... the present day, although since 1800 the major area of change has been in vocabulary rather **(10)** .... grammar. Events **(11)** .... as the Industrial Revolution and the two World Wars are among the reasons for the expansion of vocabulary. **(12)** .... factor is the growing influence of the media.

17 Fill in the following collocation grids.

	an invitation	saying sth	an accusation	help	an offer	knowledge	to work	responsibility
refuse	✓							
deny								

	passport	hand	teeth	lights	flowers	promise	alarm	statement
false	✓							
artificial								

	sky	hands	voice	house	view	clothes	record	conscience
clean								
clear								

Consolidation 1

18 Use the words in capitals to form a word that fits in the space in the same line.

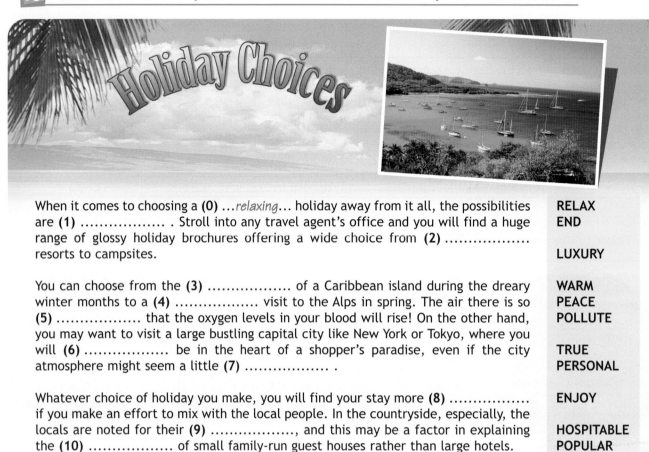

Holiday Choices

When it comes to choosing a **(0)** ...*relaxing*... holiday away from it all, the possibilities are **(1)** .... Stroll into any travel agent's office and you will find a huge range of glossy holiday brochures offering a wide choice from **(2)** .... resorts to campsites.

RELAX
END

LUXURY

You can choose from the **(3)** .... of a Caribbean island during the dreary winter months to a **(4)** .... visit to the Alps in spring. The air there is so **(5)** .... that the oxygen levels in your blood will rise! On the other hand, you may want to visit a large bustling capital city like New York or Tokyo, where you will **(6)** .... be in the heart of a shopper's paradise, even if the city atmosphere might seem a little **(7)** ....

WARM
PEACE
POLLUTE

TRUE
PERSONAL

Whatever choice of holiday you make, you will find your stay more **(8)** .... if you make an effort to mix with the local people. In the countryside, especially, the locals are noted for their **(9)** ...., and this may be a factor in explaining the **(10)** .... of small family-run guest houses rather than large hotels.

ENJOY

HOSPITABLE
POPULAR

19 Complete the sentences using the words in bold. Use two to five words.

0 A kind woman told us how to get to the museum.
directions We ...*were given directions to*... the museum by a kind woman.

1 It's not necessary to defrost this pie before cooking it.
needn't The pie .... before cooking.

2 I'm sure you had a great time in the Bahamas.
enjoyed You .... the Bahamas.

3 The twins are so alike that you can't tell them apart.
difference The twins are so alike that you can't .... them.

4 The worst time to go into town is in the rush hour.
worse There .... to go into town than the rush hour.

5 Thieves entered the building by force.
broken The building .... thieves.

6 I have never had such an exciting holiday.
far This is .... holiday I have ever had.

7 You ought to have apologised.
better It .... you had apologised.

8 My brother said I could borrow his car.
permission My brother .... borrow his car.

The Infinitive / -ing form / Participles 2

	Forms of the Infinitive		Forms of the -ing form	
	Active Voice	Passive Voice	Active Voice	Passive Voice
Present	(to) play	(to) be played	playing	being played
Present Continuous	(to) be playing		–	–
Perfect	(to) have played	(to) have been played	having played	having been played
Perfect Continuous	(to) have been playing		–	–

* Passive Present Continuous and Perfect Continuous Infinitives are rarely used.

Forms of the infinitive corresponding to verb tenses	
Verb tenses	**Forms of the Infinitive**
Present Simple/Future Simple she cleans/she will clean	**Present** (to) clean
Present Continuous/Future Continuous she is cleaning/she will be cleaning	**Present Continuous** (to) be cleaning
Past Simple/Present Perfect/Past Perfect/Future Perfect she cleaned/she has cleaned/she had cleaned/she will have cleaned	**Perfect** (to) have cleaned
Past Continuous/Present Perfect Continuous/Past Perfect Continuous/Future Perfect Continuous she was cleaning/she has been cleaning/she had been cleaning/ she will have been cleaning	**Perfect Continuous** (to) have been cleaning

1   Write the appropriate form of the infinitive.

1   she finished   ...(to) have finished...
2   he was driving   ....
3   it has been taught ....
4   they had come   ....
5   she tries   ....

6   it is brought   ....
7   they are studying   ....
8   it will be accepted ....
9   it was written   ....
10 she has left   ....

2   Fill in the correct form of the infinitive.

1   I've looked everywhere, but the file appears ...*to have been misplaced*... (**misplace**).
2   He is not old enough .... (**allow**) to stay out late.
3   Since her illness, she seems .... (**find**) work difficult.
4   Although Jane hopes .... (**invite**) to the embassy dinner, it is unlikely that she will be.
5   The little dog seems .... (**lose**) its master.
6   I don't think I'll be able to make it tomorrow. I'm supposed .... (**meet**) Jane for lunch.
7   She was only pretending .... (**read**); she was really daydreaming.
8   No one is .... (**admit**) to the concert without a ticket.
9   The team is said .... (**win**) the match through sheer luck.
10 I need you .... (**help**) me prepare the food for the party.
11 The accident is believed .... (**cause**) by reckless driving.
12 The newspaper received many calls from people claiming .... (**see**) UFOs.
13 He was the first British writer .... (**award**) the Nobel prize for literature.
14 Aren't you supposed .... (**look after**) your sister at the moment?

2 The Infinitive / -ing form / Participles

The to-infinitive is used

- to express purpose.
  *You should take a few days off **to recover**.*

- after certain verbs (agree, appear, decide, expect, hope, plan, promise, refuse etc).
  *He **agreed to meet** us tonight.*

- after certain adjectives (happy, glad, sorry etc).
  *I was **sorry to hear** about your accident.*

- after I would like/would love/would prefer to express specific preference.
  ***I'd love to visit** India.*

- after certain nouns. *It's such a **pleasure to be** with you.*

- after too/enough constructions.
  *It's **too early to leave** the party.*
  *He's **rich enough to afford** a Porsche.*
  *There's **enough food to go** round.*

- with: it + be + adjective (+ of + noun/pronoun).
  ***It was unkind of her to say** that.*

- with: so + adjective + as.
  *Would you be **so kind as to pass** the sauce?*

- with "only" to express an unsatisfactory result.
  *He won in the lottery **only to lose** at the casino.*

- after: be + the first/second etc/next/last/best etc.
  *She was **the first to congratulate** him.*

- in the expression: for + noun/pronoun + to -inf.
  ***For John to lend** you his car was very unusual.*

- in expressions such as: to tell you the truth, to begin with, to be honest etc.
  ***To be honest**, I didn't know how to react.*

Note: If two infinitives are joined by "and" or "or", the "to" of the second infinitive can be omitted. *I'd prefer to go to a disco **and dance or talk** to my friends.*

The -ing form is used

- as a noun. ***Smoking** is harmful.*

- after certain verbs (admit, anticipate, appreciate, avoid, consider, continue, delay, deny, discuss, enjoy, escape, excuse, fancy, finish, forgive, go (physical activities), imagine, involve, keep (= continue), mention, mind, miss, object to, postpone, practise, prevent, quit, recall, recollect, report, resent, resist, risk, save, stand, suggest, tolerate, understand etc).
  *They have **postponed moving** house till next week.*

- after: dislike, enjoy, hate, like, love, prefer to express general preference. *I **like swimming**. (in general)*
  * Note: like + to-inf = it's a good idea
  *I **like to help** people.*

- after: I'm busy, it's no use, it's (no) good, it's (not) worth, what's the use of, can't help, there's no point (in), can't stand, have difficulty (in), in addition to, as well as, have trouble, have a hard/difficult time.
  *There's **no point in arguing**.*
  *What's the **use of crying**? It was your fault.*

- after: spend/waste (time, money etc).
  *You **waste** too much **time watching** TV.*

- after prepositions. *He became rich **by working** hard and **without borrowing** from anyone.*

- after: look forward to, be/get used to, be/get accustomed to, object to, admit (to) etc
  *I **object to being told** what to do with my life.*

- after: hear, listen, notice, see, watch, to express an incomplete action, an action in progress or a long action. *I **saw** him **throwing** rubbish out of the window. (I saw part of the action. I didn't wait until he had finished. Perhaps he threw more rubbish.)*
  BUT hear, listen, see, watch + infinitive without "to" express a complete action, something that one saw or heard from beginning to end. *I **saw** him **throw** rubbish out of the window. (I saw all of the rubbish being thrown out of the window.)*

The infinitive without to is used

- after most modal verbs (can, could, may etc). *He **can go** if he wants to.*
- after had better/would rather/would sooner. *You**'d better go** to bed.*
- after make/let/see/hear/feel in the active. *She **made** the baby **eat** all his soup.*
  But in the passive: be made/be heard/be seen + to-inf. *The baby **was made to eat** all his soup.*
  Note that "let" turns into "was/were allowed to" in the passive.
  *Her parents **let** her **stay** out till midnight. She **was allowed to stay** out till midnight.*
  Note: The **subject of the infinitive** or **the -ing form** is omitted when it is the same as the subject of the main verb. *I **would like to help** with the preparations.* When it is different, however, it is not omitted. The subject of the infinitive can be an object pronoun, a name or a noun. *I would like **her/Mary/my assistant to help** with the preparations.*

16

The Infinitive / -ing form / Participles 2

3 Write what each word is followed by: F.I. (full inf.), B.I. (bare inf.) or -ing form.

1	refuse	+ *F.I.*	7	promise	+ ....
2	finish	+	8	be known	+ ....
3	dislike	+	9	would like	+ ....
4	would rather	+	10	it's no use	+ ....
5	would	+	11	admit	+ ....
6	object to	+	12	let	+ ....

13 hear + ...
14 it's no good + ...
15 decide + ...
16 deny + ...

4 Fill in the blanks with the correct form of the infinitive or the -ing form. Mind the tenses.

1 The police made the bank robbers ...*give*... (give) themselves up.
2 He is not likely .... (return) before five o'clock.
3 The criminals were forced .... (surrender).
4 They might not .... (complain) about the meal if the service hadn't been so dreadful.
5 Man is said .... (invent) the wheel about ten thousand years ago.
6 You must .... (starve) to have eaten such a big dinner last night.
7 She'd better .... (have) a good excuse for being so late.
8 They hope .... (make) a lot of money in their new business.
9 The wind tends .... (increase) just before sunset.
10 He should .... (tell) his parents the truth when they asked him.
11 Imagine .... (live) in a big house like that!
12 I'd rather not .... (visit) my parents this weekend.
13 She's too tired .... (concentrate) on her work today.
14 You should .... (see) his face when she told him the news.
15 It was such a shock .... (hear) from her after all these years.
16 Ann would love .... (lie) on a beach now, instead of typing reports.
17 The doctor worked for fifteen hours without .... (take) a break.
18 John's father let him .... (borrow) his car for the weekend.
19 There's no point .... (get) there early because the gates don't open till 10 am.
20 Jim doesn't have enough patience .... (be) a teacher.

5 Fill in the blanks with the correct form of the infinitive or -ing form.

BEIJING

No visit to China would be complete without 1) ...*going*... (go) to Shanghai, where you can expect 2) .... (find) a fresh, sophisticated new city awaiting you. While its sights may not 3) .... (be) as grand or historical as cities such as Beijing or Xi'an, there's certainly enough 4) .... (keep) you enchanted during your visit to this rich and cosmopolitan city, which is said 5) .... (have) a shining future as Asia's major centre of economy and trade.

No one anticipated the pace of change in Beijing 6) .... (be) quite as fast as it has been! In 1985, Shanghai had one skyscraper, now it has around 3,000, in addition to 7) .... (have) literally hundreds of new air-conditioned shopping centres and convenience stores.

As well as 8) .... (drink) in the city's vibrant atmosphere, don't forget 9) .... (spend) some time 10) .... (look) around the Old City to the west of the Huang Pu River that divides Shanghai in two.

Above all, enjoy your trip! However, let me 11) .... (give) you a word of warning – it is perhaps best 12) .... (avoid) Shanghai altogether during Chinese New Year, but if you do decide 13) .... (go) during this time, be prepared 14) .... (have) a hard time 15) .... (get) around in the crowds for most shops, businesses and tourist attractions will be closed 16) .... (make) shopping difficult.

6 Put the verbs in brackets into the -ing form or the infinitive with or without "to".

When Gilbert decided **1)** ...*to give up*... **(give up)** his job and **2)** .... **(sell)** all his possessions, everyone thought he was mad. But, as it turned out, he was just the first of many of my friends **3)** .... **(do)** this. In fact, escaping the pressures of everyday working life has become a priority for many people these days. They can't stand the idea of **4)** .... **(work)** until they are 65, only **5)** .... **(retire)** to some boring country village and **6)** .... **(waste)** their time **7)** .... **(dig)** the garden or **8)** .... **(gossip)** with the neighbours. They would rather **9)** .... **(live)** life to the full now, before they are too old **10)** .... **(enjoy)** it. **11)** .... **(buy)** a motorcycle and **12)** .... **(tour)** the world is a popular option. Other, less adventurous types might prefer **13)** .... **(buy)** a small farmhouse and live off the land. Personally, I fancy **14)** .... **(sail)** around the world in a yacht. As for Gilbert, he bought a house in a little country village and spends his time **15)** .... **(walk)** around the village and **16)** .... **(talk)** with the neighbours.

7 Put the verbs in brackets into the -ing form or the infinitive without "to".

1 I watched her ...*get up*... **(get up)** and walk slowly out of the room.
2 I heard the phone .... **(ring)** twice and then stop.
3 Tim saw Jill .... **(stand)** outside the butcher's as he was driving to work.
4 Jane stopped to watch the river .... **(flow)** down the mountainside.
5 Listen to the wind .... **(blow)** through the trees.
6 We heard the workmen .... **(drill)** in the road as we were eating breakfast.
7 The witness saw the burglar .... **(break into)** the house and steal the television.
8 Listen to her .... **(sing)** the song and then tell us what you think of it.

Verbs taking to-infinitive or -ing form without a change in meaning

● begin, continue, intend, start + to-inf or -ing form. We don't normally have two -ing forms together.
  *He began **speaking/to speak**. NOT: He is beginning speaking.*
● advise, allow, encourage, permit, require + object + to-inf. *She doesn't **allow them to talk** in class.*
● advise, allow, encourage, permit, require + -ing form. *She doesn't **allow talking** in class.*
● be advised, be allowed, be encouraged, be permitted, be required + to-inf. *They **aren't allowed to talk** in class.*
● need, require, want + to-inf./-ing form/passive inf.
  *You **need to wash** the car. Your car **needs washing**. Your car **needs to be washed**.*

8 Complete the sentences using the words in bold. Use two to five words.

1 We weren't advised to book in advance.
  advise They ...*didn't advise us to*... book in advance.
2 You really need to renew your passport before you go on holiday.
  needs Your passport .... before you go on holiday.
3 They require hotel guests to vacate their rooms by twelve noon.
  are Hotel guests .... their rooms by twelve noon.
4 The dietician advised us not to eat between meals.
  eating The dietician .... between meals.
5 They need to consider the proposals more carefully.
  considered The proposals .... more carefully.

Verbs taking to-infinitive or -ing form with a change in meaning

1 **forget + to-inf** (= forget to do sth)
*He **forgot to switch off** the TV.*
forget + -ing form (= forget a past event)
*I'll never **forget meeting** Jane for the first time.*

2 **remember + to-inf** (= remember to do sth)
*I hope you'll **remember to tidy** your room.*
remember + -ing form (= recall a past event)
*I don't **remember** him ever **tidying up** his room.*

3 **mean + to-inf** (= intend to)
*She **means to start** a new life.*
mean + -ing form (= involve)
*I won't take the job if it **means moving** to Scotland.*

4 **go on + to-inf** (= finish doing sth and start doing sth else; then; afterwards)
*She finished one letter and **went on to write** another.*
go on + -ing form (= continue)
*She **went on writing** till the early hours of the morning.*

5 **regret + to-inf** (= be sorry to) *I **regret to inform** you that your services are no longer required.*
regret + -ing form (= have second thoughts about sth already done) *He **regrets misbehaving**.*

6 **would prefer + to-inf** (specific preference)
*I'd **prefer to see** you in private.*
prefer + -ing form (in general)
*I **prefer working** on my own.*
prefer + to-inf + rather than + inf without to (say you like one thing instead of another) *He **prefers to paint** the flat on his own **rather than hire** a professional.*

7 **try + to-inf** (= do one's best; attempt)
***Try to eat** less high-cholesterol food.*
try + -ing form (= do sth as an experiment)
***Try cutting down on** fat. You might get thinner.*

8 **want + to-inf** (= wish) *I **want to stop** smoking.*
want + -ing form (= sth needs to be done)
*This room **wants tidying up**.*

9 **stop + to-inf** (= pause temporarily)
*He **stopped** at the garage **to have** the tank filled.*
stop + -ing form (= finish; cease)
*He **stopped behaving** foolishly.*

10 **be sorry + to-inf** (= feel regret about sth)
*I'm **sorry to tell** you your flight has been cancelled.*
be sorry for + -ing form (= apologise for)
*He was **sorry for hurting** her feelings.*

11 **hate + to-inf** (= hate what one is about to do)
*I **hate to cut in**, but you must see the manager.*
hate + -ing form (= feel sorry for what one is doing)
*I **hate causing** you so much inconvenience.*

12 **be afraid + to-inf** (= be too frightened to do sth; hesitate) *She **was afraid to climb** the tree.*
be afraid of + -ing form (= be afraid that what is referred to by the -ing form may happen)
*When she goes swimming, she's always **afraid of being** stung by jellyfish.*

9 Put the verbs in brackets into the -ing form or the infinitive.

1 A: Oh, Mum, this programme's nearly finished. Can't I go on ...*watching*... **(watch)** TV for a while?
   B: No, I want you to do your maths homework and then go on .... **(write)** your English essay. You haven't even started it yet and it's due in tomorrow.
2 A: Your dress is filthy. It wants .... **(wash)**.
   B: I know. I wanted .... **(take)** it to the cleaner's yesterday, but they were closed.
3 A: Don't you hate .... **(not/know)** anyone here?
   B: Yes, I get very lonely, but I hate .... **(worry)** my parents, so I tell them I've made lots of friends.
4 A: I'll never forget .... **(visit)** Thailand for the first time.
   B: Yes, it was such a wonderful holiday. If only I hadn't forgotten .... **(take)** my camera.
5 A: Why don't we stop .... **(get)** something to eat on the way home?
   B: OK, but we should really stop .... **(spend)** money on junk food.
6 A: I'm sorry for .... **(spoil)** your plans last weekend.
   B: That's OK. I was sorry .... **(hear)** you weren't feeling very well.
7 A: Jane doesn't know how to work the computer, but she's afraid .... **(ask)** for help.
   B: But isn't she afraid of .... **(get)** into trouble if she breaks it?

8 A: Did you remember .... **(tell)** Tim about the party?

B: I don't remember .... **(tell)** him, but I'm sure I did.

9 A: Do you regret .... **(offer)** him the job?

B: Yes, I regret .... **(say)** he's not a reliable employee.

10 A: I think I'd prefer .... **(go)** on holiday to Greece this year and spend some time visiting ancient sites.

B: Yes, I prefer .... **(do)** something interesting to just .... **(sit)** on a beach all day. And I'd prefer .... **(go)** somewhere warm rather than .... **(stay)** in England.

11 A: Did you mean .... **(park)** so far away?

B: Yes. Otherwise, it would mean .... **(pay)** to get into a car park.

12 A: I've been trying .... **(contact)** Mr Isaacs all morning.

B: Why don't you try .... **(phone)** his club?

10 Complete the sentences using the infinitive or the -ing form of the verb in brackets.

1 His lawyer advised him ...*to take*... the journalist to court. **(take)**

2 I wouldn't advise .... that dog - it might bite you. **(touch)**

3 The boss doesn't encourage .... in the office. He's a non-smoker. **(smoke)**

4 Why do you keep .... me such stupid questions? **(ask)**

5 I would offer .... you with the housework, but I'm rather busy. **(help)**

6 Students are not allowed .... during the exam. **(talk)**

7 They don't allow .... in this park because some boys used to ride around too fast. **(cycle)**

8 I really hate .... caught in the rain. **(get)**

9 Your childish behaviour is beginning .... me. **(annoy)**

10 She is afraid .... the lift, so she uses the stairs. **(take)**

11 Remember .... the cat or she'll starve to death. **(feed)**

12 It's hot in here. Do you mind .... the window? **(open)**

13 The bank manager agreed .... me £5,000. **(lend)**

14 She put off .... her bags until a few hours before her flight. **(pack)**

15 Our dog Timmy loves .... with his ball in the garden. **(play)**

16 She wrote him a note to remind him .... his laundry at 2 o'clock. **(pick up)**

17 Steven is exhausted because he isn't used to .... so much exercise. **(do)**

18 She looked so funny in her new hat we couldn't help .... **(laugh)**

19 You should practise .... this tune on the piano until you perfect it. **(play)**

20 I regret .... you that your bank account is overdrawn. **(inform)**

Participles

Present participles (verb + ing) describe what somebody or something is.	Past participles (verb + ed) describe how someone feels.
*It was a **boring** lecture. (What kind of lecture? Boring.)*	*They were **bored** by the lecture. (How did they feel during the lecture? Bored.)*

11 Underline the correct participle.

1 He was **encouraging**/encouraged towards his children.

2 They found the film very **excited/exciting**.

3 He was **exhausting/exhausted** after the marathon.

4 They were **worrying/worried** that they would be late.

5 Her behaviour is extremely **annoying/annoyed**.

6 We were **shocking/shocked** by his behaviour.

7 She told us a very **entertaining/entertained** story.

8 They were all **surprising/surprised** when he turned up at the party.

9 That book is really **interested/interesting**.

10 They were **fascinated/fascinating** by the view.

The Infinitive / -ing form / Participles

12   Put the verbs in brackets into the infinitive or -ing form.

Scotland was the perfect place **1)** ...*to grow up*... **(grow up)**. My parents had spent years **2)** .... **(save up)** because they wanted **3)** .... **(buy)** a small farmhouse in the Scottish Highlands. Shortly after I was born, their dream came true and our new life in the country began. To begin with, I was probably too young **4)** .... **(appreciate)** the fresh air and breathtaking views, but as I grew up, I began **5)** .... **(enjoy)** exploring the unspoilt country-side. I soon got used to **6)** .... **(have)** to walk miles to the shops, and since it was too far **7)** .... **(travel)** to the nearest primary school, my parents did their best **8)** .... **(educate)** me at home. However, I never felt lonely and was usually too busy **9)** .... **(help)** my father on the land to worry about **10)** .... **(not/have)** any friends. My brothers and sisters were also starting **11)** .... **(grow up)** fast and we had no difficulty **12)** .... **(amuse)** ourselves for hours on end. When I reached the age of eleven, my parents decided it was time **13)** .... **(send)** me to secondary school as they didn't feel they were capable of **14)** .... **(provide)** me with the range of skills I would need for my future life. This would involve **15)** .... **(travel)** twenty miles to the nearest town and twenty miles back. I was sorry **16)** .... **(say)** goodbye to my old way of life, but at the same time I looked forward to **17)** .... **(mix)** with new people. After **18)** .... **(finish)** school, I was forced **19)** .... **(move)** to Edinburgh to look for work and I have now made the city my home. Although I love the cosmopolitan lifestyle, I sometimes can't help **20)** .... **(wish)** I was back in the Highlands.

 In Other Words

- It is exciting to watch a football match.
  Watching a football match is exciting.
- It's too cold for him to go swimming.
  It isn't warm enough for him to go swimming.
  It is so cold that he can't go swimming.
- They made her tell the truth.
  She was made to tell the truth.
- I prefer walking to riding a bike.
  I prefer to walk rather than ride a bike.
- Could you open the door?
  Would you mind opening the door?

- We were bored by the film.
  We found the film boring.
  The film bored us.
- He had difficulty (in) hearing the music.
  It was difficult for him to hear the music.
  He found it difficult to hear the music.
  He could hardly hear the music.
- They allowed him to attend the meeting.
  He was allowed to attend the meeting.
- It took her an hour to reach the station.
  She took an hour to reach the station.
  Reaching the station took her an hour.

13   Complete the sentences using the words in bold. Use two to five words.

1 He arrived too late to catch the 9.30 train.
   arrive   He ...*didn't arrive early enough*... to catch the 9.30 train.
2 Preparing the meal took her three hours.
   prepare   She .... the meal.

3 These trousers are too small for me.

enough   These trousers .... for me.

4 Politicians found the results of the local election surprising.

were   Politicians .... of the local election.

5 Could you pass me the cheese, please?

mind   Would .... the cheese?

6 They made her pay £2,000 tax.

to   She .... £2,000 tax.

7 She was allowed to stay at her friend's house.

her   They .... at her friend's house.

8 He wasn't tall enough to become a policeman.

short   He .... a policeman.

9 He had difficulty seeing in the dark room.

hardly   He .... in the dark room.

10 It took her six months to learn how to drive.

took   She .... how to drive.

11 I prefer going out to staying at home.

than   I prefer to .... at home.

12 Would you mind keeping quiet while she's talking?

keep   Could .... she's talking?

13 The runner could hardly keep up with the others.

had   The runner .... up with the others.

14 I think it's interesting to visit other countries.

visiting   I think .... interesting.

15 She prefers taking the train to travelling by coach.

take   She prefers .... than travel by coach.

16 Could you run through the details once more?

mind   Would .... the details once more?

17 They took ages to reach a decision.

them   It .... a decision.

18 The police let the suspect make one phone call.

was   The suspect .... one phone call.

19 The tourists found the carnival fascinating.

were   The tourists .... the carnival.

20 It was difficult for the jury to reach a verdict.

difficulty   The jury .... a verdict.

21 The 17-year-olds weren't old enough to get into the club.

too   The 17-year-olds .... into the club.

22 She prefers speaking French to writing it.

than   She prefers .... write it.

23 Learning about other cultures is important.

learn   It .... about other cultures.

24 They made him work overtime.

was   He .... overtime.

25 During the rush hour it takes me over an hour to get to work.

getting   During the rush hour, ... over an hour.

26 The instructions were so complicated that I couldn't follow them.

too   The instructions were .... follow.

27 It was difficult for me to hear what he was saying.

hardly   I .... what he was saying.

28 Could you keep the noise down?

mind   Would .... the noise down?

29 They made the passengers wait at the airport for hours.

were   The passengers .... at the airport for hours.

30 I have difficulty in understanding his accent.

find   I .... his accent.

14 Complete the sentences using the words in bold. Use two to five words.

0 John was late for work because his train was delayed.
time If the train ...*had been on time*..., John would not have been late for work.
1 Both James and Bill dislike football.
keen Neither .... on football.
2 Mother made us clean our rooms on Saturday.
made We .... our rooms on Saturday by our mother.
3 I find it difficult to stick to a diet.
difficulty I .... to a diet.
4 Let's eat out tonight.
going How .... a meal tonight?
5 She would rather not drive to London.
feel She .... to London.
6 People say learning a new language is difficult.
supposed Learning a new language .... difficult.
7 The boy wouldn't apologise for breaking the window.
sorry The boy refused .... breaking the window.
8 Mary telephoned the secretary to say she would be late.
received The secretary .... Mary to say she would be late.

Oral Development 2

The Smiths went on an excursion last Sunday. Use the list below and your own ideas to tell the story. Use infinitives or -ing forms.

look forward to, enjoy, spend time, discuss, would rather, expect, decide, easy, involve, stop, surprised, want, see, too frightened, suggest

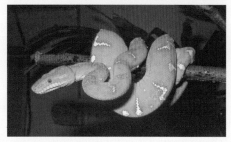

The Smiths had been looking forward to having a day out for ages ...

Consolidation 2

Phrasal Verbs

bring about: cause to happen
bring back: 1) recall, 2) reintroduce
bring down: 1) cause to fall, 2) reduce prices
bring forward: suggest an idea
bring on: cause, usu sth unpleasant
bring out: publish, release sth to the public
bring round: 1) help sb regain consciousness; bring to, 2) persuade sb to change opinion
bring up: 1) raise a child, 2) vomit, 3) introduce a subject, 4) mention

be/get carried away: be/get excited
carry off: do sth successfully
carry on (with): continue esp despite difficulties
carry out: perform, complete
carry over: postpone
carry through: 1) complete despite difficulties, 2) help sb survive during troubled times

15 Fill in the correct particle(s).

1 The corruption scandal brought ...*down*... the government.
2 The cold weather probably brought .... her illness.
3 Stephen King's publisher is bringing .... his new book next month.
4 A wet cloth helped to bring the unconscious man ....
5 She's brought .... five children on her own.
6 My father didn't want to let me buy a car, but in the end, I managed to bring him ....
7 Jane carried .... her part in the play without difficulty.
8 "Carry .... your work please," said the teacher.
9 Tom got carried .... by the music and wouldn't stop singing.
10 If we don't pay the ransom, the kidnappers will carry .... their threats.

16 Look at Appendix 1, then fill in the correct preposition.

1 They congratulated him ...*on*... getting his degree.
2 The airport was crowded .... holidaymakers.
3 She keeps boasting .... her new house.
4 The Prime Minister refused to comment .... the rumours about his resignation.
5 He's very clever .... solving crosswords.
6 She's capable .... answering all the questions herself.
7 The cause .... the fire was never discovered.
8 Don't put the blame .... him. It's not his fault.
9 He blamed John .... stealing the money.
10 They were astonished .... the number of candidates who had succeeded.
11 Which political party do you belong ....?
12 Concentrate .... what you're doing.
13 He charged me £10 .... the repairs.
14 She was charged .... murder.
15 The police are holding three suspects .... connection .... the bombing in Brighton last week.
16 Is there any connection .... sunbathing and skin cancer?
17 More money is needed to help care .... the homeless.
18 He cares deeply .... the welfare of his students.
19 Italian is frequently compared .... French as they are from the same language family.
20 The standard of education at Mount Carmel College compares favourably .... the standards elsewhere.

17 Complete the sentences using the words in bold. Use two to five words.

1 I'm sure he didn't steal the money.
 stolen He ...*can't have stolen*... the money.
2 It is likely that he will travel to Europe.
 probably He .... travel to Europe.
3 He didn't manage to catch any fish.
 succeed He .... any fish.
4 Whatever you say to Julie, she doesn't listen.
 matter Julie doesn't listen, ... you say to her.
5 The car was so expensive that we couldn't buy it.
 for The car .... to buy.

6 Please turn the lights off before you leave.
forget Before you leave, ... turn the lights off.
7 She tends to get very excited at office parties.
carried She .... at office parties.

How to treat Multiple Choice Cloze Texts

● Read the whole passage at least once to understand as much of the general meaning as possible.
● Look at the four choices given for each gap and try to reduce the choices you have to make by eliminating the obviously incorrect ones.
  He .... the world record for the long jump in 1992.
  A *did*   **B** *broke*   **C** *made*   **D** *reached*
  The word "record" is not used with "do" or "make". Also we do not say "reach" a record - you "reach" a destination. Therefore **B: broke** *is the correct answer.*
● When you have finished, read the text again to see if it makes sense and is grammatically correct.

18 Read the text below and decide which word A, B, C or D best fits each space. There's an example at the beginning (0).

The Lost Art of Old Masters

The three **(0)** ...C... spaces along the wall of the Frankfurt Schirn Gallery have probably been photographed more than the old paintings which **(1)** .... there until last Thursday. That was the day when thieves **(2)** .... two paintings by JMW Turner, which were on **(3)** .... from London's Tate Gallery.

In fact, as art theft increases, empty walls are becoming an increasingly familiar **(4)** .... in Europe's galleries. The thieves are usually members of professional **(5)** .... who study the layout of their target in **(6)** .... beforehand. They are becoming better at overcoming the tightest security. The thieves in Frankfurt **(7)** .... until the gallery closed at 10 pm, overpowered the security guard before he could **(8)** .... on the alarm system and escaped with the paintings to a **(9)** .... car. The paintings are valued at £37.7 million and, since they are too famous to sell, police suspect that the thieves will hold them to ransom. A £62,800 reward is being **(10)** .... for information.

Unfortunately, European Union policy has made it easier for thieves to **(11)** .... borders and harder for police to follow them. To discourage thieves, galleries may have to **(12)** .... themselves into high security fortresses.

	A		B		C		D	
0	A vacant	B open	(C) empty	D free
1	A hung	B waited	C held	D fixed
2	A robbed	B stole	C burgled	D borrowed
3	A advance	B trial	C credit	D loan
4	A sight	B scene	C site	D look
5	A groups	B gangs	C teams	D bands
6	A fact	B addition	C detail	D general
7	A stayed	B remained	C hung	D waited
8	A turn	B go	C rely	D set
9	A lingering	B resting	C waiting	D pausing
10	A given	B offered	C provided	D presented
11	A enter	B break	C pass	D cross
12	A become	B continue	C turn	D move

19   Use the words in capitals to form a word that fits in the space in the same line.

Insurance Risks

Paying an **(0)** ...*insurance*... premium may seem like a waste of money, but on the other hand, it can also be an **(1)** .... wise investment, saving you from serious **(2)** .... difficulties in the future.

INSURE
EXTREME
FINANCE

There are various kinds of insurance policies covering such things as houses, cars, personal **(3)** .... and healthcare. Some forms of insurance are compulsory and others are **(4)** ....

POSSESS
OPTION

One example of insurance which many people have a **(5)** .... not to bother with is holiday and travel insurance. They feel that spending extra money to cover themselves in the **(6)** .... event of something going wrong while on holiday is not an **(7)** .... idea. They prefer to risk it and hope that all will be well while they are away. So, **(8)** .... they avoid this kind of insurance, but more **(9)** .... types will be willing to pay the premium to feel covered in any **(10)** .... that may arise.

TEND

LIKELY
ATTRACT

UNDERSTAND
CAUTION
SITUATE

20   Complete the sentences using the words in bold. Use two to five words.

0 I had never met John's sister before.
    first   It ...*was the first time*... I had ever met John's sister.
1 Please don't mention the subject of food when I'm on a diet!
    rather   I'd .... the subject of food when I'm on a diet!
2 After being out in the rain, Sally caught a cold.
    down   Sally .... a cold after being out in the rain.
3 Mary called me when she got home.
    call   I received .... when she got home.
4 Michael is very sorry he bought a second-hand car.
    regrets   Michael .... a second-hand car.
5 This washing machine is inefficient and expensive.
    only   This washing machine is .... expensive.
6 It's your duty to deal with clients.
    responsible   You .... with clients.
7 Although we worked late, we still didn't finish the project.
    fact   In .... we worked late, we still didn't finish the project.
8 You will find Jimmy very different from the last time you saw him.
    difference   You will find .... Jimmy from the last time you saw him.

21   Fill in the following collocation grids.

	a bus	a sailing boat	a car	a horse	a camel	a bike	a yacht	a limo
drive	✓							
ride								
sail								

Part 1

For questions 1 - 12, read the text below and decide which answer (A, B, C or D) best fits each gap. There is an example at the beginning (0).

Eccentric or mad?

Traditionally, the British have always been very **(0)** ...C... of their eccentrics. Even today, British eccentrics are considered to be the strangest, **(1)** .... to American psychologist, David Weeks.

(2) .... the Leopard Man, for example. He lives alone in a cave on the Isle of Skye. He is tattooed from **(3)** .... to toe with leopard spots, and **(4)** .... a living selling seafood. But is this bizarre behaviour a type of mental illness? It has long been believed that creativity and insanity are **(5)** .... In the last 30 years or so, psychologists have tried to find evidence to support this belief. One study found that creative people have a lot in **(6)** .... with eccentrics, and also, that they are more **(7)** .... to suffer from extreme depression, which is often associated with mental illness.

But during David Weeks' detailed **(8)** .... into the personalities of eccentrics, he found that they are **(9)** .... the happiest and healthiest of people. Not only do they visit their doctors much less often than the **(10)** .... of us, but they are also usually **(11)** .... in several things at one time, so they always have a(n) **(12)** .... in life.

0	A loving	B caring	C fond	D warm
1	A concerning	B considering	C responding	D according
2	A Take	B See	C Watch	D Look
3	A head	B hair	C skull	D top
4	A creates	B makes	C gets	D has
5	A joined	B connected	C combined	D attached
6	A same	B alike	C common	D similar
7	A likely	B probable	C possible	D available
8	A search	B research	C check	D look
9	A among	B between	C with	D apart
10	A least	B most	C remainder	D rest
11	A excited	B attracted	C interested	D invested
12	A goal	B reason	C score	D aim

Part 2

For questions 13 - 24, read the text below and think of the word which best fits each gap. Use only one word in each gap. There is an example at the beginning (0).

NIGHTMARES

Nightmares, like most dreams, occur during the stage of sleep **(0)** ...*when*... the brain is very active and sorting through experiences and new information for learning and memory. The vivid images the brain is processing can seem **(13)** .... real as the emotions they **(14)** .... trigger.

This part of sleep **(15)** .... known as the rapid eye movement or REM stage because the eyes are rapidly moving beneath closed eyelids. Nightmares tend to happen during the second half of a night's sleep, **(16)** .... REM intervals are longer.

No one knows exactly **(17)** .... causes nightmares. Dreams and nightmares seem to be one way kids process thoughts and feelings **(18)** .... situations they face, and to work through worries and concerns.

Most times nightmares occur **(19)** .... no apparent reason. At other times, they happen when a child is experiencing stress **(20)** .... change. Events or situations that might feel unsettling – such as moving, attending a new school, the birth of a sibling, or family tensions – might also **(21)** .... reflected in unsettling dreams. For some kids, **(22)** .... those with a good imagination, reading scary books or watching scary movies or TV shows just **(23)** .... bedtime can cause nightmares. Parents can't prevent nightmares, but can help kids **(24)** .... a good night's sleep, by soothing them before bedtime.

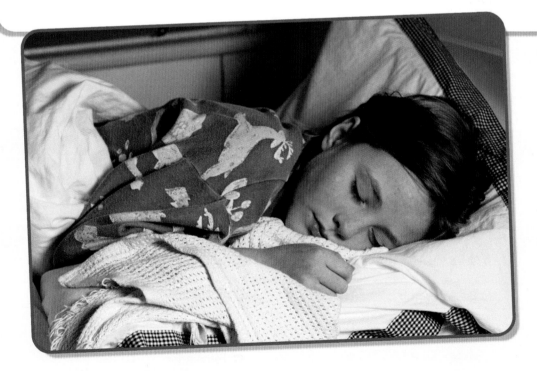

Part 3

For questions 25 - 34, read the text below. Use the word given in capitals at the end of some of the lines to form a word that fits in the gap in the same line.

Teens Go Without Meat

The **(0)** ...*decision*... to become a vegetarian is a **(25)** .... one, made for any number of reasons. There are many different **(26)** .... that teens in particular give for choosing a meatless lifestyle.

DECIDE
PERSON
EXPLAIN

One group claims that their choice is based on certain food **(27)** ....; they simply don't enjoy the taste of meat. Others are concerned about animal rights and the way animals are treated in the meat **(28)** .... process. Yet more young people may be influenced by **(29)** .... or cultural beliefs which prohibit the consumption of meat. A further reason is that teenagers feel that it is **(30)** .... not to eat meat and that they can control their weight more **(31)** .... as vegetarians. In many cases, too, it may be a **(32)** .... family decision in order to reduce food bills!

LIKE

PRODUCE
RELIGION

HEALTHY
EASE

JOIN

However, it is important to note that in some cases, teens who adopt a strictly vegetarian diet may be in danger of developing an eating **(33)** .... such as anorexia. If parents have any **(34)** .... of this kind, they should contact their child's doctor.

ORDER
SUSPECT

Part 4

For questions 35 - 42, complete the second sentence so that it has a similar meaning to the first sentence, using the word given. Do not change the word given. You must use between two and five words including the word given. There is an example at the beginning (0).

0 They worked hard on the project.
effort
They ...*put a lot of effort*... into the project.

35 You'll have no difficulty getting out of the country.
easy
You'll find .... out of the country.

36 He did the same job as his father, as it was expected of him.
footsteps
He followed ...., as it was expected of him.

37 They should have told him the truth.
better
It .... they had told him the truth.

38 I'm afraid there's no milk left.
run
I'm afraid we .... milk.

39 She spent ages planting the new flowers.
took
It .... the new flowers.

40 I prefer watching westerns to watching romances.
preference
I have .... romances.

41 They made him work overtime.
was
He .... overtime.

42 People say this is the best film ever made.
supposed
This .... the best film ever made.

Present Forms

Present Simple	Present Continuous	Present Perfect	Present Perf. Continuous
permanent situations or states *She **works** in a bank.* permanent truths or laws of nature *The sun **rises** in the east.*	temporary situations *He **is spending** the week with his mother.* changing or developing situations *She **is getting** more and more impatient.*	recently completed actions *She **has dyed** her hair black.* *(The action is complete - her hair is now dyed black - evidence in the present)*	actions started in the past and continuing up to the present. *She **has been doing** her homework for an hour. (She started an hour ago and she's still doing it.)*
repeated/habitual actions (especially with frequency adverbs: often, usually, always etc) *He **always goes** to bed at 11 o'clock. (Here "always" means every day.)*	frequently repeated actions with always, constantly, continually, expressing annoyance or criticism *He's **always getting** into trouble. (Here "always" means constantly.)*	complete past actions connected to the present with stated or unstated time reference *He **has bought** a house. (Now he owns a house.)* *He **has just returned** from Paris. (stated time reference)*	past actions of certain duration having visible results or effects in the present *He **has been running**. That's why he's out of breath.*
reviews/sports commentaries/ dramatic narrative *Smythe **serves** the ball and Lanyon **misses** it ...*	actions happening at or around the moment of speaking *The sun **is shining** now.* *He **is studying** for the exams.*	personal experiences/ changes which have happened *I **have lost** weight recently.*	to express anger, irritation, annoyance, explanation or criticism *She **has been using** my make-up. (annoyance)*
timetables/programmes (future reference) *The train **leaves** at 8.00.* in exclamatory sentences *There **goes** the bus!*	fixed arrangements in the near future *I'm **going** to the theatre this evening.*	emphasis on number *He **has seen three** films this week.* *She **has had four** cups of coffee since she woke up.*	Present Perfect Continuous is normally used with for, since or how long to put emphasis on duration *He **has been feeling** unwell for days.*

Time expressions usually used with Present Forms

Present Simple	Present Continuous	Present Perfect & Present Perfect Continuous
every day/week/month/ year, usually, sometimes, always, rarely, never, often, in the morning/ evening/afternoon, at night, on Mondays etc	now, at the moment, at present, nowadays, today, tonight, always, still etc	just, ever, never, already, yet (negations & questions), always, how long, so far, recently, since (= from a starting point in the past), for (= over a period of time), today, this week/month etc **For** and **since** are usually used with Present Perfect Continuous to emphasise the duration of an action.

1 Put the verbs in brackets into the correct present forms.

"Well, I **1)** *...have never won...* **(never/win)** anything like this before! I **2)** .... **(only/enter)** a few competitions in my life, so this is a big surprise. Of course, I **3)** .... **(watch)** TV quiz shows for years, but now I **4)** .... **(think)** of taking part in more. The prize is wonderful. We **5)** .... **(stay)** here in Hawaii for ten days now, and we **6)** .... **(have)** a great time. We **7)** .... **(already/see)** all the sights and my wife **8)** .... **(buy)** lots of souvenirs. We **9)** .... **(send)** postcards to all our friends to show them how we **10)** .... **(spend)** our time. Yes, we really **11)** .... **(enjoy)** ourselves. In fact, we **12)** .... **(want)** to stay forever."

3 Tense Forms

Stative verbs express a permanent state rather than an action and are not used in the continuous forms. These are: **verbs of the senses** used to express involuntary actions (feel, hear, see, smell, taste etc), **verbs of feelings and emotions** (adore, detest, dislike, enjoy, forgive, hate, like etc), **verbs of opinion** (agree, believe, suppose, understand etc) and **other verbs** (belong, concern, depend, know, mean, own, possess, need, prefer, want etc) *I see someone coming. She hates pop music. I don't agree with you. He knows a lot about computers.* **Note: feel** and **hurt** can be used in either continuous or simple forms. *She feels/is feeling better.* **Look, watch** and **listen** express deliberate actions and can be used in continuous forms. *He is listening to some records.*

Some **stative verbs** (be, love, see, smell, taste, think etc) have continuous forms but there is a difference in meaning.

STATE	ACTION
● I **see** them coming towards us. (= I have the ability)	● She**'s seeing** her doctor today. (= she's visiting)
● These flowers **smell** nice. (= they have a nice smell)	● Why **are you smelling** the food? Has it gone off? (= why are you checking the smell of)
● This soup **tastes** delicious. (= its flavour is good)	● She**'s tasting** the soup. (= she's testing the flavour)
● It **feels** like velvet. (= it has the texture of)	● He**'s feeling** the cloth. (= he's touching the cloth)
● He **has** a house. (= he possesses)	● We**'re having** a nice time. (= we're enjoying ourselves)
● **Do you like** his new car? (= Is it nice?)	● How **are they liking** the party? (= are they enjoying)
● I **think** he has left. (= I suppose, I believe)	● I**'m thinking** about his suggestion. (= I'm considering)
● Ann **is** polite. (= her character is)	● Tom **is being** very impolite. (= he is behaving impolitely)
● It **looks** as if it's going to snow. (= it appears)	● They **are looking** at the statue. (= they're viewing it)

2 Fill in with Present Simple or Continuous.

1 A: I **1)** ...*see*... **(see)** there's a great film on at the cinema tonight. Would you like to go?
   B: No, I **2)** .... **(see)** the dentist about my toothache.
2 A: I **1)** .... **(think)** about going on a picnic this afternoon.
   B: I wouldn't bother. I **2)** .... **(think)** it's going to rain.
3 A: Is John feeling OK? He **1)** .... **(look)** very red in the face.
   B: Yes, I know. I **2)** .... **(look)** for the doctor's telephone number now.
4 A: How **1)** .... **(you/like)** your stay in Budapest?
   B: I am really enjoying myself. I particularly **2)** .... **(like)** the Hungarian food.
5 A: Why **1)** .... **(you/taste)** the stew?
   B: I think you need to add some spices; it **2)** .... **(taste)** a bit bland.
6 A: Why **1)** .... **(you/feel)** the radiator, Dad?
   B: I don't think it's working; it **2)** .... **(feel)** very cold in here.
7 A: Tom **1)** .... **(be)** usually a very quiet boy.
   B: Yes, but he **2)** .... **(be)** very noisy today.
8 A: **1)** .... **(you/have)** a car?
   B: Yes, but I **2)** .... **(have)** some problems with it, so it's at the garage.
9 A: Why **1)** .... **(you/smell)** the roses?
   B: They always **2)** .... **(smell)** so wonderful at this time of year.

3 Put the verbs in brackets into the correct present forms.

Jane,
Thanks for agreeing to look after my flat while I'm away. I **1)** ...*have cleaned*... **(clean)** the flat thoroughly, but as I **2)** .... **(work)** late all week, I **3)** .... **(not/have)** time to cook any food for you. My dog, Rover, **4)** .... **(eat)** a tin of dog food every night, and the plants **5)** .... **(need)** watering once a week. Tonight, I **6)** .... **(stay)** at the Hutton Hotel so you can contact me there if you need me.

Donna

Have gone to / Have been to / Have been in

He **has gone to** Scotland. (He's on his way to Scotland or he's there now. He hasn't come back yet.)
He **has been to** Munich once. (He has visited Munich, but he isn't there now. He has come back.)
He **has been in** Rotterdam for two years. (He lives in Rotterdam now.)

4   **Fill in** has/have been to/in, has/have gone to.

1 Bertha's not here. She ...*has gone to*... the library.
2 I .... Madrid, but I only spent a few days there.
3 "How long .... you .... Birmingham?" "For nearly two years."
4 Tom is alone because his parents .... the seaside for the weekend.
5 Julia .... the supermarket – she'll be back in about an hour.

Since expresses a starting point. *I've been here* **since** *March.*
For expresses the duration of an action. *We've been here* **for** *three months.*

5   **Fill in** since **or** for**.**

Sue Wilson has been involved in sports **1)** ...*for*... more than 25 years. Her first interest was gymnastics, which she has been actively involved in **2)** .... she was ten, but she has also been interested in other forms of sport **3)** .... many years. She has been a keen cyclist **4)** .... 1980, when she made her first bicycle tour of Europe, and **5)** .... her marriage to all-round sportsman Tom Wilson in 1985, she has tried her hand at climbing, sailing and skydiving. Her talent as a writer has kept her busy **6)** .... the past ten years, and she has become familiar to TV viewers as a sports commentator **7)** .... her first TV appearance in 1988. Her plans for the future? "I've been interested in the role of women in sports ever **8)** .... I was a teenager. Now, after being so busy **9)** .... all these years, I've decided to take some time off so I can write a book about it." Since Sue has been part of the sporting world **10)** .... so long, her book should be fascinating.

6   **Look at the notes below, then write an article using the appropriate present forms.**

For many years researchers – try – determine whether animals – share with humans the ability to use language/One particular researcher in America – spend – sixteen years exploring the degree to which a parrot – understand – what he – say/He – find that the bird – be able to – answer questions about objects and also – understand numbers/At the moment the researcher – try – to determine whether the bird actually – know what it – say – or whether it – simply imitate – a collection of sounds.

...For many years, researchers have been trying to determine whether animals ...

7   **Put the verbs in brackets into the correct present forms.**

Dear John,

First of all, sorry I **1)** ...*haven't written*... (**not/write**) for so long, but I was on holiday. **2)** .... (**you/get**) your exam results yet? I'm sure you **3)** .... (**pass**) them all since you always **4)** .... (**study**) so hard. I **5)** .... (**wait**) for mine at the moment, and I **6)** .... (**try**) not to worry! Well, I **7)** .... (**write**) from my new flat. Yes, I **8)** .... (**move**) house! Now, we **9)** .... (**paint**) and **10)** .... (**clean**) the place to make it look nice. When it's finished, I am going to have a party and because I **11)** .... (**not/see**) you for weeks, I **12)** .... (**want**) you to come. Write soon and let me know if I'll see you there.

Love,
Mary

3 Tense Forms

Put the verbs in brackets into the correct present forms.

1 Alan ...*is flying*... **(fly)** to Barcelona tonight. He .... **(already/pack)** his suitcase, but he .... **(not/call)** a taxi yet. His plane .... **(leave)** at 8 pm.
2 Ann and Sally .... **(be)** flatmates. They sometimes .... **(argue)** because Sally .... **(always/make)** a mess in the kitchen.
3 "Look over there! It's John Cooper." "Oh yes! But he .... **(look)** so different! He .... **(put on)** at least 15 kilos, and I .... **(think)** he .... **(wear)** a toupée."
4 Ever since the accident, Susan .... **(be)** afraid to drive. Next week, she .... **(see)** a psychologist who .... **(specialise)** in that sort of problem.
5 "What a great match! Johnson .... **(pass)** the ball to Green, who .... **(shoot)** and .... **(score)**!"
6 "What on earth .... **(you/do)**? Your clothes are all dirty!" "Well, I .... **(work)** in the garden all day. Look! I .... **(already/plant)** a lot of flowers. I .... **(plan)** to cut the grass now.

La Sagrada Familia

Past Forms

Past Simple	Past Continuous	Past Perfect	Past Perf. Continuous
past actions which happened one immediately after the other *She woke up, got out of bed and made a cup of tea.*	action in the middle of happening at a stated past time *This time last week I was travelling across Africa.*	past action which occurred before another action or before a stated past time *By his second day at camp he had made several friends.*	action continuing over a period up to a specific time in the past *She had been saving for a whole year before she bought her ticket to Australia.*
past habit or state *He rode his bike to school every day when he was a child.* complete action or event which happened at a stated past time *She sold her car last week. ("When?" "Last week." - stated past time)*	past action in progress interrupted by another past action. The longer action is in the Past Continuous, the shorter action is in the Past Simple. *I was taking a shower when I heard the telephone ring.*	complete past action which had visible results in the past *She felt much safer after she had locked all the doors.*	past action of certain duration which had visible results in the past *He had been shouting so loudly that he had a sore throat.*
complete past actions not connected to the present with a stated or implied time reference *Shakespeare wrote at least 36 plays.* *(Shakespeare is dead - he won't write any more.)*	two or more simultaneous past actions of certain duration *I was washing up while he was drying the dishes.* background description to events in a story/narration *I was walking along ...*	the Past Perfect is the past equivalent of the Present Perfect *The room was empty - everyone had gone out. (Present Perfect: The room is empty - everyone has gone out.)*	the Past Perfect Cont. is the past equivalent of the Present Perfect Cont. *The party was a great success because he had been preparing for it all week. (Present Perfect: The party is a great success because he has been preparing for it all week.)*

Time expressions usually used with Past Forms

Past Simple	Past Continuous	Past Perfect	Past Perf. Continuous
yesterday, last week etc, (how long) ago, then, just now, when, in 1992 etc	while, as, the moment that etc	for, since, already, after, just, never, yet, before, by, by the time etc	for, since

34

9 Put the verbs in brackets into the correct past forms.

Last year, Tom and Fiona **1)** ...*decided*... **(decide)** to buy a house. They **2)** .... **(save up)** for ages, and by the end of May, they **3)** .... **(put by)** enough for the deposit on a house. They **4)** .... **(live)** in a tiny flat at the time and Fiona **5)** .... **(insist)** that she **6)** .... **(want)** a house with a big garden. They **7)** .... **(search)** for only a few days when they found exactly what they **8)** .... **(look for)** – a two-bedroomed house in nearly an acre of garden. Unfortunately, the owner **9)** .... **(ask)** much more than they **10)** .... **(be)** willing to pay, and when they **11)** .... **(look)** more closely at the interior, they **12)** .... **(see)** that whoever **13)** .... **(live)** there before, **14)** .... **(make)** an absolute mess of the walls and floors. Still, Fiona **15)** .... **(like)** the garden and the location so much that she **16)** .... **(manage)** to convince Tom that, despite the price, it **17)** .... **(be)** the perfect house for them.

10 Put the verbs in brackets into the correct past forms.

Last summer, some friends and I **1)** ...*arranged*... **(arrange)** to go camping. We **2)** .... **(look)** forward to going for weeks when finally the date of departure **3)** .... **(arrive)**. We **4)** .... **(load)** the car with our luggage and **5)** .... **(set off)** early in the morning. The weather was perfect, the sun **6)** .... **(shine)** brightly and the wind **7)** .... **(blow)** gently. There **8)** .... **(not/be)** a cloud in the sky! Shortly afterwards, while we **9)** .... **(travel)** along the motorway, we **10)** .... **(notice)** that the car **11)** .... **(make)** a strange noise. Pete, who **12)** .... **(drive)** very fast, suddenly **13)** .... **(stop)** the car. Everyone **14)** .... **(get out)** and **15)** .... **(go)** round to the back of the car. To our surprise the boot was wide open – whoever **16)** .... **(load)** the luggage **17)** .... **(not/close)** it properly, and everything **18)** .... **(fall out)**!

Present Perfect	Past Simple
• *He **has left**. (unstated time; we don't know when he left)*	• *He **left** a minute ago. (stated time - When? A minute ago.)*
• *She **has been** in Rome for two months. (she's still in Rome - action connected to the present)*	• *She **was** in Rome for two months. (she isn't in Rome any more - action not connected to the present)*
• *He's **been** to the cinema five times this month. (it's still the same month - action connected to the present)*	• *He **went** to the cinema five times last month. (action not connected to the present - it's the following month now)*
• *I've **seen** Matt Dillon. (action connected to the present - he's still alive)*	• *I **saw** Sir Lawrence Olivier. (action not connected to the present - he's dead)*
• *The Queen **has decided** to give up the throne. (announcing news)*	• *She **announced** her decision this morning. (giving details of the news - stated time in past)*

11 Fill in with Present Perfect or Past Simple.

1 A: "Is Paul there, please?"
  B: "Sorry, he **1)** ...*left*... **(leave)** about 10 minutes ago". I think he **2)** .... **(go)** to the library.
2 A: I **1)** .... **(live)** in Lisbon for two years now.
  B: Really? What a coincidence! I **2)** .... **(live)** there for a year before moving to America.
3 A: I need a holiday. I **1)** .... **(only/have)** two days off this year.
  B: Yes, but last year you **2)** .... **(go)** on holiday four times!
4 A: My father once **1)** .... **(see)** Elvis Presley in Las Vegas.
  B: Well, I **2)** .... **(see)** his daughter, Lisa, many times. She lives near me.
5 A: The chairman **1)** .... **(decide)** to retire.
  B: Yes, actually he **2)** .... **(inform)** the managing director of his decision this morning.

3 Tense Forms

- **Used to** expresses past habitual actions and permanent states. (Note that stative verbs are not used with "would".)

  When I was young, I used to go climbing once a month. (also: would go)
  He used to live in Paris. (NOT: would - state)

- **Would** expresses past repeated actions and routines - not states.

  When I was a child, I would go to the cinema every Sunday. (also: I used to go ...)

- **Be used to** means "be accustomed to", "be in the habit of".

  Little children are used to going to bed early in the evening.

- **Was going to** expresses actions one intended to do but didn't do.

  He was going to buy a house but he lost all his money at the racetrack.

---

12 Complete the sentences using the words in bold. Use two to five words.

1 Sally went to ballet classes three times a week.
   go   Sally ...*used to go to*... ballet classes three times a week.
2 It was my intention to phone you last night, but I forgot.
   going   I .... you last night, but I forgot.
3 Lying on the beach all day is an unusual experience for me.
   used   I .... on the beach all day.
4 When I was young, I used to visit my grandmother every day after school.
   would   When I was young, ... every day after school.

---

13 Read the notes, then write the story of Beatrix Potter using appropriate past forms.

When she – grow up Beatrix Potter – be – very fond of animals and – always draw – pictures of her pet rabbit/She – earn a living as an illustrator for several years before her dream of becoming an author come true/It – be the result of a letter – she – send to a sick child describing the adventures of four rabbits/She – later publish it – as "The Tale of Peter Rabbit"/It – become – an instant success and more tales – follow/By the time Beatrix – die – she – write over twenty-five tales and – achieve recognition as one of the greatest children's writers.

When she was growing up, Beatrix Potter was very fond of animals...

---

14 Put the verbs in brackets into the appropriate past forms.

1 Bill ...*was painting*... **(paint)** his front door when the telephone .... **(start)** ringing. He .... **(answer)** the phone and .... **(speak)** to his friend. Later, he .... **(notice)** that he .... **(leave)** red fingerprints all over the phone.
2 .... **(Tony/ring)** you last night?" "Yes. He .... **(wait)** for days for you to phone him, but since you .... **(not/phone)** he .... **(sell)** his motorbike to someone else."
3 "Your hair .... **(look)** different last night." "I know – I .... **(want)** to dye it red, but I .... **(not/pay)** attention when I .... **(buy)** the dye and I .... **(not/realise)** until it .... (be) too late that I .... **(buy)** the wrong colour."
4 One day, my sister .... **(call)** me. She .... **(not/know)** what to cook for a dinner party she .... **(give)** that evening and she .... **(want)** some advice. I .... **(give)** her some simple recipes, but I .... **(be)** surprised that she .... **(not/contact)** our mother. When I .... **(ask)** why, she .... **(reply)**, "She's one of the guests."
5 Last Friday, I .... **(walk)** to work when I .... **(see)** an old friend I .... **(not/ see)** for a long time. I .... **(throw)** my arms around him. He .... **(stare)** at me with an open mouth. To my horror, I .... **(realise)** I .... **(mistake)** him for my friend.

Future Forms

Future Simple	Be going to	Future Continuous	Future Perfect
decisions taken at the moment of speaking (on-the-spot decisions) *I'm hungry. I'll cook something to eat.*	actions intended to be performed in the near future *I'm going to join a gym on Saturday.*	actions in progress at a stated future time *This time next year, she'll be running her own business.*	actions finished before a stated future time *They will have emigrated to Canada by Christmas.*
hopes, fears, threats, offers, promises, warnings, predictions, requests, comments etc, esp. with: expect, hope, believe, I'm sure, I'm afraid, probably etc *I promise I'll be on time.*	planned actions or intentions *Now that she's passed her exams, she's going to train to be a solicitor.*	actions which are the result of a routine (instead of the Present Continuous) *I'll be playing tennis on Sunday. (I play tennis every Sunday - it's part of my routine.)*	**Note: by** or **not ... until/till** are used with Future Perf. **Until/till** are normally used with Future Perf. only in negative sentences. *He will have completed his studies by the end of the year. (NOT: till/until) He won't have arrived until tonight.*
actions or predictions which may (not) happen in the future *He'll probably pass his driving test.* or actions which we cannot control and will inevitably happen *Summer will be here soon.*	evidence that something will definitely happen in the near future *Those dark clouds mean it's going to rain soon. It's so hot - I'm going to faint.*	when we ask politely about people's arrangements to see if they can do sth for us or because we want to offer to do sth for them *Will you be going shopping at the supermarket today? Can you buy me some milk?*	**Future Perf. Continuous** duration of an action up to a certain time in the future *By his sixtieth birthday, he will have been teaching for 35 years.*
things we are not yet sure about or we haven't decided to do yet *Perhaps I'll move house.*	things we are sure about or we have already decided to do in the near future *They are going to operate on his leg. (It has been decided.)*	**Present Simple (with future meaning)** timetables/programmes *The play begins at 7 o'clock this evening.*	**Present Continuous (with future meaning)** fixed arrangement in the near future *She's meeting her aunt this weekend.*

Shall is used:	Will is used:
with I/we in questions, suggestions, offers or when asking for advice. ***Shall** we go home now? What **shall** I wear?*	to express offers, threats, promises, predictions, warnings, requests, hopes, fears, on-the-spot decisions, comments (mainly with: think, expect, believe, I'm sure, hope, know, suppose and probably). *I **hope** you **will keep** in touch with me.*

Time expressions used with:

Future Simple & Be going to	Future Perfect	Future Perfect Continuous
tomorrow, tonight, next week/month, in two/three etc days, the day after tomorrow, soon, in a week/month etc	before, by, by then, by the time, (**until** is used only in negative sentences with this tense)	by ... for

15 Fill in the correct future forms.

Technology has made such dramatic advances in the past decade that by the year 2100 who knows what changes **1)** ...*will have taken*... **(take)** place? It is quite likely that by 2020, we **2)** .... **(use up)** most of the earth's natural resources, and so, we **3)** .... **(rely)** on wind power and hydropower for our energy needs. As a result of this shortage of energy, it is quite probable that scientists **4)** .... **(find)** a way for us to live on another planet. By the next century, it's possible that people **5)** .... **(live)** in cities on the Moon or perhaps in cities on the seabed. It is hoped that scientists **6)** .... **(discover)** cures for fatal diseases such as Aids and, due to the advancement of genetic engineering, hereditary diseases passed down from generation to generation **7)** .... **(exist)** no longer. It is quite possible that by 2100, life expectancy **8)** .... **(increase)** to 100 and that we **9)** .... **(be able to)** enjoy a healthier existence than is now possible. Another area likely to have been further affected by technology in the next years is education. In schools, computers **10)** .... **(replace)** teachers and many students **11)** .... **(stay)** at home to complete their education. We **12)** .... **(see)** changes in the work-place too. The two main areas of employment **13)** .... **(be)** the so-called creative and caring professions, and the disappearance of jobs in manufacturing **14)** .... **(result)** in massive unemployment.

- We never use future forms after: as long as, as soon as, after, before, by the time, if (conditional), unless, in case, until/till, when (time conjunction), whenever, while, once, suppose/supposing, on condition that etc.
  Let's buy some extra food in case they **call** *round. (NOT: in case they will call round)*
- **When** used as a question word and **if** meaning "whether" (especially after I don't know, I doubt, I wonder etc) can be used with future forms.
  When will he bring *the books back? We don't know* **if he will be appointed** *to the post or not. (= whether)*

16 Fill in the correct present or future forms.

When you **1)** ...*take*... **(take)** a holiday with Activity Wales, you **2)** .... **(have)** the time of your life. As soon as you **3)** .... **(arrive)**, you **4)** .... **(feel)** as if you **5)** .... **(be)** in a different world. While you **6)** .... **(stay)** with us, we **7)** .... **(do)** our best to ensure that your holiday **8)** .... **(run)** smoothly and you **9)** .... **(not/get)** bored. Activity Wales **10)** .... **(have)** something to offer for all ages and tastes. If you **11)** .... **(want)** to play golf, ride, sail or fish, our staff **12)** .... **(be)** happy to make the necessary arrangements, or if you simply **13)** .... **(want)** to relax and enjoy the breathtaking view, we **14)** .... **(be)** delighted to organise some guided walks. Before your holiday **15)** .... **(be)** over, you **16)** .... **(already/plan)** your next visit.

17 Fill in will or be going to.

1 A: Why do you need so much sugar?
  B: I ...*'m going to*... make a cake.
2 A: Oh no! I've left my purse at home and I haven't got any money on me!
  B: Don't worry. I .... lend you some.
3 A: I don't know how to use this mixer.
  B: That's OK. I .... show you.

4   A: Why are all these people gathered here?
    B: The Prime Minister .... open the new hospital ward.
5   A: Did you remember to buy the magazine I asked for?
    B: Sorry, I didn't. I .... buy it when I go out again.
6   A: What's that on your curtains?
    B: It's a stain. I .... take them to the dry cleaner's tomorrow.
7   A: These bags are very heavy. I can't lift them.
    B: I .... carry them for you.
8   A: I hear you're going to Leeds University in September.
    B: Yes, I .... study French and German.
9   A: Why don't you tidy your room?
    B: I .... play football in ten minutes, so I haven't got time.
10 A: How can we get all this home?
    B: I .... ask James to come and help.

18   Put the verbs in brackets into the appropriate future forms.

A. From 14 - 20 June, Liverpool **1)** ...*will be holding/is holding*... **(hold)** its International Garden Festival. Tickets **2)** .... **(be)** on sale to the public from Saturday 1 May, and this year, we **3)** .... **(offer)** special family tickets at the discount price of £15. The gates **4)** .... **(open)** at 9 am and the first event **5)** .... **(start)** at 9.30.

B. Kenwhite's one-day sale **1)** .... **(start)** this Monday. The store **2)** .... **(open)** at 8 am and early morning shoppers **3)** .... **(be able to)** enjoy shopping in peace and quiet before the crowds **4)** .... **(arrive)**. We **5)** .... **(offer)** substantial discounts on ladieswear and you **6)** .... **(come across)** some real bargains in our menswear range. By the end of the day, we are sure that all of our customers **7)** .... **(find)** what they are looking for.

C. Anne Mayton's latest book "The S-Plan Diet" **1)** .... **(be)** available in bookshops next week. The new S-plan diet **2)** .... **(help)** you lose weight safely and quickly. You **3)** .... **(not/need)** to miss meals and you **4)** .... **(not/have to)** spend hours measuring out portions of food. By the end of the diet, the author guarantees you **5)** .... **(lose)** at least 7 kilos or she **6)** .... **(give)** you your money back.

Time Words

- **Ago:** back in time from now (used with Past Simple) *Ann left an hour* **ago**.
- **Before:** back in time from then. *Tony told me that Ann had left an hour* **before**. **Before** is also used with present or past forms to show that an action preceded another. *He'll come* **before** *you leave. He had cooked dinner* **before** *she came home.*
- **Already** is used with Perfect tenses in mid or end position in statements or questions. *He had* **already** *fixed the tap when the plumber arrived. Have you got dressed* **already**?
- **Yet** is used with Perfect tenses in negative sentences after a contracted auxiliary verb or at the end of the sentence. *He* **hasn't yet** *called. He hasn't called* **yet**. It can also be used at the end of questions. *Have they arrived* **yet**?
- **Still** is used in statements and questions after the auxiliary verb or before the main verb. *She can* **still** *dance well.* **Still** comes before the auxiliary verb in negations. *She* **still hasn't** *replied to my letter.*
- **Just** + present /past perfect - *She has* **just** *finished studying.*
  Just now + past simple - *She finished studying* **just now**.

19   Underline the correct item.

1   I'm sorry, I'm not ready to go out – I haven't finished doing the washing-up **already/<u>yet</u>**.
2   I don't think I've ever met her **yet/before**.
3   He's **still/yet** got a good memory even though he's almost eighty.
4   I used to live here six years **before/ago**.

5 He's lived in Rome all his life and he **yet**/**still** lives there.
6 I've **before**/**already** read this book – I don't want to read it again.
7 The last time I fed the goldfish was two days **before**/**ago**.
8 I can't believe I've been here nearly a year **yet**/**already**.
9 I'm afraid the plumber hasn't arrived **still**/**yet**.
10 He can **still**/**already** speak and he's only one year old.

20 Put the verbs in brackets into a correct tense.

A. Last summer, I **1)** ...*visited*... **(visit)** the United States. I **2)** .... **(look forward)** to the trip for ages, and I **3)** .... **(enjoy)** myself very much. On the 4th of July, a friend **4)** .... **(suggest)** we go and watch the fireworks. I **5)** .... **(see)** fireworks before, but I **6)** .... **(never/experience)** anything like the spectacle we **7)** .... **(witness)** that night.

B. Sarah **1)** .... **(leave)** school two years ago, and for the last year, she **2)** .... **(look)** for a decent job. She **3)** .... **(hope)** to find work as a secretary, but as she **4)** .... **(never/do)** a secretarial course before, I think she **5)** .... **(have)** some difficulty in finding such a job.

C. A: "Where **1)** .... **(you/be)** lately? The last time I **2)** .... **(see)** you **3)** .... **(be)** two years ago."
B: "I **4)** .... **(move)** to London 18 months ago – I **5)** .... **(work)** as a nurse there since then."
A: "Oh really! How **6)** .... **(it/go)**?"
B: "Great! I **7)** .... **(enjoy)** it very much at the moment, although at first, it **8)** .... **(be)** very hard."

D. A: "I **1)** .... **(have)** a party tonight. Would you like to come?"
B: "I'd love to, but unfortunately, I **2)** .... **(already/arrange)** to go out for dinner."
A: "What **3)** .... **(you/do)** tomorrow?"
B: "Not much. I think a friend **4)** .... **(come)** to visit me in the morning, but I **5)** .... **(not/have)** any plans for later in the day. **6)** .... **(you/fancy)** going for a drive?"

E. Peter **1)** .... **(drive)** to work yesterday when a dog **2)** .... **(run)** into the middle of the road. Peter **3)** .... **(manage)** to stop in time, but the car which **4)** .... **(follow)** behind him **5)** .... **(crash)** into the back of his car. Then, the two cars **6)** .... **(collide)** with a police car which **7)** .... **(travel)** in the opposite direction.

F. Some thieves **1)** .... **(break into)** my house yesterday. Apparently, I **2)** .... **(leave)** the window open. This is the first time anything like this **3)** .... **(happen)** to me. The thieves **4)** .... **(get in)** through the window and **5)** .... **(steal)** all my jewellery. None of the neighbours **6)** .... **(see)** anything happen.

G. A: "What **1)** .... **(you/do)** tonight?"
B: "I **2)** .... **(study)** for my exams."
A: "What time **3)** .... **(you/finish)** studying?
B: "I **4)** .... **(finish)** by 8 o'clock, I hope."
A: "Good – let's go to the cinema then. The film **5)** .... **(start)** at 8.30."

H. A: "**1)** .... **(you/see)** 'The Cure' concert last night?"
B: "No, but I **2)** .... **(see)** them before. I **3)** .... **(go)** to one of their concerts five years ago."
A: "They **4)** .... **(improve)** a lot since then."
B: "**5)** .... **(they/still/make)** records?"
A: "Oh yes, they **6)** .... **(just/release)** a new one."

I. This time next week, I **1)** .... **(be)** on my honeymoon and I **2)** .... **(forget)** all about my problems at work. My husband and I **3)** .... **(relax)** by the pool and we **4)** .... **(look forward)** to spending romantic evenings together.

21   **Complete the sentences. Mind the correct use of tense forms.**

1   I can't see you tonight because ...*I always go to the gym*... on Mondays.
2   Simon looks happy – he .... his test.
3   I'm sorry, Mum can't come to the phone because .... at the moment.
4   I wonder where Jim is; I .... since this morning.
5   By the time we arrived at the restaurant, they .... eating.
6   You .... fatter every day – you really should go on a diet.
7   Tim .... while Pam was watching TV.
8   By the end of next year, he .... in Madrid for three years.
9   She .... in Liverpool before she came to London.
10   She locked up the house, ... and drove away.
11   She's angry with her son because .... money from her purse.
12   I promise .... as soon as I get paid.
13   I wish they'd be quiet - they .... for hours.
14   By this time next week, we .... in Lisbon.
15   He hasn't finished the work yet, but he .... by this evening.
16   Before .... the questions, make sure you read the passage carefully.
17   The president .... Ohio in a week's time.
18   She .... on the project for two days before she finished it.
19   I .... tonight; would you like to join us?
20   He hasn't driven a car since .... that accident.

 In Other Words

- I've never met such a charming girl.
  She's the most charming girl I've ever met.
- It's a long time since she wrote to me.
  She hasn't written to me for a long time.
- She started learning French two years ago.
  She's been learning French for two years.
- When did he buy the flat?
  How long ago did he buy the flat?
  How long is it since he bought the flat?
- She hasn't returned yet.
  She still hasn't returned.

- I've never seen this film before.
  It's the first time I've ever seen this film.
- She came to London a year ago.
  She has been in London for a year.
- The last time I went out was a month ago.
  I haven't been out for a month.
- He started working as soon as she left.
  He didn't start working until she had left.
  He started working when she had left.
  He waited until she had left before he started working.

22   **Complete the sentences using the words in bold. Use two to five words.**

1   It's a week since I last saw him.
  seen   I ...*haven't seen him for*... a week.
2   When did she move to France?
  since   How long .... to France?
3   He has never seen this film before.
  ever   It's the first time .... this film.
4   The last time he visited her was a week ago.
  for   He .... a week.
5   They started eating as soon as the last guests arrived.
  had   They waited until the .... they started eating.
6   They started learning computing two months ago.
  been   They .... two months.

7 It's the fastest car I've ever driven.
   never I .... fast car.
8 They haven't come back yet.
   still They .... back.
9 How long is it since he broke his leg?
   break When .... his leg?
10 It's the first time he's ever seen a skyscraper.
   never He .... before.
11 She started writing a novel a year ago.
   been She .... for a year.
12 That's the smallest car I've ever seen.
   small I have .... car.
13 They didn't go to bed until the programme had finished.
   when They .... the programme finished.
14 I haven't called Ted for a long time.
   since It's a long time .... Ted.
15 She hasn't sold the house yet.
   still She .... house.
16 This is the most delicious meal I have ever eaten.
   such I have .... meal.
17 I've never read that book before.
   first It's the .... that book.
18 She started cooking when he arrived.
   until She .... she started cooking.
19 I haven't been swimming for a week.
   was The last .... a week ago.
20 He has been learning Russian for six months.
   started He .... ago.

Oral Development 3

Below are pictures of two people - Jack, a professional skier and Alice, a studio model. Say what they're doing now, then imagine what their lives were like 5 years ago, what their lives are like now and what their lives will be like in 5 years' time. Try to use a variety of tenses.

Jack is a professional skier. He has been training for more than ten years. etc

Phrasal Verbs

come across: meet/find by chance
come by: obtain
come down with: become ill with
come into: inherit
come off: 1) happen, 2) succeed
come out: 1) be published, 2) bloom
come round: 1) visit casually, 2) regain consciousness; come to, 3) be persuaded to change opinion
come on: come along; hurry up
come through: survive
come up: be mentioned
come up to: equal
come up with: find (an answer, solution etc)

....

cut across: take a shorter route
cut back (on): reduce (production)
cut down: reduce length of sth
cut down (on): reduce amount consumed
cut in/into: interrupt (conversation)
cut off: disconnect
be cut off: be isolated
cut out: 1) leave out; remove, 2) (for) (passive) be suited for
cut up: cut into small pieces

23 Fill in the correct particle(s).

1 Tim's work failed to come ...*up to*... his boss's high standards.
2 Sue came .... her favourite doll while she was clearing out the attic.
3 She'll come .... to the idea of buying a bigger house if we explain all the advantages.
4 Lovely yellow daffodils come .... in the spring.
5 The question of expanding the company came .... at the meeting.
6 He stayed in bed after he had come .... the measles.
7 He came .... a large fortune when his uncle died.
8 Her latest book has just come ....
9 The village was cut .... by the flood.
10 I don't think she's cut .... this kind of work.
11 Our electricity was cut .... after we forgot to pay the bill.
12 If you cut .... the field, you'll save time.
13 We are advised to cut .... our smoking.
14 You need to cut your summary .... - it's fifty words longer than necessary.
15 She cut .... the conversation to remind Bob it was time to go.

24 Complete the sentences using the words in bold. Use two to five words.

1 I'm sure it wasn't Jim who phoned.
   have   It ...*can't have been*... Jim who phoned.
2 They say he was the best footballer of the decade.
   said   He .... the best footballer of the decade.
3 It wasn't necessary for us to get a visa to visit Spain.
   need   We .... a visa to visit Spain.
4 I'm sure she has already left the office.
   have   She .... the office.
5 When did you get a letter from him?
   since   How long .... a letter from him?
6 Mr Pearce didn't take up golf until he retired.
   took   It wasn't until Mr Pearce .... golf.
7 He advises people on buying and selling houses.
   advice   He .... buying and selling houses.
8 It might snow this Christmas.
   possibility There .... this Christmas.
9 The accident wasn't my fault.
   blame   I .... the accident.
10 January was the last time I saw him.
   since   I .... January.
11 The book was so difficult that I couldn't understand it.
   for   The book was .... understand.
12 Tom didn't feel like going out.
   mood   Tom wasn't .... out.

25 Look at Appendix 1, then fill in the correct preposition.

1 Success depends ...on... good organisation.
2 The old woman died .... pneumonia.
3 He had difficulty .... understanding her.
4 The helicopter crashed .... a hill.
5 She's very fond .... her grandchildren.
6 He doesn't care .... his appearance.
7 She was very disappointed .... her rise.
8 Tom is envious .... his friends.
9 He was delighted .... his presents.
10 They decided .... a quiet wedding.
11 Pisa is famous .... its Leaning Tower.
12 She was furious .... him .... being late.
13 We are grateful .... you .... your help.
14 Have you heard .... Aunt Sheila?
15 Did you hear .... the robbery?
16 Have you heard .... this singer?

17 Smoking is harmful .... one's health.
18 He was found guilty .... six robberies.
19 There's no excuse .... his terrible behaviour.
20 He's an expert .... Middle-Eastern mythology.
21 The plumber was an expert .... unblocking drains.
22 If there's a delay .... claiming the money, you'll never get it back.
23 He's experienced .... archaeology.
24 The little girl dreams .... the same fearsome monster every night.
25 I would never dream .... leaving you.
26 His failure .... appear in court led to his being fined.
27 Her failure .... the exams disappointed her.
28 She's efficient .... typing.

26 Think of the word which best fits each space. Use only one word in each space.

The town of books

Hay-on-Wye is a tiny and picturesque town **(0)** ...which... sits on the border of England and Wales. It is often described **(1)** .... the town of books since it boasts an astonishing 40 second-hand bookshops. **(2)** .... the end of May every year **(3)** .... 1988, thousands of book lovers gather **(4)** .... attend the Hay Literary Festival and meet authors, listen to readings, and of **(5)** .... purchase books.

Old books **(6)** .... to be all over the town. You can even find **(7)** .... at the old cinema and fire station and in one of the pubs. You can step into people's front rooms and search **(8)** .... books piled up on the floor or on bookcases next to their TV **(9)** .... sofa. You can visit bookshops specialising **(10)** .... natural history, poetry, children's literature, and mysteries. There's also a bookshop **(11)** .... specialty is books about bees. Not surprisingly, it is **(12)** .... town's smallest.

Expressions with "Do"	Expressions with "Make"
one's best/worst, business with sb, a crossword, damage to, one's duty, an exercise, an experiment, somebody a favour, good, one's hair, harm, homework, housework, a job, lessons, sth for a living, miracles (for), research, right/wrong, a service, the shopping, a good turn, a translation, the washing-up, wonders, work, etc	allowances for, an appointment, an acquaintance, amends for, an arrangement, a bargain, the beds, the best of, a cake, certain, changes, coffee, a deal with sb, a decision, a difference, a discovery, an effort, an enemy of, ends meet, an excuse, friends with, a fortune, haste, fun of, a fool of somebody, an impression, improvements, a joke, a mess, a mistake, money, a note, a nuisance, a noise, an offer, peace, preparations, a profit, progress, sure, a translation, trouble, war, a will etc

27 Fill in do or make in the correct form.

1 Have you ...done... the washing-up yet?
2 Will you .... me a favour?
3 She tried to .... a soufflé, but it was a complete failure.
4 Don't .... such a fuss about unimportant things.
5 She .... a very good impression at the interview yesterday.

6 They've already .... all the preparations for the party.
7 I promise I'll .... my best to make it work.
8 I don't think this .... any sense.
9 Don't take so many pills. They won't .... you any good.
10 I'm not feeling well. I'd better .... an appointment with the doctor.
11 She .... a fortune selling cosmetics.
12 After eight years of war, both countries agreed to .... peace.
13 He .... a very good job mending my roof.
14 I can't believe this is my old house. You .... wonders with it!
15 The oil-producing companies .... an agreement to keep the prices low this year.

28 **Use the words in capitals to form a word that fits in the space in the same line.**

CANOLA OIL - The New Petrol?

Imagine a motor oil that can cut car **(0)** ...pollution... by 40 percent. Duane Johnson doesn't have to imagine such a product any more. He's made it a **(1)** ....! Johnson, a new and alternative crops specialist, has developed a lubricant from canola oil, a seed crop grown in Colorado. This lubricant **(2)** .... reduces harmful emissions from car engines. Canola oil is **(3)** .... used as a cooking oil especially in Asian foods. However, with certain **(4)** ...., it is as **(5)** .... as any normal motor oil. Canola oil is **(6)** .... for several reasons. Apart from reducing air pollution, it creates a useful by-product called meal, which can be fed to animals. Another **(7)** .... point is that it can be grown as a crop every year, and this makes it a renewable energy source, **(8)** .... petrol. In the event of an oil spill, canola is **(9)** .... friendly to soil or water. Perhaps the most **(10)** .... point of all is that, when burned in an engine, canola oil smells like popcorn!

POLLUTE

REAL

DRASTIC
TRADITION
ADJUST
EFFECT
BENEFIT

FAVOUR
LIKE
ENVIRONMENT
INTEREST

29 **Complete the sentences using the words in bold. Use two to five words.**

0 Although he tried hard, he failed the exam.
   even   He didn't pass the exam *...even though he tried...* hard.
1 That car is too expensive for us to buy.
   afford   We can't .... that car.
2 My parents always stay at home at weekends.
   anywhere   My parents .... at weekends.
3 Would you like another cup of coffee?
   get   Can .... another cup of coffee?
4 I haven't visited this town for ages.
   since   It's been .... this town.
5 When did you start working here?
   been   How .... working here?
6 Barbara hasn't finished her project yet.
   still   Barbara .... her project.
7 If you don't know what to do, ask Mary.
   sure   If you .... do, ask Mary.
8 We can have lunch outside if the weather is good.
   unless   We can have lunch outside .... bad.

4 Clauses / Linking Words

Sentences can consist of main and subordinate clauses. Subordinate clauses can be:
- **noun clauses:** *I know **that he'll be a little late**.*
- **relative clauses:** *Show me the pictures **which you took**.*
- **adverbial clauses (clauses of time, place, manner, reason, concession, purpose, result, comparison, condition)** *He left early **so as not to miss the bus**.*

Relative Clauses

Relative clauses are introduced by: a) relative pronouns, i.e. **who**, **whom**, **whose**, **which** or **that** or b) relative adverbs i.e. **when**, **where** or **why**.

Relative Pronouns

	Subject of the verb of the relative clause (cannot be omitted)	Object of the verb of the relative clause (can be omitted)	Possession (cannot be omitted)
used for people	**who/that** *That's the man **who**/**that** stole the money.*	**whom/who/that** *The man **(who/whom/that)** you saw last night was my uncle.*	**whose** *That's the girl **whose** brother is a singer.*
used for things/ animals	**which/that** *I read a book **which**/**that** was written by Samuel Johnson.*	**which/that** *The cat **(which/that)** you saw lying on the sofa is my favourite one.*	**whose/of which** *That's the coat the sleeves **of which**/ **whose** sleeves are made of velvet.*

- **Whom, which, whose** can be used in expressions of quantity with **of** (some of, many of, half of etc) *She received a lot of postcards. Most of them were from her friends. She received a lot of postcards, **most of which** were from her friends.*
- **That** can be used instead of **who**, **whom** or **which** but it is never used after commas or prepositions. *She's the actress who/that was awarded first prize. The man in the corner, **who** is sitting next to Jane, is my uncle. ('that' is not possible.)*

Relative Adverbs

Time	**when** (= in/on/at which)	*1982 was the year **(when)** I moved to Wales.*
Place	**where** (= in/at/on/to which)	*That's the hotel **where** we spent our honeymoon.*
Reason	**why** (= for which)	*That's the reason **(why)** they were celebrating.*

Prepositions in Relative Clauses

We do not normally use prepositions before relative pronouns.
*The house **in which** she lives is in the suburbs. (formal - not usual)*
*The house **which** she lives in is in the suburbs. (usual)*
*The house she lives **in** is in the suburbs. (more usual)*

 Fill in: where, whose, who, which, why **or** when.

Having visited a few countries **1)** ...*where*.... the climate is different to yours, you will appreciate how important it is to plan carefully before travelling. Not planning well enough is the reason **2)** .... some holidays can go wrong. A holiday **3)** .... involves a lot of walking, for example, means you need to go at a time **4)** .... it is neither too hot nor too cold. It also means you need to plan to go with someone **5)** .... enjoys walking and **6)** .... stamina is equal to yours. A travel companion **7)** .... likes the same things as you is ideal, but it's very difficult to meet someone **8)** .... likes and dislikes are exactly the same as yours. In any case, you need to decide on a holiday **9)** .... suits both of you and a country **10)** .... climate is not uncomfortable for either of you.

2 Rewrite the sentences in as many ways as possible.

1 That's the zoo where they took the tiger.
...That's the zoo to which they took the tiger. That's the zoo they took the tiger to....

2 The place where you went is my home town.
....

3 That's the girl he gave the present to.
....

4 He's the one person on whom she can depend.
....

5 This is the park where the village fair is held.
....

Defining / Non-defining Relative Clauses

● A **defining relative clause** gives necessary information and is essential to the meaning of the main clause. It is not put between commas. *People **who hunt illegally** should be punished.*

● A **non-defining relative clause** gives extra information which is not essential to the meaning of the main clause. It is put between commas. *Her mother, **who is a kind woman**, has helped her a lot.*
Note how the commas change the meaning of the sentence.
*The players, who were involved in the fight, were sent off the pitch. **(all the players were sent off.)** The players who were involved in the fight were sent off the pitch. **(only the players who were involved in the fight were sent off)***

3 Fill in the relative pronoun adding commas where necessary. Write D for defining, ND for non-defining and whether the relative pronoun can be omitted or not.

1 That's the man ...*who/that...* I was talking about. ..*D*.. ...*omitted*...
2 Her school .... is very old is closing down. ....
3 Have you seen the pencil .... I bought yesterday? ....
4 Ann .... contract expires next week is looking for another job. ....
5 This house .... he inherited from his parents is worth a fortune. ....
6 The company .... I set up last year is expanding. ....
7 She is the singer .... latest record reached the top of the charts. ....
8 I've never met anyone before .... was quite so rude. ....
9 This jumper .... my grandmother knitted for me, is too small. ....
10 The necklace .... I bought in Egypt is very old. ....
11 They are the friends .... invited us to their daughter's wedding. ....
12 The documentary .... I saw last night was very informative. ....
13 Elephants .... are hunted for ivory are becoming extinct. ....
14 The girl .... speaks four languages is in my class. ....
15 This is the hospital .... was built in 1920. ....
16 The police are looking for a man .... car was found abandoned in Newcastle last night. ....
17 That man .... name is Bill stole my purse. ....
18 She is a person .... I shall always be grateful to. ....
19 He's the man .... she's going to marry. ....
20 This book .... is about Vietnam is fascinating. ....
21 I know few people .... are as considerate as she is. ....
22 His group .... is touring Europe is called "Blunt". ....
23 The woman .... dog was stolen is offering a reward. ....
24 I met a really interesting man .... name I have since forgotten. ....
25 She's the girl .... I'm sharing my flat with. ....
26 My team .... won the cup are going to tour America. ....
27 "Macbeth" is a play .... was written by Shakespeare. ....

4 Clauses / Linking Words

4   Use relative pronouns/adverbs to combine the following sentences as in the example.

1 That's the hotel. We stayed there last summer. ...*That's the hotel where we stayed last summer*....
2 This is the car. He drives to work in it every day. ....
3 That's the actor. He was in the film you mentioned. ....
4 She bought a brooch. It once belonged to a duchess. ....
5 That's the house. It was damaged in the earthquake. ....
6 They met a man. His fortune is believed to be around £3,000,000. ....
....
7 That's the mansion. The Queen's youngest son lives there. ....
8 They called a woman. She was a psychic. ....
9 We went back to the café. I'd left my purse there. ....
10 That's the painting. It is a Picasso masterpiece. ....

 In Other Words ————————————————————————

- That's the town I was born in.
  That's the town where I was born.
  That's the town in which I was born.
- They let us stay, which was kind of them.
  It was kind of them to let us stay.
- This is Mr Foster; his son is a famous pianist.
  This is Mr Foster whose son is a famous pianist.
- Sunday is the day when she got married.
  Sunday is the day on which she got married.
- I bought a fridge which was faulty.
  The fridge I bought was faulty.

- That man gave my brother a job.
  That's the man who gave my brother a job.
- She brought some letters, but none of them were for me.
  She brought some letters, none of which were for me.
- They arrested six men; two of them are Swiss.
  They arrested six men, two of whom are Swiss.

5   Complete the sentences using the words in bold. Use two to five words.

1 He lost his passport, which was silly of him.
  lose   It was ...*silly of him to lose*... his passport.
2 That's the hotel we are staying in.
  where   That's .... staying.
3 That woman complained to the manager.
  who   That's .... to the manager.
4 We met several people from Portsmouth, but none of them knew Dr Irons.
  whom   We met several people from Portsmouth, ... Dr Irons.
5 The car we rented was very unreliable.
  which   We .... very unreliable.
6 Clare Spender is the author; her book became a bestseller overnight.
  whose   Clare Spender is .... a bestseller overnight.
7 We bought a kilo of apples; some of them were bruised.
  which   We bought a kilo of apples, ... bruised.
8 August is the month when most people take their holidays.
  which   August .... most people take their holidays.
9 She has a class of twenty students; half of them are of Canadian origin.
  whom   She has a class of twenty students, ... are of Canadian origin.
10 Sue tried on some shoes but none of them fitted.
  which   Sue tried on some shoes, ... fitted.
11 At the film festival we saw many people; some were famous actors.
  whom   At the film festival we saw many people, ... famous actors.

Clauses / Linking Words 4

Clauses of Time

- Clauses of time are introduced by: **after, as, as long as, as soon as, just as, once, since, when, before, by the time** (= before, not later than), **while, until/till** (= up to the time when), **the moment (that), whenever, every time, immediately** etc. *He bought a villa as soon as he got the money.*
- Time clauses follow the rule of the sequence of tenses; that is, when the verb of the main clause is in a present or future form, the verb of the time clause is in a present form, and when the verb of the main clause is in a past form, the verb of the time clause is in a past form too. Note that **will** is never used in clauses of time. *I'll give it to you when you tell me why you want it. (NOT: ~~when you will tell me~~) She had finished reading before they came home. (NOT: ~~before they come home~~)*
- When the time clause precedes the main clause, a comma is used. When the time clause follows, no comma is used. *When he finishes, he can go home. He can go home when he finishes.*
- when (time conjunction) + present tense   *When he comes, he'll tell you.*
  when (question word) + will/would   *When will he come?*
- **If** is used for things which may happen. *Wait for me if I'm late.*
  When is used for things which are sure to happen. *I'll be back when I finish shopping.*

6 Underline the appropriate time phrase and put the verbs into the correct tense.

New research offers proof that global warming is a direct consequence of man's activity on earth and not a result of some unidentified natural phenomenon. **1)** (**After/As soon as**) noting climate changes on a computer, researchers **2)** .... (**show**) that the Earth's average temperature has risen by 0.7°C **3)** (**before/ since**) the Industrial Revolution. **4)** (**While/As soon as**) the results were published, climate changes once again **5)** .... (**become**) headline news.
Other research predicts that **6)** (**by/by the time**) the end of the century, average rainfall will be 30% higher than today as a result of a warmer climate. Air pollution is blamed for the sharp rise in the Earth's temperature and **7)** (**until/whenever**) strict laws **8)** .... (**be/introduced**), the problem will continue to get worse. Something needs to be done **9)** (**the moment/before**) it **10)** .... (**be**) too late.
11) (**When/Whenever**) EU countries **12)** .... (**meet**) last month, they agreed to cut down on pollution levels. **13)** (**Just as/Once**) alternative sources of power **14)** ....
(**be/developed**), we will have taken the first steps towards stopping global warming.

7 Fill in **if** or **when** and put the verbs into the correct tense.

1 Tom will phone you ...*when*... he ...*wakes up*... (**wake up**).
2 .... do you think you .... (**finish**) the project?
3 .... there .... (**be**) any problems, I will phone you.
4 .... the exams .... (**be**) over, we will have a party.
5 .... Ted .... (**apply**) for the job, I'm sure he will get it.
6 .... we .... (**arrive**) late at the theatre, there will be no tickets left.
7 I have no idea .... he .... (**return**) from his trip to Paris.
8 .... (**you/stop**) interfering in my life?
9 Please let me know .... you .... (**hear**) from them, will you?
10 .... we .... (**have**) nothing else to discuss, we can all leave now.

8 Complete the sentences in any meaningful way using an appropriate time word.

1 They had finished packing ...*before/by the time we returned from work.* ...
2 A door-to-door salesman turned up ....
3 She came across her childhood diary ....
4 ...., the baby had already been born.
5 ...., he realised he was being followed.
6 .... the report, I will have it typed.

49

4 Clauses / Linking Words

Clauses of Reason

- Clauses of reason are introduced by: **as, since, because, for, the reason for, the reason (why), on the grounds that** etc. *As he was late for work, he got a taxi.*
- **Because** usually answers a why-question. *"Why did you lie to him?" "Because I was afraid of being punished."* **For** always comes after a comma in written speech or a pause in oral speech. *I didn't tell him anything, for I don't trust him.*
- Other ways of expressing reason:
  Because of/Due to + noun/-ing form *She was late because of/due to heavy traffic.*
  Because of/Due to + the fact that ... *Because of the fact that/Due to the fact that it had been snowing for four days, all roads were closed.*

Clauses of Result

- Clauses of result are introduced by: **that** (after **such/so ...**), **(and) as a result, (and) as a consequence, consequently, so** etc. *The sea is so cold that they can't swim.*

such a(n) + (adjective) + singular countable	It was **such a nice dress** that she bought it.
such + (adjective) + uncountable /plural noun	It was **such bad weather** that we stayed indoors.
such + a lot of + noun	There were **such a lot of people** on the bus that there were no seats left.
so + adjective/adverb	He speaks **so quickly** that hardly anyone can understand him.
so + much/many/little/few + noun	She won **so much money** in the lottery that she bought a mansion.
so + adjective + a(n) + noun	It was **so delicious a cake** that we ate it all. *(not usual)*
as a result/therefore/consequently/so + clause	He didn't have a visa and **as a result he couldn't enter the country**.

9   **Fill in** so, such **or** such a(n).

Mandy was getting **1)** ...*so*.... bored one afternoon that she decided to go shopping. She always took **2)** .... pleasure in buying things for herself that she would often spend lots of money in just one day. She set out feeling really excited. After two hours, she had bought **3)** .... many things that she could hardly carry them. The shops were closing and there was **4)** .... lot of traffic in the streets that she couldn't find a taxi. She started feeling frustrated as the parcels and bags she was carrying were getting in everyone's way. She was **5)** .... anxious to get back home that she decided to take the underground. She took **6)** .... long time to find her purse among her things that people waiting behind her in the queue started muttering. When she finally found it, there was **7)** .... little money in it that she didn't have enough to buy a ticket. Mandy was **8)** .... embarrassed that she just wanted to disappear. She left the station and was in **9)** .... desperate state that she didn't know what to do. "I've spent **10)** .... much money," she thought, "that I've made a fool of myself in front of complete strangers." Mandy eventually got home with all her shopping after getting a lift in a pizza delivery van!

10   **Join the sentences using the words in brackets.**

1 It was a hard job. We were exhausted by the time we had finished. **(such...that)**
   ...*It was such a hard job that we were exhausted by the time we had finished*....
2 He'd forgotten to bring the report with him. He had to go home and get it. **(because)**
   ....

50

3 The food was bad. We complained to the manager. **(Since ...)**

....

4 It was a long journey. They packed some food to take with them. **(due to the fact)**

....

5 I hate sailing. I get seasick. **(the reason)**

....

6 Their house is too small. They are going to look for a larger one. **(consequently)**

....

7 Sharon is busy this weekend. She can't come to the seaside with us. **(Since)**

....

8 The exam was difficult. Many students failed. **(such ... that)**

....

9 They fell behind with the project. They had to work overtime. **(as a result)**

....

10 Their flight was delayed. They spent the night in a hotel. **(as)**

....

 In Other Words

- He was so busy that he couldn't talk to me.
  He was too busy to talk to me.
- It's such an expensive dress that I can't buy it.
  The dress is too expensive for me to buy.
- No one knows the reason for his absence.
  No one knows (the reason) why he is absent.

- It was such a nice day that we went out.
  It was so nice a day that we went out.
- The flight was cancelled because there was a strike.
  The flight was cancelled due to/because of a strike.
- He lost his ticket so he couldn't board the plane.
  He lost his ticket and as a result/consequently/therefore he couldn't board the plane.

11 Complete the sentences using the words in bold. Use two to five words.

1 The team were so good that we couldn't beat them.
such   They were ...*such a good team that*... we couldn't beat them.
2 It was such a boring film that we left in the middle of it.
so   It was .... we left in the middle of it.
3 No one knows why they are emigrating.
for   No one knows .... emigration.
4 Our car broke down so we were very late.
consequently Our car broke down, ... very late.
5 She was so insistent that we couldn't ignore her.
too   She was .... ignore.
6 They couldn't go to the post office because of a snowstorm.
as   They couldn't go to the post office .... snowstorm.
7 She had a very bad night's sleep, so she was exhausted.
result   She had a very bad night's sleep, ..., she was exhausted.
8 Do you know the reason for her leaving her job?
why   Do .... her job?
9 The coffee was so strong that I couldn't drink it.
such   It .... that I couldn't drink it.
10 He was such a skilful player that he seldom lost a game.
so   He was .... he seldom lost a game.
11 He didn't get the job because he was inexperienced.
to   He didn't get the job .... experience.

Oral Development 4

Use the notes below and your own ideas to talk about Clare Harvard. Try to link your ideas together using relative pronouns/adverbs, time words, and words introducing clauses of reason or result.

Clare Harvard from Portsmouth

- wanted a career in management
- studied hard - got a place at university
- worked extremely hard at university - passed all her exams
- got a Management degree
- graduated - was offered a job in a large multinational company
- ambitious and was promoted within a year
- well-respected by her colleagues for her hard work and dedication

S1: *Clare, who comes from Portsmouth, wanted a career in management.*
She studied hard so that she could get a place at university ...

12 Complete the sentences using the words in bold. Use two to five words.

1 She gave us a lift, which was kind of her.
  of   It was ...*kind of her to give*... us a lift.
2 That's the college my son got his degree from.
  where   That's .... got his degree.
3 I bought several dictionaries, but none of them are really up to date.
  which   I bought .... are really up to date.
4 This is Emma Thompson; her husband is an Oscar nominee.
  whose   This is Emma Thompson, ... nominee.
5 The reason for his resignation is strictly personal.
  why   The reason .... strictly personal.
6 It was such an appalling event that we'd rather forget about it.
  so   It was .... we'd rather forget about it.
7 It was so late that I couldn't get to the meeting.
  too   It was .... get to the meeting.
8 He forgot to post his application, so he didn't get called for an interview.
  result   He forgot to post his application, ..., he didn't get called for an interview.
9 He came into his inheritance and immediately after he bought a bigger house.
  soon   He bought a bigger house .... into his inheritance.
10 The children were so polite that everyone took to them.
  such   They were .... everyone took to them.
11 When he got the phone call, he left the house immediately.
  moment   He left the house .... the phone call.
12 The last time I saw Peter was 14 February.
  since   I .... 14 February.
13 Careless drivers should be punished.
  carelessly People .... should be punished.
14 One of the five students he interviewed was Spanish.
  whom   He interviewed .... was Spanish.

Expressing Purpose - Clauses of Purpose

Purpose is expressed with:

● to/in order to/so as to + inf	*I'll leave home early **to get** to work on time. **(informal)*** *She's studying **so as to qualify** as a lawyer. **(formal)***
● so that + can/will (present/future reference) ● so that + could/would (past reference)	*She works hard **so that** she **will** have better career prospects.* *He gave me directions **so that** I **could** find his house easily.*
● with a view to/with the aim of + -ing form	*He did a Master's degree **with the aim of applying** for a managerial post when he had finished.*
● for + noun/-ing form	*This is a knife **for cutting** bread.*
● in case + Present Simple (present/future reference) ● in case + Past Simple (past reference)	*I'll write it down **in case** I **forget** it.* *He took an umbrella **in case** it **rained**.*

Negative Purpose is normally expressed with:

● so as not/in order not + to -inf	*She studied hard **so as not/in order not to fail** her test.* *(NOT: She studied hard ~~not to fail~~ her test.)*
● so that + can't/won't (present/future reference) so that + couldn't/wouldn't (past reference)	*Tie up the dog **so that** it **won't** get out of the garden.* *She locked the door **so that** burglars **couldn't** get in.*
● for fear/lest + might/should for fear of sth/doing sth	*He didn't say where he was going **for fear** he **might** be followed.* *He gave them all his money **for fear of being** shot.*
● prevent + noun/pronoun + (from) + -ing form	*She put on her raincoat to **prevent herself (from) getting soaked**.*
● avoid + -ing form	*He took a taxi to work to **avoid being** late.*

● **Clauses of Purpose** follow the rule of the sequence of tenses.
*She's **going to buy** a dictionary **so that** her spelling **will improve**. They **tied** him up **so that** he **wouldn't escape**.*

13 Rephrase the following sentences in as many ways possible as in the example.

1 I brought her a present. I wanted to cheer her up. ...*I brought her a present so as to cheer her up. I brought her a present in order to cheer her up. I brought her a present to cheer her up. I brought her a present so that I could cheer her up. I brought her a present with the aim of cheering her up.... etc*

2 She didn't answer the phone. She didn't want to have to talk to anyone. ....
....
....

3 They bought a bigger house. They wanted to have more room. ....
....
....

4 He always kept a spare tyre in the boot. He might have a puncture. ....
....
....

5 The hospital staff went on strike. They wanted to protest about working conditions. ....
....
....

6 Pauline didn't go to the party. She didn't want to bump into Ian. ....
....
....

---

14 Use the notes below to write the letter. Use purpose words where possible.

Dear Mr Bowes,

1 I write/invite you/attend/interview/27th May/Edge Hill College.
....

2 We hold interviews/view/appoint/Senior Lecturer/English Department.
....

3 If you be unable/attend/please phone/college as soon as possible/we arrange/alternative date.
....

4 You/be requested/read/enclosed information/avoid waste time on the day of the interview.
....

5 The day last/9 am to 3.30 pm/give interviewees time/familiarise themselves/college.
....

6 When you arrive/college/please report/reception/you be shown/staff common room.
....

I look forward to meeting you shortly.

Yours sincerely,
M. Davies
(Head of English Dept.)

---

15 Complete the sentences using the words in bold. Use two to five words.

---

1 I didn't tell her the bad news. I didn't want to upset her.
   avoid   I didn't tell her the bad news ...*to avoid upsetting*... her.
2 Mary wrote out a shopping list. She didn't want to forget anything.
   that   Mary wrote out a shopping list .... forget anything.
3 Paul trained hard every day. He wanted to be the best.
   as   Paul trained hard every day .... the best.
4 Lee gave up her job. She planned to continue her education.
   view   Lee gave up her job .... her education.
5 She turned the oven off. She didn't want to burn the cakes.
   might   She turned the oven off .... burn the cakes.
6 He was saving all his money. He intended to buy a house.
   aim   He was saving all his money .... a house.
7 Peter left the office early. He wanted to be at the cinema on time.
   in   Peter left the office early .... at the cinema on time.
8 This is a pencil sharpener. You use it to sharpen pencils.
   for   This is a pencil sharpener. It is used .... pencils.
9 I'll bring a pack of cards. We might want to play later.
   case   I'll bring a pack of cards .... play later.
10 We didn't want to get stuck in a traffic jam so we bypassed the city centre.
   avoid   We bypassed the city centre .... in a traffic jam.

11 Before we went to Africa we had injections so we wouldn't get malaria.
prevent   Before we went to Africa, we had injections .... malaria.
12 He's taking his camera on holiday. He might want to take some photos of the wildlife.
case   He's taking his camera on holiday .... to take some photos of the wildlife.
13 Peter goes to night school. He wants to learn French.
order   Peter goes to night school .... French.
14 If you want him to remember to phone the bank, leave a note on his desk.
that   Leave a note on his desk .... to phone the bank.
15 She tries her best. She wants to stand out in her field.
as   She tries her best .... in her field.

Oral Development 5

Peter has decided to go on a mountaineering holiday. Look at the list below then decide, in order of importance, which things he should take with him and why. You can mention items which are not in the list. Use words of purpose to link your ideas together.

map, compass, rope, thick jacket, sleeping bag, climbing boots, warm clothes, insect repellent, swimming trunks, evening suit, suntan lotion, thick socks, suitcase, waterproof

Peter should take a map and a compass in case he gets lost.

Expressing Concession - Clauses of Concession

Concession is expressed with:

- although/even though/though + clause
- despite/in spite of + noun/-ing form
- despite/in spite of the fact + that-clause
- while/whereas/but/on the other hand/yet + clause
- nevertheless/however + clause
- however/no matter how + adj/adv + subject (+ may) + verb
- whatever/no matter what + clause
- adj/adv + though + subject + verb/(may + bare inf)
- adj/adv + as + subject + verb

Although it was expensive, she bought it.
Despite his wealth/being rich, he never lends money.
In spite of the fact that he's rich, he never lends money.
*She swam fast, **yet she finished third**.*
*He is bright; **however, he is rather lazy**.*
However clever you are, you won't solve this puzzle.
However fast he runs, he won't catch the robbers.
Whatever you do, you won't succeed.
Loudly though he knocked on the door, nobody heard.
Exhausted as she was, she went to the party.

- Note that a comma is used when the clause of concession either precedes or follows the main clause.
Whatever she says, he won't believe her. He won't believe her, whatever she says.

16 Underline the correct item.

1 **However/Despite** the great danger, we decided to attempt the rescue.
2 **In spite of the fact that/Despite** she is disabled, she plays a lot of sports.
3 He decided not to do the computer course, **although/whereas** it would have been useful to him.
4 He knows he is damaging his health, **despite/yet** he continues to smoke.
5 **Even though/In spite of** strong opposition from the public, the company went ahead with its plans.
6 Brilliant **though/although** the cook may be, he knows nothing about French sauces.
7 **Although/However** he ate a lot of spicy food at the reception, he didn't suffer from indigestion.
8 I can't agree with you on this subject, **however/whatever** hard you may try to convince me.
9 I arrived late at the cinema, **but/as** I still got a good seat.
10 **No matter how/No matter what** measures the government takes against hooliganism, there will still be fans who overreact.

17 Rephrase the sentences in as many ways as possible in order to express concession.

1 He prepared the meal very quickly. Everyone enjoyed it. ...*Although/Even though he prepared the meal very quickly, everyone enjoyed it. Despite/In spite of his having prepared the meal very quickly, everyone enjoyed it. etc...*
2 She disliked the book. She read all of it. ....
   ....
3 He has a good income. He only rents a small flat. ....
   ....
4 She's been having French lessons for years. She doesn't speak French very well. ....
   ....
   ....
5 She went shopping yesterday. The cupboards are already bare. ....
   ....
   ....
6 He set his alarm for 6 am. He was still late for work. ....
   ....
7 They took their costumes with them. They didn't go swimming. ....
   ....
   ....

18 Fill the gaps with the following words.

whatever, no matter how, although, nevertheless, in spite of, whereas

Pirates of the Caribbean: At World's End

Our favourite pirates are back again in this third and final film in the *Pirates of the Caribbean* trilogy! The adventure starts with Will (Orlando Bloom) and Elizabeth (Keira Knightly) going to rescue Captain Jack Sparrow (Johny Depp) from the dead. Depp is as convincing as ever as Captain Jack. **1)** ...*In spite of*... his good heart, he can be cunning and mean. But he is so funny and crazy that you just can't help loving him, **2)** .... he does! Knightly and Bloom also give spectacular performances. The film is a bit scary in parts, **3)** .... other parts are quite sentimental and romantic. **4)** ...., kids will love it! But *Pirates of the Caribbean* isn't just for kids. You're sure to enjoy it **5)** .... old you are! All in all, **6)** .... it's a little long (almost three hours), this is a great film. If you only see one film this year, this should be it!

19 Complete the sentences using the words in bold. Use two to five words.

1 She tried hard, but she couldn't solve the problem.
   as   Hard ...*as she tried*...,she couldn't solve the problem.
2 However much you complain, they won't give you a refund.
   how   No .... complain, they won't give you a refund.
3 He's a writer, but he often makes spelling mistakes.
   being   In .... a writer, he often makes spelling mistakes.
4 Although she exercises a lot, she's not very strong.
   fact   Despite .... a lot, she's not very strong.
5 In spite of his leaving home early, he was late for the appointment.
   though   Even .... early, he was late for the appointment.
6 The plot was complicated, but I enjoyed the film a lot.
   though   Complicated ...., I enjoyed the film a lot.
7 John works as a travel agent, but he's never been abroad.
   of   In .... a travel agent, John has never been abroad.
8 However hard he tried, he didn't succeed.
   matter   He didn't succeed, ... he tried.
9 In spite of having a good voice, he could never be a professional singer.
   has   Although ...., he could never be a professional singer.
10 She did her best. She failed the exam.
   yet   She .... failed the exam.

Look at the pictures below and the information given. Talk about each of the women using words expressing concession as in the example. You may also use your own ideas.

Mary

Jane

housewife/used to teach before her children were born
children have now grown up/decided not to go back to work
enjoys gardening/garden is too big to look after on her own
would like to become more involved in community life/not have much free time

managing director/doesn't find work very stressful
lives alone/doesn't feel lonely
loves cooking/not much time to spend in the kitchen
quite enjoys entertaining clients in the evenings/prefers spending time on her own

Although Mary's a housewife now, she used to teach before her children were born ...

Clauses of Manner

● **Clauses of manner** are introduced by: **as if/as though** (after the verbs act, appear, be, behave, feel, look, seem, smell, sound, taste), **as**, **how**, **(in) the way**, **(in) the way that**, **the way in which**, **(in) the same way**, **(in) the same way as**.
*It **smells as if** they are frying chicken. Do **as** you like.*

● **Were** can be used instead of **was** in formal English in all persons in clauses introduced with **as if/as though**.
*She behaves **as if** she **were/was** the Queen.*

● The tense forms used after **as if/as though** depend on whether the ideas are true or untrue.

> **as if/as though + any tense form** (expressing similarity/probability - how sb/sth seemed)
> *She sounds **as if** she **is** Italian. (She may be Italian.)*
> *She looked **as if** she **was** tired. (She may have been tired.)*
>
> **as if/as though + Past Simple/Past Continuous** (unreal in the present)
> *She treats me **as if** she **were** my mother. (but she isn't)*
>
> **as if/as though + Past Perfect** (unreal in the past)
> *She talked about Marilyn Monroe **as if** they **had been** close friends. (but they hadn't been)*

20 Put the verbs in brackets into the correct tense.

1 Does he ever have a holiday? It seems as though he ...*works*... **(works)** seven days a week!
2 My father is so proud of his cooking - he behaves as though he .... **(be)** a trained chef.
3 The boy was staring at the motorbike as if he .... **(never/see)** one before.
4 She is so skinny! She looks as though she .... **(never/eat)** a proper meal in her life!
5 He slept for ten hours last night, but today he's acting as though he ....
(not/have) any sleep at all.
6 She isn't a member of the aristocracy, but she acts as though she .... **(be)**.
7 My brother isn't rich but he spends money as if he .... **(be)** a millionaire.
8 He talked about Hawaii as if he .... **(be)** there, but we knew he hadn't.
9 The boy was so hungry that he ate the food as though he .... **(not/eat)** for a week.
10 The hand-painted bowl was quite cheap, but it looked as though it .... **(be)** expensive.
11 You look as though you .... **(have)** some good news recently.
12 It seems as if the burglar .... **(break in)** through the study window.
13 As Mansell rounds the last corner, it looks as if he .... **(win)** the race easily.
14 I talked to him on the phone and he sounded as though he .... **(just/wake up)**.
15 The baby seems as if it .... **(have)** a temperature; why don't you get the thermometer?

21 Complete the sentences using the words in bold. Use two to five words.

1 He was hungry. He felt like he could eat a horse.
   as   He was so hungry he ...*felt as though he could*... eat a horse.
2 Someone must have added too much salt to the soup.
   though   The soup tasted .... too much salt.
3 He seems to have put on weight since I last saw him.
   if   He looks .... on weight since I last saw him.
4 She had a feeling that she had been in that house before.
   if   She felt .... in that house before.
5 I installed the computer as he had instructed me.
   way   I installed the computer .... instructed me.
6 He isn't a rock star but he behaves like one.
   though   He behaves .... a rock star.
7 She seemed to need a rest.
   if   She looked .... a rest.

Exclamations

- **Exclamations** are used to express anger, fear, shock, surprise etc. They always take an exclamation mark (!). Some exclamations are: **Oh dear!**, **Ah!**, **Oh!**, **Good gracious!** etc.

. . . .

- **What + a(n) + (adjective) + singular countable noun**   *What a nice day!*

- **What + (adjective) + uncountable/plural noun**   *What awful weather!* *What nice manners!*

- **How + adjective/adverb**   *How clever he is!* *How slowly he speaks!*

- **You + (adjective) + noun**   *You (filthy) liar!*

- **such (a/an) + (adjective) + noun**   *It's such an old car!*

- **so + adjective/adverb**   *He's so nice to us!*

- **adverb/adverbial particle + subject + verb of movement**   *Off he went!*

- **Here/There + subject + verb**   *There she goes! BUT:* ***There** goes Mary! (when the subject is a noun, it follows the verb)*

- **Interrogative - negative question at the beginning of the sentence**   *Isn't it awful!*

---

22   Rephrase the following as in the example.

1   What fantastic photos!
...Aren't these photos fantastic! / These photos are so fantastic! / How fantastic these photos are! / These are such fantastic photos!...

2   This beach is so crowded!
3   He has such an expensive car!
4   How polite they are!
5   What a spoilt boy!

6   This is such a beautiful view!
7   The exam was so difficult!
8   It's been such a hot summer!
9   Don't they look angry!

10   What a helpful assistant!
11   She's so conscientious!
12   This is such nice weather!
13   How talented you are!

---

23   Fill in: what (a/an), how, so or such (a/an).

1   *...What a...* wonderful opportunity!
2   .... funny he is!
3   This is .... healthy meal!
4   .... friendly staff!
5   He has .... expensive taste!
6   .... miserable he looks!
7   She works .... hard!
8   .... terrible liar!
9   It's .... tragedy!
10   She's .... easy to talk to!
11   .... fantastic costume!

12   .... sad music!
13   .... enthusiastic she is!
14   He's .... imaginative artist!
15   They're .... helpful!
16   .... lucky man!
17   .... wonderfully she sings!
18   .... tasteful decorations you've got!
19   He's .... irresponsible employee!
20   .... amazing achievement!
21   They have .... much money.
22   .... ridiculous hairstyle!

---

24   Fill in: what (a/an), how, so or such (a/an).

Don: Have you seen the new drama teacher?
John: Yes. She is **1)** *...so...* beautiful!
Don: She certainly is. She's got **2)** .... lovely eyes!
John: And **3)** .... gracefully she moves!
Don: Have you heard her speak? She has **4)** .... soft voice!
John: **5)** .... pity we don't do drama!
Don: Yes, we're **6)** .... unlucky!

4 Clauses / Linking Words

Linking Words

Linking words show the logical relationship between sentences or parts of a sentence.

25 Rewrite the sentences from the table in as many ways as possible. Whenever this is not possible, make up a new sentence so that other linking words can be used.

She is both young and successful. She's not only young but she's also successful. etc

Positive Addition	and, both ... and, not only...(but also/as well), too, moreover, in addition to, furthermore, further, also, not to mention the fact that, besides	*She is young **and** successful.*
Negative Addition	neither ... nor, nor, neither, either	***Neither** Jane **nor** Paula has any desire to meet him again. Jane has no desire to meet him again. **Nor** does Paula.*
Contrast	but, not ... but, although, while, whereas, despite, even if, even though, on the other hand, in contrast, however, (and) yet, at the same time	*She can speak Russian fluently; **however**, she is unable to read or write it.*
Similarity	similarly, likewise, in the same way, equally	*When you move house, you must notify the post office of your change of address. **Similarly**, you must register with the local county council.*
Concession	but, even so, however, (and) still, (and) yet, nevertheless, on the other hand, although, even though, despite/in spite of, regardless of, admittedly, considering, whereas, while, nonetheless	*She applied for the job **even though** she wasn't suitably qualified.*
Alternative	or, on the other hand, either ... or, alternatively	*They could take a holiday now **or alternatively** they could wait until the summer.*
Emphasis	besides, not only this but ... also, as well, what is more, in fact, as a matter of fact, to tell you the truth, actually, indeed, let alone	*I find him pushy and demanding and, **what is more**, he is self-centred.*
Exemplification	as, such as, like, for example, for instance, particularly, especially, in particular	*I enjoyed all the books you lent me, but **in particular**, I liked "Wild Swans".*
Clarification	that is to say, specifically, in other words, to put it another way, I mean	*He needs to concentrate more on his schoolwork. **Specifically**, he has to pay more attention in the classroom.*
Cause / Reason	as, because, because of, since, on the grounds that, seeing that, due to, in view of, owing to, for, now that, so	*The company has decided to take on more staff **now that** sales are increasing.*

Manner	as, (in) the way, how, the way in which, (in) the same way (as), as if, as though	*The manager explained **how** the organisation could increase productivity.*
Condition	if, in case, assuming (that), on condition (that), provided (that), providing (that), unless, in the event (that), in the event of, as/so long as, granted/granting (that), whether, whether...or (alternative condition), only if, even if, otherwise, or (else), in case of	*Please notify us **in the event that/in case** you are unable to attend the meeting.*
Consequence of a condition	consequently, then, under those circumstances, if so, if not, so, therefore, in that case, otherwise, thus	*I may take a long lunch break tomorrow. **If so**, I can go to the hairdresser's then.*
Purpose	so that, so as (not) to, in order (not) to, in order that, for fear (that), in case	*I took plenty of magazines with me **in case** I got bored during the flight.*
Effect / Result	such/so...that, consequently, for this reason, as a consequence, thus, therefore, so	*The room at The Ritz was double-booked, and **as a consequence**, we were moved to another hotel.*
Comparison	as...as, than, half as...as, nothing like, the...the, twice as...as, less...than	*You look **nothing like** your sister.*
Time	when, whenever, as, while, now (that), before, until, till, after, since	*As a freelance writer, she can choose to work **whenever** she wants.*
Place	where, wherever	*She makes friends **wherever** she goes.*
Exception	but (for), except (for), apart from	*We have sent invitations to everyone **apart from** the Fords.*
Relative	who, whom, whose, which, what, that	*Let me introduce you to the man **whose** ideas have revolutionised the workplace.*
Chronological	**beginning:** initially, first..., at first, to start/begin with, first of all **continuing:** secondly ..., after this/that, second.., afterwards, then, next, before this **concluding:** finally, at last, in the end, eventually, lastly, last but not least	***First of all**, we need to decide what the problem is.* ***Then**, we need to consider all possible solutions.* ***Finally**, we must decide on the best alternative.*
Reference	considering, concerning, regarding, with respect/regard/reference to, in respect/regard/reference to this/to the fact that	***Considering** the length of time he took to write the report, it is not up to standard.* ***With reference to** what we agreed last week, I would like to remind you that the deadline has been brought forward to 1 June.*
Summarising	in conclusion, in summary, to sum up, as I have said, as (it) was previously stated, on the whole, in all, all in all, altogether, in short, briefly, to put it briefly	***To sum up**, the film was a complete waste of time.*

26 Join the sentences, then identify the functions of the linking words in brackets.

1 You could leave now. You could wait and ride with us. **(either ... or)**
   ...*You could either leave now or wait and ride with us. (alternative)*...

2 He's not a very good tennis player. He practises all the time. **(considering)**
   ....

3 He decided to change jobs. He wanted a chance to be more creative. **(on the grounds that)**
   ....

4 I don't feel like going out tonight. I never enjoy myself at discos. **(besides)**
   ....

5 He's afraid of heights. He wants to go rock climbing. **(and yet)**
   ....

6 You should write down your appointments. You won't forget them. **(so that)**
   ....

7 We're going to go on with the project. They say it's no longer necessary. **(even if)**
   ....

8 This house is exactly what we are looking for. It's a real bargain. **(moreover)**
   ....

9 She hardly ever practises the piano. She plays very well. **(even though)**
   ....

10 It was an interesting conference. There was one speaker who was boring. **(in spite of)**
   ....

11 She always gives money to poor people. She's extremely generous. **(in other words)**
   ....

12 I enjoy her company. She's been a great help to me. **(not only ... but also)**
   ....

13 She sings like an opera star. She isn't a star though. **(as if)**
   ....

14 Exercising will help you feel better. Eating less will improve your health. **(likewise)**
   ....

15 He isn't qualified for the job. He hasn't had much practical experience. **(what is more)**
   ....

16 You can play tennis for free here. You have to book in advance though. **(provided)**
   ....

17 I received a letter today. It was about my insurance policy. **(regarding)**
   ....

18 You should always wear a seatbelt. You may have an accident. **(in case)**
   ....

27 Replace the underlined words with synonymous ones.

Attention all staff: **1) First of all** complaints have been made to the management by the company chairman concerning the making of personal phone calls. **2) In view of the fact that** this year's bill is double last year's, some action has to be taken. **3) Consequently**, no members of staff **4) except for** senior management may use the phone for such purposes. **5) Secondly**, we have received complaints from the contract cleaners claiming that staff preparing coffee are making too much mess. **6) Concerning** this matter, we kindly request that staff clean the coffee area after use, **7) in other words**, wipe away any stains and dispose of paper cups in the bins provided. **8) Finally**, it has come to our attention that certain employees persist in smoking in the designated non-smoking areas. This must stop, **9) otherwise** there will be a total ban on smoking in all areas. Thank you for your cooperation in these matters.

Oral Development 7

Students look at the picture, then one after the other continue the story using the following linking words:
To begin with, consequently, then, not only ... but also, in order to, which, only if, on the other hand, because, what is more, since **etc**

Harry is a man in his early thirties who seems to be in trouble. It all started when ...

28 Complete the sentences using the words in bold. Use two to five words.

1 I was born in that hospital.
was That's ...*the hospital where I was*... born.

2 He has decided to emigrate to Australia; we can't stop him.
prevent We can't .... to Australia.

3 I didn't tell her the news because I didn't want to upset her.
so I didn't tell her the news .... her.

4 He couldn't get a credit card because he owed the bank money.
result He owed the bank money, ..., he couldn't get a credit card.

5 It was such a rude remark that we all felt insulted.
so It was .... we all felt insulted.

6 He bought a computer as he intended to work from home.
view He bought a computer .... from home.

7 She seldom left the house because she was afraid of being attacked.
fear She seldom left the house .... attacked.

8 Whatever you say, I will never trust that man.
what I will never trust that man .... you say.

9 That's the shop where he used to work when he was young.
in That's the shop .... when he was young.

10 You must phone work if you are ill.
event You must phone work .... you are ill.

11 She was tall, but she couldn't reach the top shelf.
though Tall .... not reach the top shelf.

12 There was heavy traffic on the motorway, so we arrived late.
due We arrived late .... on the motorway.

13 I like all my dresses, but the red one is my favourite.
particular I like all my dresses, but the red one .... favourite.

14 Once they all arrived, she began the seminar.
had She waited .... before she began the seminar.

15 Gary was the only one who didn't enjoy the meal.
   except   Everyone .... Gary.
16 What a slow worker you are!
   slowly   How .... work!
17 I'm not going to work today because I've got a cold.
   owing   I'm not going to work today .... I've got a cold.
18 His second film is very different to his first.
   like   His second film .... his first.
19 I'm writing concerning the advertised position.
   reference   I'm writing .... the advertised position.
20 This is Mr Jones; you will be seeing him tomorrow.
   who   This is Mr Jones .... tomorrow.
21 It looked like it was going to rain.
   if   It looked .... to rain.
22 Although he knew it was rude, he couldn't help laughing.
   prevent   Although he knew it was rude, ... from laughing.
23 The holiday was too expensive; we couldn't afford it.
   such   It was .... we couldn't afford it.
24 Take your book; you may get bored.
   case   Take your book .... bored.
25 Always check the dictionary if you don't want to make spelling mistakes.
   avoid   Always check the dictionary .... spelling mistakes.

---

29   Use the words in capitals to form a word that fits in the space in the same line.

The Silkworm

When you wear a silk shirt, scarf or tie you might not **(0)** ...*immediately*... think where the material came from. The silkworm which produces it is not **(1)** .... a worm at all, but a kind of butterfly or moth. From its body, it spins its own **(2)** .... cocoon which can be up to one mile in **(3)** ....

For more than 4,000 years, these silk threads have been **(4)** .... into luxurious fabrics to provide clothes for the **(5)** .... Today, in China, more than 10 million farmers raise silkworms, supplying more than one half of the world's **(6)** ....

When the caterpillars are hatched from the eggs, they spend about a month eating mulberry leaves, before being put into **(7)** .... in their own separate boxes. Here, they spin a cocoon around **(8)** .... After about two weeks, the caterpillars change into moths, and the cocoons are ready to receive a hot steam bath **(9)** .... to loosen the thread. This is carefully unravelled and wound into skeins of silk. This simple **(10)** .... process gives us our pure thread.

IMMEDIATE	
REAL	
PROTECT	
LONG	
WEAVE	
WEALTH	
REQUIRE	
ISOLATE	
THEY	
TREAT	
NATURE	

Phrasal Verbs

do away with: abolish
do down: speak badly of sb
do in: kill
do out: clean
do up: 1) fasten; tie, 2) redecorate
do with: 1) need; want, 2) have a connection with
do without: manage to live or continue without

....

fall back: move back; retreat
fall back on: use sth in the absence of sth else; turn to
fall behind: 1) fail to keep up with, 2) be late with payment
fall for: 1) be tricked, 2) fall in love with sb
fall in with: accept sb's plans, ideas
fall off: decrease
fall on: 1) attack, 2) eat (food) hungrily
fall out (with): quarrel
fall through: fail to be completed

30 Fill in the correct particle(s).

1 No one can do ...*without*... water for more than two days.
2 The death penalty was done .... in Britain many years ago.
3 You'd better do your shoes .... or you'll trip over your laces.
4 He was arrested for doing ...... a woman with a gun.
5 It's so hot, I could do .... a nice cool drink.
6 Theatre attendance has fallen .... because of the rise in ticket prices.
7 Our holiday plans fell .... when all the airlines went on strike.
8 After some disagreement, they finally fell .... our suggestions.
9 Once we'd spent all our money, we fell .... our credit card.
10 John fell .... the rest of the class after being ill for three weeks.
11 George always falls .... girls with blonde hair.
12 I fell .... one of my friends and haven't spoken to her for weeks.

31 Look at Appendix 1, then fill in the correct preposition.

1 If you insist ...*on*... going against their orders, you must be prepared to face the consequences.
2 There has been a noticeable increase .... staff turnover.
3 She bought a house with a garden as she's very keen .... gardening.
4 George is very keen .... start university.
5 His openness and sincerity are the key .... his political success.
6 Factories have a negative impact .... the environment.
7 When I was at university, I lived .... a student grant.
8 I am always being mistaken .... my cousin.
9 Julie has been married .... Bill for nearly ten years.
10 She's notorious .... telling incredible lies.
11 I didn't expect so many people to object .... the scheme.
12 We hoped you would be more obedient .... the rules.
13 Most people are indifferent .... the welfare of the homeless.
14 He asked her to write him a cheque .... £75.

15 Poor working conditions are believed to have caused a decrease .... production.
16 Don't disturb him as he's busy ...... his assignment.
17 The criminal was assured .... a fair trial.
18 Christine got engaged .... her boyfriend Ted.
19 The class is engaged .... a discussion about politics.
20 The interviewee made a good impression .... the manager.
21 What we lack .... our flat is enough storage space.
22 They were very impressed .... his ability.
23 The workers were protesting .... the wage cuts.
24 Gary prides himself .... his honesty.
25 Do you take pride .... your work?
26 I've never had the pleasure .... meeting her before.
27 He is jealous .... his younger brother's success.
28 He was nervous .... the forthcoming exams.
29 The hostess was pleasant .... each of her guests.
30 I'm really pleased .... your performance.
31 We always take pleasure .... their company.

Consolidation 4

32

For questions 1 - 12, read the text below and decide which word (A, B, C or D) best fits each space. There's an example at the beginning (0).

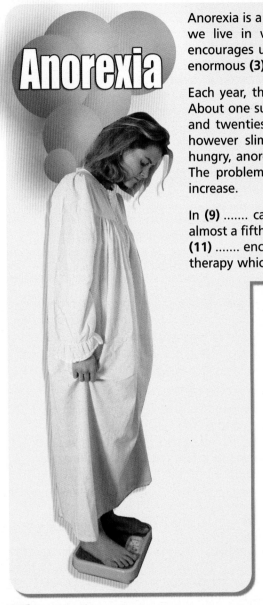

Anorexia is a comparatively new illness that seems to be **(0)** ...*B*... to the society we live in which increasingly **(1)** .... us on our appearance. The media encourages us to try to be **(2)** .... and beautiful. Falling short of this can put enormous **(3)** .... on the majority of us who are less than perfect.

Each year, there are estimated to be at **(4)** .... 2,000 new cases of anorexia. About one sufferer in ten is male, but most anorexics are females in their teens and twenties who **(5)** .... from a distorted self image, feeling fat and ugly, however slim and attractive they may appear to others. Though constantly hungry, anorexics attempt to **(6)** ..... control of their lives by **(7)** .... to eat. The problem commonly **(8)** .... in the teenage years, when responsibilities increase.

In **(9)** .... cases, it can **(10)** .... anaemia, heart and kidney problems, and, in almost a fifth of the cases, death by starvation or secondary infection. Treatment **(11)** .... encouraging patients to **(12)** .... weight by providing counselling and therapy which, in essence, guides the sufferers towards a normal life.

	A	B	C	D
0	resulted	(B) linked	caused	developed
1	watches	judges	measures	criticises
2	narrow	slight	light	slim
3	pressure	tension	weight	force
4	minimum	less	least	more
5	experience	suffer	go	pain
6	achieve	gain	win	earn
7	forbidding	refusing	rejecting	denying
8	develops	delivers	grows	evolves
9	enlarged	extended	prolonged	expanded
10	lead	catch	cause	give
11	considers	involves	concerns	deals
12	put	win	earn	regain

33 Complete the sentences using the words in bold. Use two to five words.

1 Are you likely to see him again?
   chance   Is there ...*any chance of your seeing*... him again?
2 He was late because there was an accident on the motorway.
   due   He was .... on the motorway.
3 He definitely won't pass his driving test.
   hope   There's .... his driving test.
4 I am disappointed with your exam results.
   let   You .... with your exam results.
5 I left home early so as to be on time for work.
   would   I left home early .... on time for work.
6 In Austria we visited Mozart's birthplace.
   where   We saw the .... while we were in Austria.

34 Use the words in capitals to form a word that fits in the space in the same line.

Teleworking

An **(0)** ...*increasing*... number of people nowadays are choosing to work from the **(1)** .... environment of their own homes rather than undergo the **(2)** .... process of travelling to work every day. The emergence of teleworking, as it is **(3)** .... called, is due to the **(4)** .... use of computers in the workplace.

Working conditions at home are more relaxed and can **(5)** .... be timed to suit oneself. There is no **(6)** .... need to get to the office on time, no **(7)** .... caused by the rush-hour traffic as with commuting, and it isn't necessary to face **(8)** .... colleagues on a daily basis.

However, there is a negative side. For example, some people might suffer from **(9)** .... if they spend all day at home, or they might feel the **(10)** .... to spend time doing other jobs around the house.

INCREASE
COMFORT

TROUBLE

COMMON
EXTEND

ACT
STRESS
FRUSTRATE

PLEASANT

BORE

TEMPT

35 Complete the sentences using the words in bold. Use two to five words.

0 Mark's mum didn't let him watch TV until he had finished his homework.
made Marks's mother ...*made him finish his homework*... before he watched TV.
1 When I got home, I did not realise I had lost my key.
idea When I got home, I .... lost my key.
2 They are going to demolish the building this weekend.
pulled The building .... down this weekend.
3 You might get thirsty on the trip, so take some water with you.
case Take some water with you .... thirsty on the trip.
4 He apologised for losing his temper.
sorry He .... for losing his temper.
5 Pam's worried she won't be able to keep up with her lessons.
behind Pam's worried she'll .... her lessons.
6 He didn't open the door because he was afraid of robbers.
fear He didn't open the door .... robbed.
7 Children can damage their eyesight if they play too many computer games.
result Playing too many computer games .... children's eyesight.
8 It was unfair that the teacher told Ann off.
deserve Ann .... told off.

Part 1

For questions 1 - 12, read the text below and decide which answer (A, B, C or D) best fits each gap. There is an example at the beginning (0).

Creative therapy is now (0) ...A... as a worthy alternative to the more conventional forms of treatment such as psychoanalysis. Art, music and dance are some of the forms of therapy now (1) ..... . These therapies are thought to be (2) ..... in relieving stress, depression and even emotional problems caused by tensions in relationships.

Art therapy (3) ..... painting, sculpting and modelling as a(n) (4) .....of expressing one's hidden feelings. The good news is that no particular talent is needed; once you have (5) .... your work of art, there is the opportunity to (6) ..... it through with a therapist. Those who find it difficult to immediately start up a conversation find this (7) .....of therapy useful. Music therapy involves singing or the playing of a musical instrument, (8) ..... sound to bring hidden emotions to the (9) .... Again, no special skill is required; you don't have to be Pavarotti to (10) ..... from this type of therapy.

This technique is often used to promote self-confidence in the physically or mentally disabled. And for those among you who (11) ..... too much time on intellectual pursuits, dance therapy may prove (12) ..... . It encourages spontaneity and helps the deep thinker become more bodily aware.

0	(A) regarded	B	considered	C	thought	D	felt
1	A accessible	B	available	C	handy	D	ready
2	A active	B	capable	C	efficient	D	effective
3	A contains	B	implies	C	involves	D	requires
4	A means	B	attempt	C	process	D	effort
5	A completed	B	worked	C	ended	D	achieved
6	A talk	B	discuss	C	tell	D	speak
7	A category	B	class	C	variety	D	form
8	A consisting	B	having	C	using	D	trying
9	A surface	B	top	C	front	D	side
10	A profit	B	win	C	gain	D	benefit
11	A have	B	spend	C	use	D	spare
12	A invaluable	B	priceless	C	precious	D	worthy

Part **2**

For questions 13 - 24, read the text below and think of the word which best fits each gap. Use only one word in each gap. There is an example at the beginning (0).

Mountain Biking

Mountain biking is becoming an increasingly popular sport, as people become **(0)** ...*more*... interested in keeping **(13)** .... and doing activities which take them out of their homes. It is not only a pleasurable way of improving your fitness, but **(14)** .... one of the most rewarding ways to explore the countryside.

However, it is important to follow a **(15)** .... simple rules, otherwise you could destroy the environment and spoil **(16)** .... people's enjoyment. Cyclists can use any road, but they must **(17)** .... attention to the type of path they are on. Some paths **(18)** .... only designed for people who are **(19)** .... foot, so if you are cycling on these, you could cause inconvenience to walkers as **(20)** .... as ending up being taken to court by the owner of the land you are on. On any other path, you should still respect walkers and be careful **(21)** .... you are passing horse riders.

Other things which you are asked to do are to close gates behind you, so **(22)** .... farm animals cannot escape, and to take your rubbish home with you. Always **(23)** .... someone know where you are going and have the right equipment and clothing for the conditions, **(24)** ...., you could create unnecessary problems for yourself.

For questions 25 - 34, read the text below. Use the word given in capitals at the end of some of the lines to form a word that fits in the gap in the same line. There is an example at the beginning (0).

The Boiled Egg Device

The Englishman Simon Rhymes **(0)** ...*recently*... thought up an idea for boiling an egg to **(25)** ...., something which is not as **(26)** .... as it seems. A **(27)** .... problem is that the yolks are either too soft or too hard, but with Rhymes' new **(28)** ...., your boiled eggs are now guaranteed to be cooked **(29)** .... the way you want.

RECENT
PERFECT
EASE
TYPE
INVENT

EXACT

After the **(30)** .... of over 600 experiments with eggs, Rhymes got the **(31)** .... idea of using the heat from a halogen light bulb to cook them. Of course, the light bulb had to be **(32)** .... reduced in size to fit into Rhymes' machine, which cooks your egg in around six minutes.

COMPLETE
EXCEPT

CONSIDER

According to personal **(33)** ...., you can change the cooking time, depending on how hard or soft you like your egg. The only **(34)** .... is that it takes slightly longer than the standard three minutes!

PREFER

ADVANTAGE

Part **4**

For questions 35 - 42, complete the second sentence so that it has a similar meaning to the first sentence, using the word given. Do not change the word given. You must use between two and five words including the word given. There is an example at the beginning (0).

0 They worked hard on the project.
effort
They ...*put a lot of effort*... into the project.

35 It was a mistake for us to move to London.
should
We .... to London.

36 I can't decide where to go on holiday.
mind
I can't .... where to go on holiday.

37 They worked fast in the hope of finishing sooner.
so
They worked fast .... sooner.

38 The house is completely empty.
left
There's .... in the house.

39 Considering that Sam is so young, you must admit he's making excellent progress as a doctor.
account
If you .... young Sam is, you must admit he's making excellent progress as a doctor.

40 You shouldn't put down your friends.
wrong
It's .... about your friends.

41 She had never been promoted before.
first
It .... she had ever been promoted.

42 They enjoyed themselves a lot at the party.
time
They .... at the party.

Revision 1

A   Choose the correct item.

1 I am sorry .... you that you're suspended.
   A informing   **C** to inform
   B inform   **D** have informed

2 I'll .... some research before writing my essay.
   A do   **C** work
   B make   **D** have

3 She's been working at Supersave .... 1990.
   A for   **C** since
   B ago   **D** before

4 Can you .... me a favour and babysit tonight?
   A make   **C** create
   B do   **D** have

5 Please stop .... I can't concentrate.
   A talk   **C** to talking
   B to talk   **D** talking

6 Take a drink in case you .... thirsty.
   A get   **C** would get
   B will get   **D** got

7 He's used .... with children.
   A to coping   **C** coping
   B cope   **D** to cope

8 .... he lives in Italy, he can't speak Italian.
   A As   **C** In spite of
   B Despite   **D** Although

9 He objects to people .... in his house.
   A smoked   **C** smoking
   B smoke   **D** had smoked

10 Most children prefer playing .... doing their homework.
   A from   **C** to
   B rather than   **D** rather

11 He .... an excuse to avoid helping us.
   A made   **C** claimed
   B did   **D** worked

12 .... its high price, she bought the Porsche.
   A As   **C** Though
   B Although   **D** Despite

13 We spent two weeks .... on the project.
   A to working   **C** working
   B work   **D** to work

14 If you .... an effort, you will succeed.
   A try   **C** do
   B have   **D** make

15 We .... haven't finished painting the house.
   A still   **C** already
   B before   **D** yet

16 We heard him .... the whole sonata.
   A play   **C** to play
   B to playing   **D** played

17 He gave us .... useful information!
   A too   **C** such
   B so   **D** such a

18 I really appreciate your .... me in hospital.
   A visiting   **C** to visit
   B visit   **D** to visiting

19 The management does not allow ....
   A to smoking   **C** to smoke
   B smoke   **D** smoking

20 Louisa has .... learnt to ride a bike.
   A yet   **C** already
   B still   **D** before

21 Will you remember .... the tickets?
   A to collect   **C** to collecting
   B collect   **D** collecting

22 The dog made .... much noise that we couldn't sleep.
   A such   **C** too
   B such a   **D** so

23 School groups are permitted .... the museum free.
   A visiting   **C** visit
   B to visiting   **D** to visit

24 The suspect was seen .... the house at 2 am and drive away.
   A to leave   **C** left
   B leave   **D** to leaving

B   Put the verbs in brackets into the correct tense.

Last summer, Gordon **1)** .... **(start)** university. He **2)** .... **(apply)** to various institutions for months and **3)** .... **(begin)** to wonder if he would ever succeed. He **4)** .... **(study)** hard every day since he started and, for that reason, he still **5)** .... **(not/make)** many friends. However, he **6)** .... **(begin)** to feel more at home now, and he thinks he **7)** .... **(be)** quite happy here. Next week, he **8)** .... **(start)** revising for the end-of-term tests.

C   Put the verbs in brackets into the correct tense.

Janet and John **1)** .... **(just/get)** married. They **2)** .... **(go out)** with each other for three years before they **3)** .... **(decide)** to get engaged. John **4)** .... **(buy)** her a ring last week. At the moment, they **5)** .... **(travel)** around Europe on a motorcycle. They both **6)** .... **(love)** motorcycles. When the honeymoon is over, they **7)** .... **(buy)** a house in Oxford. I think they **8)** .... **(be)** very happy.

D   Complete the sentences using the words in bold. Use two to five words.

1 She didn't start typing until her boss asked her.
   started   She waited until her boss asked her .... typing.
2 It would be a good idea to lock the door before you leave.
   had   You .... before you leave.
3 He's the most intelligent person I've ever met.
   never   I .... intelligent person.
4 The exercise was so difficult that we couldn't finish it.
   too   The exercise was .... finish.
5 Going on trips abroad alone is sometimes boring.
   go   It is sometimes boring .... abroad alone.
6 Mike prefers going by train to flying.
   than   Mike prefers to .... fly.
7 My grandmother is too ill to make the journey.
   enough   My grandmother .... make the journey.
8 He made me promise that I would keep it a secret.
   to   I .... that I would keep it a secret.
9 How long is it since you found out about it?
   find   When .... about it?
10 I've never seen this picture before.
   first   It's the .... this picture.
11 It's ages since we went out.
   been   We .... ages.
12 I'm sure Louise didn't lose her temper.
   have   Louise .... her temper.
13 I didn't call her because I didn't want to upset her.
   avoid   I didn't call her .... her.
14 Helen's been dieting for three weeks.
   started   Helen .... ago.
15 Perhaps they will give us their new address.
   give   They .... their new address.
16 He isn't the boss, but he acts like he is.
   were   He acts .... the boss.
17 It was difficult for them to find a flight.
   had   They .... a flight.
18 He'll probably get to Paris before we do.
   likely   He .... Paris before we do.

Revision 1

19 She found his reaction surprising.
    was   She .... reaction.
20 He wore sunglasses to avoid being recognised.
    that   He wore sunglasses .... be recognised.

E   Fill in the blanks with the correct particle(s).

1 He came .... a fortune on his father's death.
2 He came .... his car through dishonest means.
3 He brought .... his child alone.
4 The village was cut .... for weeks because of the snow.
5 John and Sue broke .... after their argument.
6 I took the bus because my car broke ....
7 We fell .... our neighbours because of their constant noise.
8 I'm thirsty. I could do .... a drink.

F   Fill in the blanks with the correct preposition(s).

1 She's very attached .... her pet hamster.
2 You're jealous .... me because I won the prize.
3 She was charged .... assault.
4 The beaches were crowded .... people.
5 It's so noisy - I can't concentrate .... my work.
6 The President congratulated the diplomat .... his work.
7 Is June well? I haven't heard .... her for months.
8 Catwalk models take a lot of pride .... their appearance.

G   Complete the sentences using the words in bold. Use two to five words.

0 Jane was late for work because her train was delayed.
   time   If the train ...*had been on time*..., Jane wouldn't have been late for work.
1 I wish to complain to the manager.
   make   I wish .... to the manager.
2 Percy couldn't understand what Peter was saying.
   clear   What Peter was saying .... Percy.
3 We have lived in Germany since we were children.
   home   Germany has .... since we were children.
4 Jeremy couldn't sit the exam because he was ill.
   prevented   Jeremy's illness .... the exam.
5 But for the help of the teacher, the students would have had difficulty understanding the lesson.
   helped   If the teacher .... have understood the lesson.
6 I can't believe Jake did all the work himself.
   difficulty I .... Jake did all the work himself.
7 No one said you were to blame for the accident.
   fault   No one said the accident .... of yours.
8 Although Sue exercises every day, she isn't losing any weight.
   despite   Sue isn't losing any weight, ... exercise.

74

- **Adjectives** describe nouns and are the same in singular and plural. *They are* **close** *friends. (What kind of friends? Close.)* They can be **factual** (small, round, yellow etc) or **opinion** (awful, ugly etc). Note that after **appear, be, become, get, feel, look, seem, smell, sound, stay, taste** we use adjectives, not adverbs. *It tastes* **awful**. *(NOT:* ~~awfully~~*)*

- Most common adjectives (long, late etc) do not have a particular ending. However, there are certain common endings for **adjectives which are formed from nouns and verbs**. These are:

-able	*fashionable*	**-ent**	*persistent*	**-ical**	*mechanical*	**-like**	*woman-like*
-al	*magical*	**-esque**	*picturesque*	**-ious**	*rebellious*	**-ly**	*deathly*
-ant	*hesitant*	**-ful**	*successful*	**-ish**	*stylish*	**-ory**	*sensory*
-ar	*spectacular*	**-ian**	*Iranian*	**-ist**	*racist*	**-ous**	*humorous*
-ary	*disciplinary*	**-ible**	*terrible*	**-ive**	*selective*	**-some**	*bothersome*
-ate	*considerate*	**-ic**	*melodic*	**-less**	*faultless*	**-y**	*sandy*
-ial	*artificial*						

- The most common prefixes used with adjectives are:

a	-	*amoral*	**im**	-	*immoral*	**pre**	-	*prearranged*
ab	-	*abnormal*	**in**	-	*inactive*	**pro**	-	*pro-war*
anti	-	*antisocial*	**ir**	-	*irresponsible*	**sub**	-	*sub-zero*
dis	-	*disrespectful*	**mal**	-	*maladjusted*	**super**	-	*superhuman*
hyper	-	*hyperactive*	**non**	-	*non-existent*	**un**	-	*unavailable*
il	-	*illegible*	**over**	-	*overweight*	**under**	-	*understaffed*

- **Compound adjectives** are formed with:
  1 **present participles**. *a long-playing record, a fee-paying student*
  2 **past participles**. *cut-off jeans, undercooked meat, a rolled-up carpet*
  3 **cardinal numbers + nouns**. *a three-year contract, a ten-minute journey, a two-week course*
  4 **prefixes and suffixes**. *a modern-day costume, an open-ended discussion*
  5 **well, badly, ill, poorly + past participle**. *a poorly-kept garden, a well-timed joke, a badly-furnished room*

- **Present** and **past participles** can be used as adjectives. *The lecture was* **boring**. *We were* **exhausted**.

---

1   Use the words in capitals to form a word that fits in the space in the same line.

The Oscars

Most people agree that the Oscars are the **(0)** ...biggest... film awards in the world. They are the most **(1)** .... awards anyone in the film business can win. The first Oscars were awarded in 1929.

They are called the Oscars after the **(2)** .... statue which is given out to the **(3)** .... Why the statue is named Oscar remains **(4)** ...., but it is rumoured to be because one of the Academy members thought the statue bore a **(5)** .... to her Uncle Oscar, and the name stuck.

Oscars are of great **(6)** .... because winning one can really help a film to be **(7)** .... or an actor to achieve **(8)** .... As a result, an actor often gets offered lots more work and better films once he/she has won an award, as people take him/her more **(9)** .... Another benefit is that arty films which have not done that well at the box office suddenly gain **(10)** .... once they have won an Oscar.

BIG
PRESTIGE

GOLD
WIN
CERTAIN
RESEMBLE

IMPORTANT
SUCCESS
RECOGNISE

SERIOUS

POPULAR

5 Adjectives / Adverbs / Comparisons

2 Use the words in capitals to form a word that fits in the space in the same line.

Bag Snatching

The **(0)** ...*increasing*... amount of street crime is something we are all aware of. In recent years bag snatching in particular has made walking alone in the street in certain areas quite **(1)** ....
There are several pieces of **(2)** .... you should keep in mind. Firstly, if you are walking alone on a pavement and a motorcyclist comes near you, you should keep your **(3)** .... by walking on the side of the pavement furthest from the road. If the motorcyclist asks for **(4)** ...., you should respond **(5)** .... but keep walking.
If you need help but no one pays **(6)** ...., don't be afraid to yell "Thief!" People will rush to see, and someone will get involved and ensure your **(7)** ....
Bags should be carried under your arm and NOT diagonally across your chest as you may have been **(8)** .... recommended. Hooking your bag across your chest does make it more difficult to steal, but a determined thief will not be **(9)** .... by this and you may get **(10)** .... hurt.

INCREASE

HAZARD
ADVISE

DISTANT

DIRECT
NORMAL
ATTEND
SAFE

PREVIOUS

COURAGE
SERIOUS

---

3 Write the opposites of the following adjectives.

1	active	...*inactive*...	4	legible	....	7	available	....
2	existent	....	5	religious	....	8	responsible	....
3	well-adjusted	....	6	moral	....	9	respectful	....

---

4 Make compound adjectives to describe the following:

1 An award that is well deserved. ...*a well-deserved award*...
2 A product that lasts a long time. ....
3 A suit that isn't made well. ....
4 A story that never ends. ....
5 A meal that has three courses. ....
6 An employee who isn't paid well. ....
7 A house that has two storeys. ....
8 An office that isn't organised well. ....

● Certain adjectives are used with **the** as nouns to talk about groups of people in general. These are: the elderly, the middle-aged, the old, the young, the blind, the deaf, the disabled, the living, the sick, the poor, the rich, the homeless, the hungry, the strong, the weak, the unemployed etc.
Young people are full of curiosity./*The young* are full of curiosity. *(refers to young people in general)*
The young people in our town are planning a concert. *(refers to a specific group of young people)*

---

5 Fill in the where necessary.

1 The Government is cutting benefits for ...*the*... unemployed and .... unemployed people all over the country are organising protest marches.
2 .... homeless in our town are being helped by .... young people, who are organising a sale to raise money for .... needy people in general.
3 A friend of mine works in a school for .... deaf, where she teaches .... deaf children.
4 .... middle-aged people tend to criticise .... young for their disrespectful attitude.

Order of Adjectives

- When there are two or more adjectives, they normally go in the following order:

	Opinion adjectives	Fact Adjectives							
		size	age	shape	colour	origin	material	used for/ be about	noun
It's a	beautiful	big	old	round	brown	Italian	oak	dining	table.

- Afraid, alike, alive, alone, ashamed, asleep, content, ill, glad etc are never followed by a noun.
  The baby is asleep. (NOT: the asleep baby)
- Nouns of **material**, **purpose** or **substance** can be used as adjectives. a cotton skirt, a winter dress, a shopping bag. However, certain adjectives derived from such nouns are used metaphorically. *silky hair* (hair like silk) **BUT** *a silk scarf* (a scarf made of silk), *a stony expression* (cold expression) **BUT** a *stone cottage* (a cottage made of stone), *golden hair* (hair like gold) **BUT** a *gold pen* (a pen made of gold), *feathery leaves* (leaves which look like feathers) **BUT** a *feather duster* (a duster made of feathers), *metallic colour* (colour that looks like metal) **BUT** a *metal chair* (a chair made of metal), *leathery skin* (skin looking/feeling like leather) **BUT** a *leather wallet* (a wallet made of leather), *a leaden feeling* (an unpleasant feeling) **BUT** *lead pipes* (pipes made of lead), *a steely look* (a strong, determined look) **BUT** *steel framework* (framework made of steel)

6 Rewrite the sentences putting the adjectives into the correct place. Identify what kind of adjectives they are.

1 He was carrying a briefcase. **(leather, nice, black, new)**
   ...*He was carrying a nice new black leather briefcase. (opinion/age/colour/material)*...
2 He gave her a scarf. **(silk, fantastic, French, red)** ....
3 I bought chairs from an antique shop. **(American, three, oak, old)** ....
4 She is an actress. **(English, intelligent, young, dramatic)** ....
5 The table lamp was broken by the children. **(metal, white, small)** ....
6 She bought a carpet. **(expensive, Persian, antique, woollen)** ....
7 He crashed his car yesterday. **(sports, brand new, yellow)** ....
8 It was a dress. **(hand-made, gorgeous, wedding, lace)** ....
9 I saw a film on TV last night. **(Italian, exciting, detective)** ....
10 They live in a house. **(big, lovely, country, old-fashioned, brick)** ....
11 She is a salesperson. **(young, computer, successful)** ....
12 I bought a book. **(old, poetry, Latin)** ....
13 We watched a programme. **(short, English, interesting, educational)** ....
14 She bought a raincoat. **(plastic, long, cheap)** ....
15 They found a trunk. **(wooden, rectangular, antique, interesting)** ....
16 He bought a yacht. **(Swedish, second-hand, huge)** ....

7 Underline the correct adjective.

1 She gave him a **stone/stony** look when he criticised her daughter.
2 These **metal/metallic** chairs are suitable for outdoor use as they are weatherproof.
3 The sky was full of light **feather/feathery** clouds.
4 She is admired for her **gold/golden** hair and **meta/metallic** blue eyes.
5 The old farmer had dark **leather/leathery** skin.
6 This new body milk gives you smooth, **silk/silky** skin in a matter of days.
7 She had a **lead/leaden** expression on her face.
8 The **gold/golden** candlesticks were very expensive, so we bought some **silver/silvery** ones instead.
9 He wears **woolly/woollen** suits and expensive **leather/leathery** shoes.
10 She has a **steel/steely** manner towards her colleagues.

Adjectives / Adverbs / Comparisons

8   Put the adjectives in the correct order.

Dear Louisa,

We've nearly finished furnishing the cottage, and I must say I'm very pleased with it. Yesterday, they delivered an **1)** *...antique French oak...* **(oak, antique, French)** cupboard which Peter had bought as a surprise for me. It looks lovely in the **2)** .... **(upstairs, front, big)** bedroom. We've put up **3)** .... **(plain, linen, off-white)** curtains and I found two **4)** .... **(woollen, old, beautiful, flower-patterned)** carpets for the sitting room. We've made friends with our **5)** .... **(new, charming, next-door)** neighbours. He is a **6)** .... **(well-known, fiction, popular)** writer, and she is a garden designer. I'm hoping she'll help us with our **7)** .... **(old, overgrown, big)** garden. There's a **8)** .... **(thirty-year old, beautiful, cherry)** tree at the bottom of the garden and we're planning to build a **9)** .... **(stone, small, square)** patio, so we can sit outside in the summer. You must come over soon and enjoy a **10)** .... **(home-made, delicious)** meal in our new home.

Best wishes,
Natalie

● **Adverbs normally describe verbs, adjectives, other adverbs or whole sentences.** *She dances well. (How does she dance? Well.)* They say **how** (adverbs of manner - *slowly*), **when** (adverbs of time - *yesterday*), **where** (adverbs of place - *next door*), **how often** (adverbs of frequency - *usually*) or **to what extent** (adverbs of degree - *absolutely*) something happens. There are also **sentence adverbs** (*possibly etc*) and **relative adverbs** (*where, why, when*).

Formation of Adverbs from Adjectives

Adverbs are formed from **adjectives + -ly**. *quick ➡ quickly, calm ➡ calmly*
● adjectives ending in **consonant + -y ➡ -ily**. *sleepy ➡ sleepily, weary ➡ wearily, weepy ➡ weepily*
● adjectives ending in **-ic** add **-ally**. *tragic ➡ tragically, frantic ➡ frantically,* **BUT** *public ➡ publicity*
● adjectives ending in **-le** drop **-le** and add **-ly**. *irritable ➡ irritably, reliable ➡ reliably*
● adjectives ending in **-e** add **-ly**. *false ➡ falsely,* **BUT** *whole ➡ wholly, true ➡ truly*
● adjectives ending in **-ly** (elderly, fatherly, friendly, lively, lonely, lovely, motherly, silly, ugly etc) form their adverb with **in a(n) ... way/manner**. *in a motherly manner, in a lively way etc.*

Adjectives and Adverbs which have the same form

best, better, big, cheap*, clean*, clear*, close*, cold, daily, dead, dear*, deep, direct, dirty, early, easy, extra, far, fast, fine*, free, further, hard, high, hourly, inside, kindly, last, late, long, loud*, low, monthly, past, quick*, quiet*, right, slow, straight, sure, thin*, thick, tight, weekly, well, wide, wrong, yearly etc
*Ann was our **last** guest. She came in **last**.* Those adverbs with an asterisk (*) can be found with **-ly** ending without a difference in meaning, but then they are more formal. *Walk slow! (informal)* ALSO *Walk slowly! (formal)*

9   Identify the underlined words as adjectives or adverbs.

1 He felt uncomfortable because his jeans were too **tight**.   *...adjective...*
2 I buy Time Magazine **weekly** whereas he subscribes to it on a **yearly** basis.   ....
3 I couldn't get the book down from the top shelf because it was too **high**.   ....
4 If you want to find the post office, go **straight** down the high street and
    you'll see it on your left.   ....
5 Tom constantly arrives **late** for work.   ....
6 The **late** Prime Minister was a collector of antiques.   ....
7 The walls were so **thin** you could hear the next-door neighbours.   ....
8 He worked **hard** all day to finish painting the house.   ....

9 She bought this rug **cheap** from the market.   ....

10 He kicked the ball **high** into the air.   ....

Adverbs with two forms and differences in meaning

deep = a long way down	**full** = exactly; very	**late** = not early	**sure** = certainly
deeply = greatly	**fully** = completely	**lately** = recently	**surely** = without a doubt
direct = by the shortest route	**hard** = intently; with effort	**near** = close	**wide** = off-target
directly = immediately	**hardly** = scarcely	**nearly** = almost	**widely** = to a large extent
easy = gently and slowly	**high** = at / to a high level	**pretty** = fairly	**wrong** = incorrectly
easily = without difficulty	**highly** = very much	**prettily** = in a pretty way	**wrongly** = unjustly (wrongly
free = without cost	**last** = after all others	**short** = suddenly	goes before verbs/past part. -
freely = willingly	**lastly** = finally	**shortly** = soon	wrong/wrongly go after verbs)

---

10 Underline the correct item.

1 **Lately**/**Late** there has been a rise in the price of vegetables; they are not **near**/**nearly** as cheap as they used to be.

2 I can **hard**/**hardly** believe that he has gone. **Surely**/**Sure** he wouldn't have left without me!

3 It is **wide**/**widely** believed among scientists that we will **short**/**shortly** run out of natural resources.

4 He is very **high**/**highly** thought of at the office because he works so **hardly**/**hard**; that's why he **full**/**fully** deserves a promotion.

5 You **wrong**/**wrongly** accused him of stealing the pen without hearing his explanation first - now he is **deep**/**deeply** offended.

6 He managed to get to Lisbon **easily**/**easy** by flying there **direct**/**directly**.

7 It is not **wide**/**widely** known that students can get medication **free**/**freely**.

8 She was **prettily**/**pretty** embarrassed when she realised that she had arrived **lastly**/**last** at the party.

9 He **hard**/**hardly** ever studies, yet he always produces a **high**/**highly** standard of work.

10 I **fully**/**full** understand your concern.

Quite - Fairly - Rather - Pretty

● **Quite** (fairly, to some degree) is used in **favourable comments**. *She's quite good at painting.* **Quite** meaning "completely" is used with adverbs, some verbs and adjectives such as: alone, amazing, brilliant, certain, dead, dreadful, different, exhausted, extraordinary, false, horrible, impossible, perfect, ridiculous, right, sure, true, useless etc. *I'm quite sure he stole the money.* **Quite** is used before **a/an**. *She's quite a good dancer. I quite enjoyed the film.*

● **Rather** is used: a) in **unfavourable comments**. *He's rather mean with money.* b) in **favourable comments** meaning "to an unusual degree". *The lecture was rather informative. (It was more informative than we expected)* and c) with **comparative degree**. *It's rather sunnier today than yesterday.* **Rather** is used before or after **a/an**. *He's a rather rude person. He's rather a rude person.*

● **Fairly** and **pretty** are synonymous with **quite** and **rather**. They can be used after **a**. *He's a fairly/pretty well-behaved person.*

---

11 Complete the sentences using quite, fairly, rather **or** pretty.

1 It's ...*quite*... wet out today. You'd better wear your boots.

2 The party on Saturday was .... enjoyable. I'm glad I went.

3 The food in this restaurant is .... good although it's .... expensive.

4 His new film is .... interesting, but it's .... a long one.

5 That exercise may be .... difficult, but it will be .... good for your vocabulary.

6 Although his speech was .... short, it was still .... boring.

7 We .... enjoyed our holiday in Finland though the weather was .... cold.

8 John is .... a short man, but he's .... good looking.

9 She's a .... intelligent girl, but she is .... difficult to get to know.

10 We wanted to walk, but it was .... a long way to go on foot.

Word Order of Adverbs

● Adverbs can be used in front, mid or end position in a sentence. **Front position** is at the beginning of a sentence. **Mid position** is normally before the main verb or after the auxiliary. **End position** is at the end of a sentence.

Front	Mid	End
At university I often	*saw her walking around*	**confidently**.

● Adverbs of manner can go in any position. When placed in front position, they give emphasis.
*He climbed up the stairs **quickly**. **Quickly** he climbed up the stairs. (emphasis)*

● When there is more than one adverb in the sentence, their usual order is manner-place-time.

subject	verb	manner	place	time
She	*was studying*	*hard*	*in her room*	*all night.*

● When there is a verb of movement, then the order is place - manner - time.

subject	verb	place	manner	time
He	*goes*	*to school*	*on foot*	*every day.*

● Time adverbs go in end position. They also go in front position to emphasise the time.

subject + verb	place	manner	time	time	subject+ verb	place	manner
He goes	*to the park*	*on his bike*	*every day.*	*Every day*	*he goes*	*to the park*	*on his bike.*

● **Adverbs of frequency** (**sometimes, always, usually, never, often, seldom, rarely** etc) go after an auxiliary but before the main verb. *You **are always** late. He **usually comes** late.* They go before the auxiliary in short answers. *"Does he help you clean the house?" "Yes, he **always does**."*

● **Adverbs of degree** (**hardly, almost, nearly** etc) go before the words they modify. *She works **quite** hard.*

12 Rewrite the sentences putting the adverbs in the right place.

1 He eats his sandwiches. (**at break time/always/quickly**)
   ...*He always eats his sandwiches quickly at break time.*....
2 Birds migrate. (**to warmer countries/usually/in winter**)
   ....
3 The plane crashed. (**into the sea/suddenly/an hour ago**)
   ....
4 Politicians prepare their speeches. (**thoroughly/at home/generally/in advance**)
   ....
5 The thief crept into the house. (**silently/at midnight**)
   ....
6 Newspapers are delivered. (**only/weekly/in remote areas**)
   ....
7 Hundreds of people are imprisoned. (**in Britain/each year/wrongly**)
   ....
8 People who sunbathe can get burnt. (**badly/on the beach/frequently**)
   ....
9 Hotplan's new washing machine has been designed to save you money. (**cleverly/now/in the home**)
   ....
10 Staff have been made aware of the consequences of a shrinking market. (**rapidly/recently/fully**)
   ....

13 Rewrite the text putting the adverbs into the correct place.

the MIRAMAR HOTEL

Our hotel is ...**conveniently**... located in the fashionable resort of Praia da Rocha in Portugal's Algarve region. (**conveniently**) The Hotel Miramar sits on top of the cliffs overlooking the beach below. (**picturesquely**) The service we offer is exceptional - the hotel staff work to make your visit memorable. (**all day / hard**) Each room is designed to enable you to rest and each has its own bathroom. (**specially / comfortably**) The rooms have been decorated to help you to relax and feel at home. (**tastefully / completely**) Sample the local dishes prepared in our hotel restaurant. (**traditionally /every evening**) We are proud of our chef who selects only the freshest fruit and vegetables and then prepares each dish for your pleasure. (**expertly / particularly / daily**) So don't delay! Reserve your rooms and spend your holiday with us. (**this summer / at once**)

Regular Comparative and Superlative Forms

Adjectives	Positive	Comparative	Superlative
of one syllable add **-(e)r/-(e)st** to form their comparative and superlative forms	short simple big	short**er** (than) simpl**er** (than) bigg**er** (than)	**the** short**est** (of/in) **the** simpl**est** (of/in) **the** bigg**est** (of/in)
of two syllables ending in **-ly, -y, -w** also add **-er/-est**	funny narrow	funn**ier** (than) narrow**er**(than)	**the** funn**iest** (of/in) **the** narrow**est** (of/in)
of two or more syllables take **more/most**	modern intelligent	**more** modern (than) **more** intelligent (than)	**the most** modern (of/in) **the most** intelligent (of/in)

- We normally use **than** with the **comparative** form. *Tim is **shorter than** Tony.* We normally use **the...of/in** ("in" refers to places, groups etc) with the **superlative** form. *She's **the smartest of** all.*
- Certain adjectives form their comparative and superlative either with **-er/-est** or **more/most**. These are: **clever, common, cruel, friendly, gentle, narrow, pleasant, polite, shallow, simple, stupid, quiet**. *quiet - quieter - quietest ALSO quiet - more quiet - most quiet*

14 Put the adjectives in brackets into the correct form.

Egypt

Come and visit one of **1)** ...*the most historical*... (**historical**) countries in the world — Egypt, where the people are **2)** .... (**hospitable**) than anywhere else. You will see some of **3)** .... (**old**) and **4)** .... (**famous**) ancient monuments in the world, as well as modern cities with **5)** .... (**good**) restaurants in the Middle East. To make travel arrangements **6)** .... (**easy**), our tour includes guided visits to all of **7)** .... (**popular**) tourist attractions in Egypt. You will also get the opportunity to go on a cruise down the River Nile – the **8)** .... (**long**) river in the world! The experience is sure to be **9)** .... (**amazing**) than anything you've experienced before, as you see first hand where one of **10)** .... (**old**) civilisations began. Our company offers tailor-made tours for **11)** .... (**small**) groups than is usual on a package holiday. We provide accommodation in intimate hotels which offer a **12)** .... (**friendly**) service than the **13)** .... (**large**), **14)** .... (**impersonal**) ones. Even **15)** .... (**frequent**) traveller will experience something new in this unique country. Book today!

5 Adjectives / Adverbs / Comparisons

Adverbs	Positive	Comparative	Superlative
adverbs having the same forms as their adjectives add **-er/-est**	fast	fast**er**	**the** fast**est**
early drops **-y** and adds **-ier/-iest**	early	earl**ier**	**the** earl**iest**
two syllable or compound adverbs take **more/most** (Compound adverbs are adjectives + -ly. *thoughtful - thoughtful***ly***)	often patiently	**more** often **more** patiently	**the most** often **the most** patiently

Irregular Forms

Positive	Comparative	Superlative
good / well	better	best
bad / badly	worse	worst
much	more	most
many / a lot of	more	most
little	less	least
far	farther	farthest
far	further	furthest

Well is the adverb of **good**. *She is a good dancer. She dances well.*

a) **further/farther** (adv) = longer (in distance)
   *His house is **further/farther** away than John's.*
   further (adj) = more
   *I need no **further** help from you.*
b) **very + positive degree** *I'm **very** happy in my job.*
c) **even/much/far/a bit + comparative degree**
   *The weather's **even** less bearable today: it's **much** worse than last year.*
d) **most + adj/adv of positive degree** = very
   *He was **most** helpful and answered all my questions.*
e) **any + comparative** (used in negatives and questions)
   *Can you write **any** quicker, please?*

---

15 Fill in the relevant adverbs in their comparative or superlative forms.

Bicycles look set to become **1)** ...*the most commonly*... **(common)** used form of transport in Britain. Not only are bicycles better for the environment than cars, but they allow you to travel **2)** .... **(convenient)**. You can get from point A to point B **3)** .... **(quick)** than by car and you can find somewhere to leave your bike much **4)** .... **(easy)**. Many younger people now ride a bike to work because they find it **5)** .... **(good)** suits their lifestyle and enables them to get around **6)** .... **(practical)**. In addition, they often arrive **7)** .... **(early)** than their colleagues who drive to work and who have to wait **8)** .... **(long)** in traffic jams than they do.

---

16 Underline the correct word.

1 She drove **very/even** quickly along the lane.
2 "We will give you **further/farther** news as we receive it," the newsreader said.
3 Her parents were **more/most** pleased when she won the prize.
4 Can't he speak **any/much** louder than that? No one can hear him.
5 She plays **very/much** more noisily than any child I've ever met.

---

17 Put the adjectives in their comparative or superlative forms.

If you want to own **1)** ...the fastest... **(fast)**, **2)** .... **(powerful)** car on the road, you can't go wrong with a Tornado. You will not only have **3)** .... **(comfortable)** ride you've ever experienced, you'll also be **4)** .... **(safe)** than in any other car on the market. No other manufacturer is **5)** .... **(careful)** than we are to ensure that its safety features are of **6)** .... **(high)** possible standard. So if you want to be **7)** .... **(proud)** car owner in your neighbourhood, come and test drive the Tornado today!

Type of Comparisons

● **as ... (positive degree) ... as** **not so/as ... (positive degree) ... as** **such a(n)/so ...as**	For hair **as soft as** silk, try this new shampoo. The service is**n't as good as** it used to be. It's **not such a** long way **as** we thought.
● **twice/three times etc/half as ... (positive degree) ... as**	She earns **twice as much as** me. She's only **half as well-qualified as** her sister.
● **the same as**	The Orion costs **the same as** the Golf.
● **look, sound, smell, taste + like**	That **sounds like** a good idea.
● **less ... (positive degree) ... than** **the least ... (positive degree) ... of/in**	I have **less free** time **than** Cathy, but Laura has **the least free** time of all.
● **the + comparative ..., the + comparative**	**The busier** the roads are, **the longer** it will take to get there. **The less** you sleep, **the more** tired you get.
● **comparative + and + comparative**	Jobs are getting **harder and harder** to find.
● **prefer + -ing form or noun + to + -ing form or noun** (general preference)	She **prefers living** for the moment **to thinking** about the future. Most people **prefer summer to winter**.
● **would prefer + to-inf + rather than + inf without to** (specific preference)	I **would prefer to book** our tickets now **rather than wait** until the last minute.
● **would rather/sooner + inf without to+ than + inf without to**	He'd **sooner go** alone **than go** with Edward.
● **clause + whereas/while + clause** (comparison by contrast)	Carole enjoys adventure **while/whereas** her sister prefers peace and quiet.

18 Complete the sentences using the words in bold. Use two to five words.

1 Wouldn't you prefer to get a takeaway rather than have to cook tonight?
sooner   Wouldn't you ...*sooner get a takeaway than*... have to cook tonight?
2 If we stay longer, we can spend more time sightseeing.
the   The .... time we can spend sightseeing.
3 I'd rather go home than go to the cinema.
than   I'd prefer .... go to the cinema.
4 In some countries, men and women are paid the same.
as   In some countries, women .... men.
5 Crisps are not as nutritious as nuts.
less   Crisps .... nuts.
6 No other job is as well-paid.
best   It .... job.
7 John and I have received the same number of job offers.
many   I have received .... John.
8 Last night I felt more tired than ever.
as   I have .... I did last night.
9 Tony finds history easier than geography.
not   Geography .... history for Tony.
10 As he gets older, he becomes less tolerant.
the   The .... tolerant he becomes.

11 I love going to football matches, but my sister prefers going to tennis tournaments.
whereas   I love going to football matches .... to tennis tournaments.

12 Helen had twice as much work as Janet.
half   Janet had .... Helen.

13 I like being self-employed. It's better than working for someone else.
to   I prefer .... for someone else.

14 My grandfather is getting less and less patient as he gets older.
impatient   My grandfather is getting .... as he gets older.

15 Laura is a less sensitive girl than her sister.
such   Laura isn't .... her sister.

16 Airships are not as dangerous as they used to be.
than   Airships .... they used to be.

17 My father is spending less time at the office now that he's nearing retirement.
as   My father is .... at the office now that he's nearing retirement.

18 Martha and Julie have the same views.
as   Martha's views .... Julie's.

19 I think I would prefer to leave rather than wait until he comes.
sooner   I think I .... until he comes.

20 If we climb higher, the view will be better.
the   The .... the view will be.

Like is used	As is used
● for similarities. *He works **like** a mule. (He isn't a mule.)*	● to say what sb or sth really is (jobs or roles) *He works **as** a dentist. (He's a dentist.)*
● after **feel, look, smell, sound + noun.** *She looks **like** her mother.* *It smells **like** burnt toast.*	● in certain expressions: **as usual, as...as, as much, such as, the same as.** *She was late **as usual.***
● with nouns, pronouns or the -ing form to express similarity. *Frogs' legs are supposed to taste just **like chicken**.* *Is that your Mum? You look **like her**.* *It's **like walking** on air.*	● after: **accept, be known, class, describe, refer to, regard, use.** *He's **regarded as** an expert on computers.*
	● in clauses of manner to mean 'in the way that'. *We must write the essay **as** they have shown us.*

19 Fill in as or like.

1 ...*As*... you mentioned, they are .... two peas in a pod. Jack looks exactly .... his twin brother Jim. They even have the same personality .... each other.

2 Ugh! This soup tastes just .... water. Didn't you make it .... I told you?

3 He treats his friends .... dirt. I detest people behaving .... that. He should treat people .... he'd like to be treated himself.

4 .... he didn't know what his relations looked ...., they sent him a photo so he would recognize them at the airport.

5 I have been working .... a tour guide for two years now, but I don't really regard it .... a serious career. It's time to do something different. I might even go back to college .... my sister has done.

6 .... usual, it looks .... if it's going to rain. It's no wonder Lancashire is described .... the wettest county in Britain.

7 He drinks .... a fish and smokes .... a chimney and, ... we all keep telling him, he won't live long.

8 .... much .... I admire his work, I don't think he deserves to be known .... the greatest novelist of the century.

In Other Words

- Jane is more beautiful than Mary.
  Mary isn't as beautiful as Jane (is).
  Mary is less beautiful than Jane.
- Can't you buy a cheaper coat than that?
  Is that the cheapest coat you can buy?
- Joe's got the same number of suits as Ted.
  Ted has got as many suits as Joe.
- He's the fastest driver of all.
  No one else drives as fast as he does.
  He's faster than any other driver.
  He is a faster driver than anyone else.
  He drives faster than anyone else.

- I've never seen such a tall man.
  He's the tallest man I've ever seen.
- He's a good tennis player.
  He plays tennis well.
- As he gets older, he becomes more sensible.
  The older he gets, the more sensible he becomes.
- That dress is similar to this one.
  That dress and this one are alike.
- Tom is very fatherly to his children.
  Tom behaves in a fatherly way to his children.

20 Complete the sentences using the words in bold. Use two to five words.

1 Unfortunately, we couldn't find a better solution in the time available.
   best   Unfortunately, it ...*was the best solution*... we could find in the time available.
2 Spanish and Portuguese are said to be alike.
   similar   Spanish is .... Portuguese.
3 I've never eaten such a hot curry.
   the   It's .... I've ever eaten.
4 She is extremely disrespectful to her colleagues.
   way   She behaves .... to her colleagues.
5 Sheila is not as talented as her sister.
   less   Sheila is .... her sister.
6 She was the best prepared of all the candidates.
   than   She was .... all the other candidates.
7 As prices increase, the cost of living becomes higher.
   the   The .... the cost of living becomes.
8 She writes very creatively.
   creative She .... writer.
9 George made the same number of mistakes as Peter.
   as   George made .... Peter.
10 It's more expensive to live in London than in Liverpool.
   not   It's .... to live in Liverpool as in London.
11 MacMahon is the most skilful player in the team.
   as   No one else in the team .... MacMahon.
12 The seller wouldn't accept a lower offer.
   lowest   It was .... the seller would accept.
13 She's the most eccentric person I've ever met.
   never   I've .... eccentric person.
14 As she gets richer, she becomes more extravagant.
   the   The .... extravagant she becomes.
15 We've never had such a heated argument before.
   most   It .... we've ever had.
16 The boss is very friendly to her staff.
   way   The boss behaves .... to her staff.
17 She received the same number of gifts as her cousin on her birthday.
   many   She received .... her cousin on her birthday.
18 He speaks German fluently because he was born in Germany.
   a   He .... because he was born in Germany.

21   Complete the sentences using the words in bold. Use two to five words.

0   A friendly man gave us directions.
   given   We ...*were given directions by*... a friendly man.
1   You should be very careful when handling this antique vase.
   great   You should .... when handling this antique vase.
2   It would be senseless to turn down such a good offer.
   make   It wouldn't .... turn down such a good offer.
3   My grandfather suggested that idea.
   forward   That idea .... my grandfather.
4   You must be very patient if you want to teach children.
   run   You mustn't .... if you want to teach children.
5   It was the first time Michael had ever been in a helicopter.
   been   Michael .... in a helicopter before.
6   My father doesn't want me to stay out late tonight.
   objects   My father .... out late tonight.
7   Mr Jones is very proud of his ceramics collection.
   pride   Mr Jones .... his ceramics collection.
8   Peter couldn't perform well in the interview because of nerves.
   prevented   Peter's nerves .... well in the interview.

Oral Development 8

Look at the pictures below then talk about the professions using comparative and superlative forms. Use the adjectives given as well as your own ideas.
dirty, well-paid, exciting, interesting, boring, creative, challenging, stressful, dangerous, safe, hard, varied, repetitive, skilled, unskilled

A firefighter's job is the most dangerous of all.

Phrasal Verbs

get about: move around; spread
get sth across: make sth understood
get away (from): 1) escape, 2) leave
get along (with): have a friendly relationship
get at: 1) reach, 2) imply, suggest
get away with sth: avoid being punished for sth
get sb down: depress sb
get off: 1) to avoid punishment, 2) to descend from a bus etc
get on: 1) enter a bus etc, 2) manage
get on with: continue, often after interruption
get over: 1) return to usual state of health, happiness etc after sth bad, 2) overcome
get (a)round: coax; persuade sb by kindness
get through: 1) finish work, 2) reach sb by phone

....

give away: 1) give sth for free, 2) reveal
give off: emit
give back: return
give in: 1) surrender, 2) hand in
give out: distribute
give up: 1) stop (a habit etc), 2) surrender

22   Fill in the correct particle(s).

1 I can't get ...*through*... to Joan. I think there's a fault on the line.
2 He's a good speaker and gets his views .... very well.
3 It took Ted a long time to get .... the breakup of his marriage.
4 The young boys got .... with a caution because it was their first offence.
5 You must give .... smoking. It's ruining your health.
6 Please give .... your homework by next Friday.
7 The record shop has a promotion and is giving .... free CDs.
8 The milk is giving .... a horrible smell.
9 I want to get .... the city for a few days.
10 I'm afraid my father and I don't get .... at all.
11 All this bad news really gets me ....
12 How are you getting .... without a cooker?
13 Stop talking and get .... your work.
14 You have to get .... your revision tonight.
15 She gave .... my secret so I'm terribly hurt.
16 He stopped resisting and gave himself .... to the police.

23   Look at Appendix 1, then fill in the correct preposition.

1 I don't know the result ...*of*... my exams yet.
2 He made a lot of mistakes resulting .... his inexperience.
3 Her arrogance resulted .... her losing all her friends.
4 I am obliged .... you .... all your invaluable assistance.
5 Was he really involved .... the incident?
6 You can lean .... me.
7 The ladder was leaning .... the wall.
8 The guest apologised .... the hostess .... staining the sofa with wine.
9 Some people are deliberately cruel .... stray animals.
10 There are big differences .... the two cultures.
11 Claire is familiar .... the procedure.
12 That man seems familiar .... me; I must have seen him before.
13 You cannot deny there is a relationship .... crime and poverty.
14 She has a good relationship .... her children.
15 I find it hard to sympathise .... Denise.
16 She's not very sympathetic .... the poor.
17 James was suspected .... starting the riot.
18 Poor Jill suffers .... hay fever.
19 She spends a lot of money .... cosmetics.
20 I'm sorry .... forgetting our anniversary.
21 She's very sorry .... the state of the house.
22 The manager was not satisfied .... his staff.
23 That's the same car .... mine.
24 What are you so excited ....?
25 South Africa is a country rich .... gold.
26 Kindly refrain .... throwing litter in the park.
27 I am writing .... reference to your letter.
28 Don't refer .... his recent dismissal.
29 It's no use trying to reason .... her.
30 There was no reason .... him to shout like that.
31 Professor Harris specialises .... the history of the Roman empire.

24   Complete the sentences using the words in bold. Use two to five words.

1 Richard isn't too young to ride a motorbike.
   old   Richard ...*is old enough to ride*... a motorbike.

2 In general, women are shorter than men.
   as In general, men .... women.
3 I can't wait to go on holiday.
   forward I'm really .... on holiday.
4 Prices may go up next year, so you should buy now.
   case You should buy now .... next year.
5 Mark does not run as fast as he did.
   used Mark .... he does now.
6 They sunbathed all day long when they were on holiday.
   spent They .... when they were on holiday.
7 Helen hasn't tried Japanese food before.
   time It's the .... Japanese food.
8 She'd rather watch tennis than football.
   prefers She .... football.
9 The police managed to catch the bank robbers after a three-day chase.
   catching The police .... the bank robbers after a three-day chase.
10 Can't he do any better than this?
   the Is .... he can do?
11 I don't know all the facts.
   aware I .... all the facts.
12 Whose fault was the fire at the factory?
   blame Who .... the fire at the factory?
13 He came here three months ago.
   been He .... three months.
14 They decided to cancel the wedding.
   off They .... the wedding.
15 He crossed the street because he didn't want to speak to her.
   speaking He crossed the street .... to her.
16 His father doesn't want him to drink spirits.
   disapproves His father .... spirits.

25 For questions 1 - 12, read the text below and think of the word which best fits each space. Use only one word in each space.

Choose your Sport Carefully

Regular exercise such **(0)** ...*as*... jogging or swimming is good **(1)** .... the heart. It can also give you more energy to enjoy life. As a **(2)** .... of regular exercise, your body gets better **(3)** .... using oxygen. It becomes easier for your heart to pump blood **(4)** .... your body. After a while, the heart doesn't **(5)** .... to work quite as hard.

Exercise is often thought to be an easy **(6)** .... to lose weight. But in fact, exercise tends to increase your appetite. Many people discover they **(7)** .... weight with exercise alone. **(8)** .... diet and exercise are needed to achieve this.

Some people start to exercise later in life because they think it will help them to live longer. If that is your reason for exercising, then you **(9)** .... avoid short, intensive exercise. Squash, for example, **(10)** .... is a fast game, may be harmful **(11)** .... you're unfit or middle-aged.

Other sports can be dangerous too. Although both rugby and football are popular sports, a rugby player is three **(12)** .... more likely to be injured than a tennis player. It is advisable, therefore, to choose a sport that suits you.

26 Use the words in capitals to form a word that fits in the space in the same line. Write your answers in the boxes provided.

The **Importance** of Trees

Trees provide us with many **(0)** ...*valuable*... resources such as building materials, fuel, rubber, food like fruit and nuts, and pulp for paper **(1)** .... to name just a few. They also provide **(2)** .... shelter for people, animals, and other plants as well as reducing the devastating effects of flooding which can make whole communities of people and animals **(3)** ....

Most **(4)** ...., though, they protect the world's climate by absorbing massive amounts of **(5)** .... chemicals, such as carbon dioxide, from our atmosphere and in turn give off oxygen. Without trees there would be no **(6)** .... of minimising the effects of **(7)** .... warming caused by the Greenhouse Effect. As if this is not enough, trees are also a constant source of medicine. Tropical forests especially are the source of over 20,000 species of **(8)** .... plants.

(9) ...., tropical forests are disappearing at an alarming rate and man must act soon to protect our most valuable **(10)** .... resource.

VALUE

PRODUCE
ESSENCE

HOME
IMPORTANT

HARM

POSSIBLE
GLOBE

MEDICINE
FORTUNATE

NATURE

27 Complete the sentences using the words in bold. Use two to five words.

0 My favourite aunt gave me a CD player.
   given   I ...*was given a CD player by*... my favourite aunt.
1 I don't feel like going to the cinema tonight.
   mood   I'm not .... to the cinema tonight.
2 Wendy is responsible for keeping the classroom tidy.
   charge   Wendy is .... the classroom tidy.
3 He didn't get married until he was forty.
   when   He .... married.
4 You bought more milk than we needed.
   so   You needn't .... milk.
5 No one plays the guitar as well as Eric Clapton.
   better   Eric Clapton plays the guitar .... else.
6 Sally shouldn't have given up her job.
   foolish   It .... give up her job.
7 Adam is not usually rude.
   like   It .... be rude.
8 The sports coach explained the game to us fully.
   gave   The sports coach .... of the game.

6 Passive Voice / Causative Form

The passive is formed with the appropriate tense of the verb **to be + past participle**. Present Perfect Continuous, Future Continuous, Past Perfect Continuous are not normally used in the passive. Note that only transitive verbs (verbs which take an object) can be put into the passive.

	Active Voice	Passive Voice
Present Simple	They **restore** buildings.	Buildings **are restored**.
Present Continuous	They **are restoring** the building.	The building **is being restored**.
Past Simple	They **restored** the building.	The building **was restored**.
Past Continuous	They **were restoring** the building.	The building **was being restored**.
Future Simple	They **will restore** the building.	The building **will be restored**.
Present Perfect	They **have restored** the building.	The building **has been restored**.
Past Perfect	They **had restored** the building.	The building **had been restored**.
Future Perfect	They **will have restored** the building.	The building **will have been restored**.
Present infinitive	They should **restore** the building.	The building should **be restored**.
Perfect infinitive	They should **have restored** the building.	The building should **have been restored**.
-ing form	They like people **restoring** buildings.	They like buildings **being restored**.
Perfect -ing form	**Having restored** the building, ...	The building, **having been restored**, ...
Modal + be + p.p.	They **must restore** the building.	The building **must be restored**.

Note: Get is used in colloquial English instead of **be** to express something happening by accident.
*He'll **get hurt** if he plays like that.*

- when the person performing the action **(agent)** is **unknown, unimportant** or **obvious from the context**.
  *The rooms **have been searched** thoroughly. (by the police - obvious agent)*
- to **emphasise** the agent. *The maths lesson was taken **by the English teacher** yesterday.*
- when we are interested more in the action than the agent, such as in **news reports, formal notices, instructions, processes, headlines, advertisements** etc. *"Crocodiles **have been set free** ..."*
- to make **statements** more **formal** or **polite**. *The vase **has been broken**. (more polite than saying "You have broken the vase.")*

1 Write sentences in the passive as in the example:

1 (Her hair/dye/at the moment)   *...Her hair is being dyed at the moment....*
2 (The Queen/not drive/to the embassy/yet)   ....
3 (The Hay Wain/paint/Constable)   ....
4 (Most olives/grow/the Mediterranean)   ....
5 (The convict/take/to prison/now)   ....
6 (His wound/not treat/yet)   ....
7 (My car/break into/last night)   ....
8 (The trees/prune/a tree surgeon/last week) ....
9 (Reservations/can/make/by dialling 001 now) ....
10 (Our house/clean/weekly)   ....
11 (He/bring up/his grandparents)   ....
12 (The book/not write/yet)   ....
13 (The building/demolish/by next year)   ....
14 (The new school/open/next week/the mayor) ....
15 (Sally's shoes/re-heel/last Saturday)   ....
16 (The dustbins/empty/recently)   ....

2   Put the verbs in brackets into the correct passive form.

1   Polar bears ...*are hunted* ... (hunt) for their fur.
2   A lecture .... **(give)** in the main hall at the moment.
3   After .... **(award)** a medal for bravery, he became a local hero.
4   Her ankle .... **(hurt)** when she fell down.
5   She thinks her car .... **(steal)** by someone she knows.
6   The apartment .... **(sell)** last week.
7   I hate .... **(lie to)** by my friends.
8   Nurses really ought .... **(pay)** more than they are.
9   The music must .... **(turn down)** by 12 o'clock at the latest.
10 Your free gift .... **(send)** to you in the next few days.
11 I wish I .... **(teach)** how to use a computer when I was at school.
12 Human bones .... **(find)** by archaeologists yesterday.
13 My car .... **(repair)** at the moment, so I can't give you a lift.
14 New York .... **(say)** to be one of the most dangerous cities in the world.
15 Hopefully, all forms of discrimination .... **(wipe out)** by the end of this century.

Changing from Active into Passive

● The object of the active verb becomes the subject in the passive sentence. The active verb changes into a passive form and the subject of the active verb becomes the agent which is either introduced with "by" or is omitted.

	Subject	Verb	Object	Agent
Active	Kate	wrote	the story.	
Passive	The story	was written		by Kate.

● **By + agent** is omitted when the agent is **unknown, unimportant, obvious from the context** or words such as: **someone, people, I,** etc. *They will give more information soon.* ➡ *More information will be given soon. ("by them" is omitted)*
● **By + agent** is used to say who or what did the action. She was knocked down **by a lorry**. With + instrument or **material** is used to say what the agent used. *The policeman was stabbed **with a knife**.*
● Verbs followed by a preposition *(look after, accuse of etc)* take the preposition immediately after them when turned into the passive. *She looks after her daughter well.* ➡ *Her daughter **is looked after** well.*
● For verbs which take two objects, it is more usual to begin the sentence with the person.
*They gave **her all the details**.* ➡ ***She** was given all the details. (more usual than: All the details were given to her.)*
● In **passive questions** with **who, whom** or **which** we do not omit **by**.
Who offered her the job? ➡ *Who was she offered the job **by**?*
● **Make, hear, help, see** are followed by a **to-infinitive** in the passive. *They saw him **cross** the street.* ➡ *He was seen **to cross** the street.* Note that **hear, see, watch** can be followed by a **present participle** in the active and passive. *We heard him **playing** the guitar.* ➡ *He was heard **playing** the guitar.*

3   Change the sentences from the active into the passive. Omit the agent where it can be omitted.

1   The British eat over thirty million hamburgers each year.
    ...*Over thirty million hamburgers are eaten by the British each year*....
2   Who wrote "One Hundred Years of Solitude?" ....
3   The bad weather has spoiled my holiday plans. ....
4   Do they always pay their workers on time? ....
5   The children picked the strawberries. ....
6   She saw them go out. ....
7   You should wash those walls before you paint them. ....

8 Penguin have translated all her books into English. ....

9 He objects to people telling him what to do. ....

10 Tesco are converting the old bank into a supermarket. ....

11 They told him not to say anything to her. ....

12 Did they give you a reward for finding their cat? ....

13 The nurses take very good care of the patients. ....

14 Everyone heard her shouting at the students. ....

15 Why have they given him a promotion? ....

16 I love people giving me presents. ....

17 When we got to the theatre, they had sold all the tickets. ....

18 The police have just arrested the man who broke into our house. ....

19 What did he tell you to do? ....

20 Oxfam will hold a fashion show next week. ....

21 They are holding the next World Cup in France. ....

22 When did they demolish that building? ....

23 The officers took the suspect in for questioning. ....

24 Will they hand out free T-shirts at the concert? ....

25 Does the school provide accommodation for all new teachers? ....

4 Change the sentences from the passive into the active.

1 Why was James asked to leave the club? ...*Why did they ask James to leave the club?*...

2 They love being invited to parties. ....

3 The best cream cakes are made by Sayers. ....

4 By the end of the party, all the food had been eaten. ....

5 Sanchez was beaten by Graff in the Women's Tennis Final. ....

6 My glasses must have been thrown away by mistake. ....

7 The building is being examined by Health and Safety experts this week. ....

8 Who was the television invented by? ....

9 She was heard complaining about the new timetable. ....

10 She was sent a telegram by the Queen on her 100th birthday. ....

11 The English language is now spoken by over two billion people worldwide. ....

12 My overdraft is being extended by the bank tomorrow. ....

13 Hundreds of free gifts are being given away by Donels this Saturday. ....

14 Why haven't the beds been made yet? ....

15 I hate being taken for granted. ....

16 The tickets should have been booked weeks ago. ....

17 A new shopping centre is being built on the outskirts of town. ....

18 Why was I not told about the meeting? ....

19 Further information can be obtained from your local post office. ....

20 When will you be interviewed for the post? ....

5 Fill in by or with.

1 This suit was designed ...*by*... Armani.

2 This cake is filled .... fresh cream.

3 Who was Australia discovered ....?

4 Ford cars are made .... experts.

5 The baby was covered .... a blanket.

6 "Carmen" was composed .... Bizet.

7 The coat was lined .... fur.

8 The food will be provided .... caterers.

9 The stew was flavoured .... garlic.

10 The Royal Wedding was watched .... millions.

6 Change into the passive.

Last month, Samuel Block opened a restaurant in the centre of Macclesfield. He had planned it for over five years, but he only completed it after local businessmen raised a large sum of money. A top hotelier has trained the waiters and they will wear specially designed uniforms to fit in with the restaurant's modern look. They have brought in a famous chef from France and they are going to give him complete control over the daily menu.

The verbs **believe, expect, feel, hope, know, report, say, think** etc are used in the following passive patterns in personal and impersonal constructions.

- **subject (person) + passive verb + to -inf** (personal construction)

  Doctors expect he will recover soon.
  ***He is expected to** recover soon.*

- **It + passive verb + that-clause** (impersonal construction)

  ***It is expected that** he will recover soon.*

7 Turn the following into the passive as in the example:

1 They say he is a millionaire.
He *...is said to be a millionaire....*
It *...is said that he is a millionaire....*
2 They expect the plane will be landing soon.
The plane ....
It ....
3 They believe he was working illegally.
He ....
It ....
4 They say he is feeling better.
He ....
It ....
5 They thought he had been brave to do so.
He ....
It ....

6 They think he has escaped from prison.
He ....
It ....
7 They expect he'll pass his exams.
He ....
It ....
8 They say she lied to the police.
She ....
It ....
9 They say they miss too many lessons.
They ....
It ....
10 They know she was always late for work.
She ....
It ....

8 Complete the sentences using the words in bold. Use two to five words.

1 The teacher scolded Jim for not paying attention.
was   Jim *...was scolded by the teacher...* for not paying attention.
2 Her parents named her after her grandmother.
was   She .... her grandmother.
3 Most people think that broken homes cause a lot of social problems.
thought   It .... cause a lot of social problems.
4 An editor will check the article.
be   The article .... an editor.
5 The traffic warden will give you a ticket if you park there.
be   You .... if you park there.
6 A lot of men enjoy football.
is   Football .... a lot of men.
7 The builder will have finished the extension by July.
been   The .... by July.
8 The teacher has given the students their homework.
have   The .... their homework.

9 They are blaming Martin for the accident.
is   Martin .... for the accident.
10 They are going to preview the film tomorrow evening.
is   The film .... tomorrow evening.
11 They will have settled the matter by this afternoon.
been   The matter .... by this afternoon.

9 Look at the notes, then write a report using the passive.

Yet again we experienced an earthquake last night.

A remote area in northern Spain/shake/by an earthquake last night. Several villages/totally destroy/and many people/leave/homeless. The total extent of the damage/still not known/but luckily few casualties/ report as people/warn/of the danger earlier and many villages/evacuate. Victims of the earthquake now/ offer/shelter in local churches/where food and drink/provide.

10 Rewrite the following text in the passive.

After 20 years of civil war, the Lebanese government is rebuilding Beirut. They will construct new offices and hotels. The authorities must also expand Beirut airport. Luckily, bombing did not destroy archaeological sites. By the year 2000, building companies will have completed most of the work. Lebanon's new look will attract many tourists in the future. A few groups have already visited this Middle Eastern paradise.

11 Rewrite the following text in the passive.

The critics have greeted with enthusiasm "Turning Point", Marvin Morton's new play. They regard it as his most mature work. Morton wrote it after he had studied people's behaviour for a considerable time. On the opening night the audience called Morton onto the stage and applauded him loudly. They are staging the play at the Apollo Theatre where they expect thousands of people to see it. Film companies have asked Morton to write a script for a film based on the play. We do not know yet whether Morton will seriously consider the proposal.

Oral Development 9

Look at the picture and the prompts and make sentences using the passive. You can also use your own ideas.

sea/pollute - waste/dump/for years - companies/ fine/last year - action/take - new laws/ introduced/soon - protest marches/organised/ recently - people/ask not swim/at present - fishermen/advise/fish elsewhere - hope/problem solve/two years - volunteers/ask/help/clean up

The sea has been polluted. etc

Causative Form

- We use **have + object + past participle** to say that we arrange for someone to do something for us.
  *He asked the mechanic to repair his car. He **had his car repaired**. (He didn't do it himself - the mechanic did it.)*

Present Simple	She **looks after** her children.	She **has** her children looked after.
Present Continuous	She **is looking after** her children.	She **is having** her children looked after.
Past Simple	She **looked after** her children.	She **had** her children looked after.
Past Continuous	She **was looking after** her children.	She **was having** her children looked after.
Future Simple	She **will look after** her children.	She **will have** her children looked after.
Future Continuous	She **will be looking after** her children.	She **will be having** her children looked after.
Present Perfect	She **has looked after** her children.	She **has had** her children looked after.
Present Perf. Continuous	She **has been looking after** her children.	She **has been having** her children looked after.
Past Perfect	She **had looked after** her children.	She **had had** her children looked after.
Past Perf. Continuous	She **had been looking after** her children.	She **had been having** her children looked after.
Infinitive	She can **look after** her children.	She can **have** her children looked after.
-ing form	She likes **looking after** her children.	She likes **having** her children looked after.

- The verb **to have**, when used in the causative, forms its **negations** and **questions** with **do/does** (Present S.) and **did** (Past S.). *She **doesn't have** the flowers arranged. **Did** you **have** the clothes ironed?*
- **Get** can be used instead of **have** in the causative. *Did you **have/get** your hair cut?*
- The **causative** can be used instead of the passive to express **accidents** or **misfortunes**.
  *He **had** his cheek bruised in a fight. (= His cheek was bruised in a fight.)*

---

12   **Read the situations, then write sentences using the causative form.**

1 The optician is testing her eyes. What is she doing?
...*She's having her eyes tested*....
2 If he doesn't drive more carefully, the police will take away his licence. What will happen to him? ....
....
3 This time tomorrow, an artist will be painting her son's portrait. What will she be doing? ....
4 Someone is cutting down the tree in our garden at the moment. What are we doing? ....
5 They can vaccinate your children against smallpox. What can you do? ....
6 She will hire someone to build a shed for her. What will she do?
....
7 The dentist is polishing Tom's teeth. What is Tom doing?
....
8 The police are towing away his car. What is happening to him?
....
9 Someone dry-cleans his suits every month. What does he do?
....
10 He has been paying a therapist to massage his back. What has he been doing? ....
11 Sally gets a hairdresser to dye her hair every month. What does she do? ....

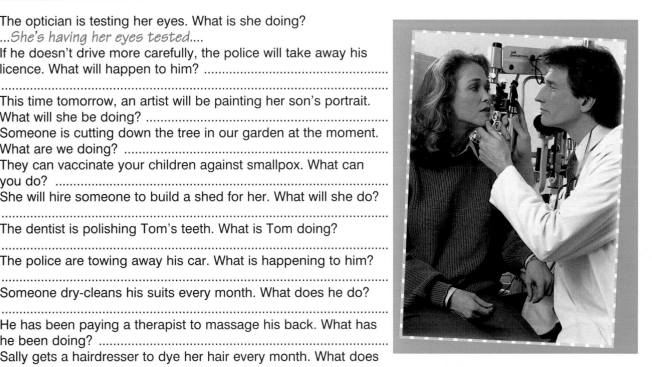

13 Write sentences in the causative form as in the example.

1 Do you ask someone to type your essays? ...*Do you have your essays typed?*....
2 Her photographs haven't been developed yet. ....
3 She doesn't like asking people to do her shopping. ....
4 Have you asked them to install a burglar alarm for you? ....
5 I didn't use to employ someone to do the housework for me. ....
6 The doctor examined her wound. ....
7 He isn't going to take his glasses to be adjusted today. ....
8 Did the detective order the constable to follow the suspect? ....
9 You should ask someone to collect your mail while you are away. ....
....
10 Did the doctor set Gary's broken leg? ....
11 Will she get someone to check her washing machine for her? ....
12 We're going to ask them to send us a copy of the contract. ....
13 Has the chauffeur been driving Mary's kids to school for years? ....
....
14 Was his arm broken in a car crash? ....
15 How many times has the plumber fixed John's tap this year? ....
....

● **Make/have + object + bare infinitive** are used to express that someone causes someone else to do something, but their meaning is slightly different.
*He **made Liz send** a fax. (He insisted that Liz should send a fax.)*
*He **had Liz send** a fax. (He asked Liz to send a fax.)*
● **Get + object + to -inf** is used to show that someone **persuades** someone else to do something.
*She **got her husband to cut** the grass. (She persuaded her husband to cut the grass.)*

14 Rephrase the following using have, make or get as in the example.

1 He insisted that Peter left immediately. ...*He made Peter leave immediately*....
2 Janet persuaded Diane to drive her to the airport. ....
3 My car radio is being fitted by Gary today. ....
4 She asked her sister to translate the article. ....
5 I finally persuaded the landlord to change the locks. ....
6 My mother insisted that I should wear a dress to the wedding. ....
7 I'll ask John to pick me up at the station. ....
8 Sue persuaded her colleagues to change their minds. ....
9 She is going to ask them to rewrite the assignment. ....
10 I can't believe he asked me to return the cheque. ....
11 He insisted that they should stay at home. ....
12 I'll try to persuade him to give you the money he owes you. ....
13 The receptionist asked her to wait outside his office. ....
14 The doctor insisted that she should go to hospital. ....
15 He asked the porter to carry his luggage. ....

15 Complete the sentences using the words in bold. Use two to five words.

1 They arranged for medical supplies to be flown into the region.
had They ...*had medical supplies flown*... into the region.
2 A shark bit Tony's leg off.
got Tony .... by a shark.

3 A lawyer will have to sign this document for you.
have   You .... this document signed by a lawyer.

4 Why did you insist that I buy this horrible cheese?
make   Why .... this horrible cheese?

5 She pays someone to clean the windows every month.
cleaned   She .... every month.

6 The labourers were forced to work seven days a week.
made   They .... seven days a week.

7 Someone will probably mug you if you walk through that part of town.
get   You .... if you walk through that part of town.

8 They will take away your licence if they catch you driving that way.
have   You .... away if they catch you driving that way.

9 She arranged for her neighbour to walk her dog while she was away.
had   She .... by her neighbour while she was away.

10 Please don't insist that I cook dinner tonight.
make   Please .... dinner tonight.

11 Someone stole their car while they were asleep.
had   They .... while they were asleep.

12 Her nose was broken in the accident.
got   She .... in the accident.

13 Did you insist they rewrite the composition?
make   Did .... the composition?

14 She hired someone to make new curtains for her house.
had   She .... for her house.

15 He got someone at the garage to adjust the brakes.
adjusted   He .... at the garage.

Oral Development 10

Architects are looking at plans for a luxurious hotel for Smithson International. In pairs comment on the jobs that have already been done, are being done, will be done, or will have been done, then make sentences using the causative. You can use your own ideas.

10 June

Things done: decorate VIP suites, build staff accommodation block, paint reception area

Things being done: build swimming pool, decorate dining room, furnish lounge, paint rooms

Things to be done: landscape gardens, build car park

Things that will have been done by the end of next month: install phones, fit bathrooms, equip sports centre

They have had the VIP suites decorated.

16   Complete the sentences using the words in bold. Use two to five words.

1   Fire has completely destroyed the left wing of the house.
    been   The left wing of the house ...*has been completely destroyed by*... fire.
2   Under no circumstances must you remove books from the library.
    removed   Under no circumstances .... from the library.
3   It's still possible to find copies of their album at selected music stores.
    found   Copies of their album .... at selected music stores.
4   Don't you object to people asking you for favours all the time?
    being   Don't you object to .... all the time?
5   The teacher insisted that all latecomers remain behind at the end of the class.
    made   The teacher .... at the end of the class.
6   I don't appreciate people not paying me on time.
    being   I don't appreciate .... on time.
7   You have to wear safety helmets at all times.
    worn   Safety helmets .... at all times.
8   These remains are believed to date back to the Bronze Age.
    these   It .... back to the Bronze Age.
9   Why did they make the decision without consulting me?
    made   Why .... without their consulting me?
10 Anne persuaded her brother to lend her the money.
    got   Anne .... her the money.
11 John has invited me to his birthday party.
    have   I .... John's birthday party.
12 I'd better get a mechanic to look over the car before we set off for Spain.
    looked   I'd better .... before we set off for Spain.
13 We have not yet finalised details for the wedding.
    been   Details .... for the wedding.
14 Aren't you going to ask someone to repair the roof before winter sets in?
    have   Aren't you .... the roof before winter sets in?
15 The office now handles all transactions on computer.
    handled   All transactions .... on computer.

17   Use the words in capitals to form a word that fits in the space in the same line.

The First Wedding Anniversary

Each year of (0) ...*marriage*... is associated with a certain   **MARRY**
anniversary gift. A couple's first anniversary is (1) ....   **TRADITION**
known as their paper anniversary. The reason why paper was
chosen is unclear, but there are a number of traditions associated with
this (2) ....

One thing the couple do on their first anniversary is to eat a piece of   **CELEBRATE**
their (3) .... wedding cake. This piece has usually been   **ORIGIN**
(4) .... after the reception and saved for the occasion. In   **FREEZE**
this way, they remember their wedding vows and the (5) ....   **CHOOSE**
they have made to spend the rest of their lives together.

Another tradition is for the couple to exchange paper gifts. A writing
set, for instance, would be a (6) .... gift. What the paper   **SUIT**
is meant to (7) .... is hard to say, but it may be a   **SYMBOL**
(8) .... that the couple have made a formal legal   **REMIND**
(9) ....   **AGREE**
Clocks and (10) .... watches are also associated with first   **SPECIAL**
wedding anniversaries, but again it is uncertain why.

Phrasal Verbs

go about with: keep company with
go ahead: go in front
go back on: break a promise, agreement, etc
go down with: become ill
go for: 1) attack, 2) apply for
go in for: enter a competition
go off: 1) explode, 2) (of food) go bad
go out: 1) be extinguished, 2) mix socially
go over: 1) examine details, 2) repeat
go round: be enough for everyone to have a share

....

hold back: 1) hesitate, 2) control, 3) keep a secret
hold on: wait
hold out: 1) endure, 2) last
hold up: 1) delay, 2) rob (sb or sth)

18 Fill in the correct particle(s).

1 Go ...*over*... the rules of the game once more.
2 You go .... and we'll follow close behind.
3 I've decided to go .... the teaching job.
4 The bomb will go .... in two minutes.
5 She is so beautiful she is going .... a beauty contest.
6 He stayed in bed after going .... the flu.
7 My father disapproves of the people I go ....
8 Bring some wood; the fire is going ....
9 You should never go .... a promise.
10 There weren't enough sandwiches to go ....
11 She went .... him with a knife.
12 The bank has been held .... twice this year.
13 Hold .... a minute while I get my jacket.
14 Will the car hold .... until we get to a garage?
15 The roadworks held .... the traffic.
16 Don't hold ...., tell me everything.
17 I was upset and unable to hold .... my tears.

19 Look at Appendix 1, then fill in the correct preposition.

1 He has absolutely no taste ...*in*... clothes.
2 He succeeded .... upsetting all his friends.
3 I think I was a bit mean .... Paula yesterday.
4 Are you having trouble .... your car?
5 Not many people have such a talent .... acting.
6 Cathy is very sensitive .... the needs of others.
7 This ticket is valid .... two days only.
8 I took pity .... the beggar and gave him £1.
9 She is completely unaware .... the trouble she has caused.
10 Children should be warned .... the dangers of drugs.
11 The government feels uneasy .... the current political situation.
12 There is no solution .... your problem.
13 Don't you have any pity .... the poor man?
14 Don't interfere .... their papers.
15 I've been longing .... some peace and quiet.
16 The detective went .... search .... the stolen painting.
17 The flat smells .... paint.
18 This ice-cream tastes .... almonds.
19 It's important to make good use .... your dictionary.
20 She's not used .... being spoken to like that.
21 This voucher is valid .... all Smiths stores.
22 Don't worry .... Garfield. He'll be OK.
23 I'm not worthy .... such an honour.
24 The children were throwing stones .... the window.

20 Complete the sentences using the words in bold. Use two to five words.

1 He had no right to treat me so rudely.
   have   He ...*shouldn't have treated me*... so rudely.
2 The conference took place in a large hotel.
   held   The conference .... hotel.
3 He has a good relationship with his parents.
   gets   He .... his parents.
4 He missed the end of the film because he fell asleep.
   due   He missed the end of the film .... asleep.
5 I'm sure the suspect is telling lies.
   be   The .... lies.
6 People believe she lives in New York.
   believed   She .... in New York.

For questions 1 - 12, read the text below and decide which answer (A, B, C or D) best fits each space.

Developing countries

There are **(0)** ..*B*... 140 countries which are **(1)** ... as 'developing', less developed and poor countries.

Although there are great **(2)** ... between them, they do have a number of **(3)** ... in common. For instance, many of the developing countries are in poverty. A few **(4)** ... to this rule are Saudi Arabia, Kuwait and Libya. However, because the economies of these three countries **(5)** ... largely on one export, oil, they are still vulnerable in the world market. Most of the developing countries **(6)** ... have very little industry.

Farming is often the only way in which the country can make money. **(7)** ... worse, many of the countries only produce enough food to **(8)** ... their own populations alive. India is a classic example of this, as no less than 70 percent of its 870 million people work the land for a **(9)** ... .

Another feature which **(10)** ... less developed countries is life expectancy. People die younger in developing countries because of the poverty in which they live. The poor have inadequate diets **(11)** ... to developed countries, and healthcare is also more **(12)** ... to be inferior.

0	**A**	mostly	**(B)**	roughly	**C**	partly	**D**	evenly
1	**A**	said	**B**	known	**C**	told	**D**	taken
2	**A**	changes	**B**	disagreements	**C**	differences	**D**	varieties
3	**A**	features	**B**	sides	**C**	faces	**D**	signs
4	**A**	separations	**B**	exceptions	**C**	differences	**D**	changes
5	**A**	decide	**B**	insist	**C**	lean	**D**	depend
6	**A**	then	**B**	although	**C**	while	**D**	still
7	**A**	Most	**B**	More	**C**	Quite	**D**	Even
8	**A**	have	**B**	keep	**C**	hold	**D**	make
9	**A**	luck	**B**	long	**C**	life	**D**	living
10	**A**	fastens	**B**	connects	**C**	attaches	**D**	combines
11	**A**	balanced	**B**	compared	**C**	matched	**D**	weighed
12	**A**	likely	**B**	probable	**C**	possible	**D**	definite

22 Complete the sentences using the words in bold. Use two to five words.

0 I'll pack some sandwiches for the picnic. We may be hungry later.
   case   I'll pack some sandwiches for the picnic ...*in case we get hungry*... later.
1 Mary is very surprised she passed her driving test.
   thought   Mary never .... her driving test.
2 I get up early so that I can avoid the traffic.
   order   I get up early .... the traffic.
3 The manager made all the staff work overtime.
   obliged   All the staff .... overtime.
4 Someone will have to replace this broken window.
   have   This broken window .... replaced.
5 All the children liked their new French teacher.
   popular   The new French teacher .... all the children.
6 You should learn to cook now.
   time   It's .... to cook.
7 There probably won't be any rain today.
   unlikely   It is .... any rain today.
8 It was easy for my team to win the match.
   difficulty   My team .... the match.

23 Use the words in capitals to form a word that fits in the space in the same line.

The Triathlon

A Triathlon consists of three sports – swimming, **(0)** ...*cycling*... and running. In the Olympics, the event is **(1)** .... made up of a 1,500m swim, a 40km bike ride and a 10km run. Elsewhere, a **(2)** .... of other events are held to test the **(3)** .... of athletes.

The first modern race was held in California as **(4)** .... as 1974. The San Diego Track Club were the **(5)** .... of the first event and the distances were slightly **(6)** .... than those in today's Olympics.

The first time the Triathlon put in an **(7)** .... at the Olympics was in the 2000 Sydney Games. What made it **(8)** .... was the grand setting of the Sydney Opera House and Harbour Bridge.

London is currently making **(9)** .... for a similar event in the 2012 Olympics. The majority of people participating will be **(10)** .... athletes, but amateurs can also take part.

CYCLE
USUAL

VARY
FIT

RECENT
ORGANISE
SHORT

APPEAR

MEMORY

PREPARE

PROFESSION

For questions 1 - 12, read the text below and decide which answer (A, B, C or D) best fits each gap. There is an example at the beginning (0).

Does the moon affect your behaviour?

For thousands of years, the moon has captured our **(0)** ...*C*... . Although it can be seen during the day, it is **(1)** .... associated with things that come out after **(2)** ...., like werewolves and witches. For thousands of years, the moon has been considered to have magical **(3)** .... and it is still a symbol of the supernatural.

Despite moon-landings in the second half of this century, the idea that the moon **(4)** .... our minds and bodies remains **(5)** .... A number of studies have reported more murders at full moon, more bleeding during surgery, a greater number of accidents and suicides, and more disturbed **(6)** .... in psychiatric hospitals. This apparent lunar influence has been called the 'Transylvania Effect'.

In **(7)** ...., the word lunacy itself promotes this belief. However, Ivan Kelly of the University of Saskatchewan and James Rotton of Florida International University have put **(8)** .... their belief that the 'Transylvania Effect' does not **(9)** .... exist at all. Furthermore, they **(10)** .... 'Transylvania Effect' theories, saying they were scientifically incorrect. Kelly claims moon moods are probably **(11)** .... by psychological factors. "If you believe the moon affects you, you alter your behaviour accordingly. There is no magic **(12)** .... at all."

0	**A** breath	**B** thoughts	**C** imagination	**D** minds
1	**A** better	**B** best	**C** more	**D** mostly
2	**A** night	**B** dark	**C** day	**D** light
3	**A** talents	**B** gifts	**C** powers	**D** strengths
4	**A** affects	**B** concerns	**C** changes	**D** alters
5	**A** contemporary	**B** popular	**C** famous	**D** fashionable
6	**A** manners	**B** ways	**C** actions	**D** behaviour
7	**A** time	**B** places	**C** fact	**D** order
8	**A** on	**B** away	**C** forward	**D** up
9	**A** frequently	**B** hardly	**C** eventually	**D** actually
10	**A** sacked	**B** rejected	**C** dropped	**D** refused
11	**A** resulted	**B** led	**C** caused	**D** occurred
12	**A** involved	**B** concerned	**C** mixed	**D** included

Part **2**

For questions 13 - 24, read the text below and think of the word which best fits each gap. Use only one word in each gap. There is an example at the beginning (0).

THE ISLE OF WIGHT

The Isle of Wight is a small island just **(0)** *...off...* the south coast of England near the towns of Portsmouth and Southampton.

Queen Victoria loved the island **(13)** .... much that she had Osborne House built there, which has not changed at all since the days when she **(14)** .... to visit with her huge family.
(15) .... tourist attractions include Butterfly World, where, **(16)** .... the name suggests, visitors can see a large range of butterflies, and two zoos. In summer it is usually warm and sunny — **(17)** .... for holidaymakers to enjoy the miles of clean beaches.

Alternatively, for those **(18)** .... want to be outdoors but don't like sunbathing, the Isle of Wight is an excellent place for cyclists. There are numerous little paths which lead to picturesque villages **(19)** .... over the island. Newport, the island's capital, is also **(20)** .... a visit. It is a busy little town with **(21)** .... of shops, boutiques, restaurants and cafés.

(22) .... the beginning of August, the island hosts the world's most famous yachting event, which takes **(23)** .... at Cowes. During Cowes Week, as it **(24)** .... known, every restaurant on the island is packed with people.

For questions 25 - 34, read the text below. Use the word given in capitals at the end of some of the lines to form a word that fits in the gap in the same line. There is an example at the beginning (0).

Hypochondriacs

There are people who spend years suffering from an **(0)** ...*illness*... which doctors are not usually **(25)** .... towards. Hypochondria is a **(26)** .... term which describes an abnormal amount of worry about your health when there is nothing **(27)** .... wrong.

Sufferers regularly visit their doctors with **(28)** .... about serious symptoms which doctors cannot explain. Hypochondriacs are always **(29)** .... about their health and often imagine that they are suffering from dangerous or incurable diseases. They waste doctors' time when they are really perfectly healthy.

The **(30)** .... between hypochondriacs and patients is that they cannot be **(31)** .... They continue to think there is something wrong with them. However, **(32)** .... to some doctors, this reaction should not be dismissed as all in their heads. Often, the pain is real and requires real **(33)** .... even when the illness is imaginary. For instance, **(34)** .... techniques and psychotherapy can help.

ILL
SYMPATHY
MEDICINE
PHYSICAL
COMPLAIN
PESSIMISM
DIFFER
ASSURE
ACCORD
TREAT
RELAX

Part **4**

For questions 35 - 42, complete the second sentence so that it has a similar meaning to the first sentence, using the word given. Do not change the word given. You must use between two and five words including the word given. There is an example at the beginning (0).

0 They worked hard on the project.
effort
They ...*put a lot of effort*... into the project.

35 It's possible that he didn't understand you.
may
He .... you.

36 I'm sure it wasn't Jim who installed the programme.
have
It .... Jim who installed the programme.

37 It wasn't necessary for Ann to tie up the dog.
tied
Ann .... the dog.

38 You can try all you want, but you'll never convince me to help you.
matter
You'll never convince me to help you, ... try.

39 I do not run as fast as I did when I was younger.
used
I .... I do now.

40 I don't really want to get up so early in the morning.
prefer
I .... up so early in the morning.

41 Although it was raining, we still went swimming.
of
In ...., we still went swimming.

42 She will probably get the job.
likely
She .... the job.

7 Reported Speech

Direct Speech gives the exact words someone said. We use inverted commas in Direct Speech. *"It's quite warm," she said.*	**Reported Speech** gives the exact meaning of what someone said but not the exact words. We do not use inverted commas in Reported Speech. *She said **it was quite warm**.*

Say - Tell - Ask

We use **say** in Direct Speech. We also use **say** in Reported Speech when **say** is not followed by the person the words were spoken to.	*"I can't help you," he **said**. ➡ He **said (that)** he couldn't help me.*
We use **tell** in Reported Speech when it is followed by the person the words were spoken to	*"I can't help you," he said to me. ➡ He **told me** he couldn't help me.*
We use **say + to-infinitive BUT** never ~~say about~~. We use **tell sb**, **speak/talk about**, instead.	*Mum **said to be** home by 10 o'clock.* *She **spoke/talked about/told us about** her adventures.*
We use **ask** in reported questions and commands, or in direct questions.	*He said to me, "Help me!" ➡ He **asked me** to help him.* *He asked, "Are you OK?" ➡ He **asked me if** I was OK.*

Expressions with say, tell and ask

Expressions with **say**	say good morning/evening etc, say something, say one's prayers, say a few words, say so, say no more, say for certain/sure etc
Expressions with **tell**	tell the truth, tell a lie, tell (sb) the time, tell sb one's name, tell a story, tell sb a secret, tell sb the way, tell one from another, tell sb's fortune, tell sb so, tell the difference etc
Expressions with **ask**	ask a favour, ask the time, ask a question, ask the price etc

1   **Fill in** say, tell **or** ask **in the correct form.**

1 My parrot can ...*say*... a few words in English.
2 Please .... me what you think of my new dress.
3 He .... that he couldn't reply to any more questions.
4 My mother used to .... me a story before I went to bed.
5 He promised to .... no more about the matter.
6 She stopped to .... the time because she thought she was late.
7 The little girl .... her prayers and then went to sleep.
8 Sally couldn't .... for certain whether or not she would be staying.
9 He had taken an oath, so he had to .... the truth in court.
10 With identical twins you can rarely .... the difference between them.
11 The old man always .... good morning to his neighbours.
12 "I'd love to go," she .... to me.
13 When I was younger I used to .... my sister all my secrets.
14 "Could you help me with these bags?" she .... me.
15 Rachel keeps .... me that she's going to change jobs, but she never does.

There are three types of Reported Speech: **statements**, **questions** and **commands/requests/suggestions**.

Statements

- Reported statements are introduced with **say** or **tell**. **Inverted commas** are omitted in Reported Speech. **That** is optional in the reported sentence.
  "She is sleeping," Tom said. ➡ *Tom **said (that)** she was sleeping.*

- **Tenses** change as follows:

	Direct Speech	Reported Speech
Present Simple	*"He **plays** well," she said.*	➡ *She said (that) he **played** well.*
Present Cont.	*"He **is playing** well," she said.*	➡ *She said (that) he **was playing** well.*
Past Simple	*"He **played** well," she said.*	➡ *She said (that) he **had played** well.*
Past Cont.	*"He **was playing** well," she said.*	➡ *She said (that) he **had been playing** well.*
Future Simple	*"He **will play** well," she said.*	➡ *She said (that) he **would play** well.*
Future Cont.	*"He **will be playing** well," she said.*	➡ *She said (that) he **would be playing** well.*
Present Perfect	*"He **has played** well," she said.*	➡ *She said (that) he **had played** well.*
Present Perf. Cont.	*"He **has been playing** well," she said.*	➡ *She said (that) he **had been playing** well.*

- Note that **Past Perfect** and **Past Perfect Continuous** remain the same in Reported Speech.

- **Tenses do not change in Reported Speech when**

the reporting verb (**said**, **told** etc) is in the Present, Future or Present Perfect.	*"The weather is hot," she **says**.* ➡ *She **says** (that) the weather is hot.*
the speaker expresses general truths, permanent states or conditions.	*"Water freezes at 0˚C," he said.* ➡ *He said (that) water **freezes** at 0˚C.*
the speaker is reporting something immediately after it was said (up to date).	*"The hotel **is** awful," he said.* ➡ *He said (that) the hotel **is** awful. (up to date)*
the reported sentence deals with unreal past, conditionals type 2/type 3 or wishes,	*"I wish I **were** rich," she said.* ➡ *She said she wished she **were** rich.*

- If the speaker expresses something which is believed to be true, the tenses may change or remain unchanged.
  "I love the place," she said. ➡ *She said she **loves**/**loved** the place.*

- However, if the speaker expresses something which is believed to be untrue, the tenses change.
  "China is a small country," he said. ➡ *He said (that) China **was** a small country.*

- The **Past Simple** changes to the **Past Perfect** or remains the **same**. When the reported sentence contains a time clause, the tenses remain unchanged.
  *"The car broke down **while I was driving** to work," he said.* ➡ *He said the car had broken down **while he was driving** to work.*
  Note: If the reported sentence is out of date, the tenses change, but if it is up to date, the tenses can remain the same. *"He **moved out** a month ago," he said.* ➡ *He said that he **had moved out** a month before. (speech reported after he had moved out - out of date)* *"I **am going** to the cinema tonight," she said.* ➡ *She said she **is going** to the cinema tonight. (speech reported before she goes to the cinema - up to date)*

- **Personal pronouns** and **possessive adjectives** change according to context.
  *"No, I won't lend **you my** new car!" he said.* ➡ *He said he wouldn't lend **me his** new car.*

- Certain words change as follows depending on the context.
  Direct Speech: this/these   here   come   *"Will you **come** to my house for dinner?" she said.*
  Reported Speech: that/those   there   go   *She asked him to **go** to her house for dinner.*

7 Reported Speech

● **Time words** can change or remain the same depending on the time reference.

Direct Speech	Reported Speech
tonight, today, this week/month/year	➡ that night, that day, that week/month/year
now	➡ then, at that time, at once, immediately
now that	➡ since
yesterday, last night/week/month year	➡ the day before, the previous night/week/month/year
tomorrow, next week/month/year	➡ the following day/the day after, the following/next week/month/year
two days/months/years etc, ago	➡ two days/months/years etc, before

*"I'm sitting an exam **tomorrow**," he said. ➡ He said he was sitting an exam **the next/following day**. (out-of-date reporting) "I'm sitting an exam **tomorrow**," he said. ➡ He said he **is sitting** an exam **tomorrow**. (up-to-date reporting)*

2 Turn the following sentences into Reported Speech.

1 "I'm visiting Greece," says Angela. **(up-to-date reporting)**
...*Angela says she's visiting Greece*....
2 "I've never been to Paris before," said John. **(out-of-date reporting)**
....
3 "I'm taking my driving test next week," she said. **(up-to-date reporting)**
....
4 "I don't speak Spanish," said Sarah. ....
5 "My house is not far from the town centre," he says. ....
6 "Water boils at 100°C," he said. ....
7 "Australia is a very big country," he said. ....
8 "If I see him, I'll invite him to the party," said Mary. **(out-of-date reporting)** ....
9 "I was locking the car when a traffic warden turned up," she said. ....
....
10 "I'm not going on holiday next week," he said. **(up-to-date reporting)** ....
11 "I've written five letters this morning," said Eddy. **(up-to-date reporting)** ....
....
12 "I saw a car accident last night," he said to me. ....
13 "I met David while I was working in Manchester," she said. ....
....
14 "I'll see you tonight," she said to him. **(out-of-date reporting)** ....
15 "It's time you got a job," his mother said to him. ....
16 "If you had studied harder, you would have passed your exam," the teacher said to Tom. ....
....
17 "If I were rich, I would buy a mansion in Beverly Hills," she said. ....
....

Reported Questions - Indirect Questions

● **Reported questions** are used to report someone else's questions, suggestions, offers or requests. In reported questions, we use affirmative word order and the question mark becomes a full stop. Inverted commas are omitted. To report a question we use: a) **ask + question word** (who, which, where, how etc) when the direct question begins with a question word; b) **ask + if/whether** when the direct question begins with an auxiliary verb (**do**, **have**, **can** etc). Tenses, personal pronouns, possessive adjectives, time words etc change as in statements.

Direct questions	Reported questions
He asked her, "What is your name?"	*He asked her **what her name was**.*
He asked her, "Do you like tea?"	*He asked her **if/whether she liked** tea.*

3   Turn the following sentences into Reported Speech.

1   "Will you be going to San Francisco next summer?" his boss asked. ...*His boss asked him if he would be going to San Francisco the following summer.*...

2   "Why were you in a hurry?" she asked me. ....

3   "Do you want a lift to work tomorrow?" he asked her. ....

4   "What time have you arranged to meet Clare?" he asked her. ....

5   "How long has Jane been working here?" she asked me. ....

6   "Who left the door open?" she asked them. ....

7   "Did you actually see the man fall?" the reporter asked the bystander. ....
....

8   "Will you give me a hand lifting the piano?" the workman asked his helper. ....
....

9   "Can you check the brakes please?" she asked the mechanic. ....
....

10   "Have they finished renovating their house?" he asked me. ....

11   "Is Mary still having a party next Saturday?" she asked me. ....
....

12   "Where does your father work?" the teacher asked him. ....

●   **Indirect questions** are used to ask for information/advice. They are introduced with: **Could you tell me...?**, **Do you know ...?**, **I wonder ...**, **I want to know ...**, **I doubt ...**, etc and the verb is in the affirmative. If the indirect question starts with **I wonder ...**, **I want to know ...** or **I doubt ...**, the question mark is omitted. Question words (**what, who, where** etc) or **whether** can be followed by an infinitive in the indirect question if the subject of the question is the same as the speaker.

Direct questions	Indirect questions
He asked me, "How old is Thomas?"	*Do you know **how old Thomas is**?*
He asked me, "Is it correct?"	*He wondered **if/whether it is/was** correct.*
He asked me, "Where can I leave it?"	*He wanted to know **where he could leave** it/**where to leave** it.*

4   Turn the following sentences into Indirect Questions. Omit question marks where necessary.

1   Where did I leave my glasses? **(I wonder ...)** ...*I wonder where I left my glasses.*...

2   Is John planning to call a meeting? **(Did you know ...)** ....

3   Have they ever had a hit single before? **(Do you know ...)** ....

4   When are you leaving? **(I want to know ...)** ....

5   Did he tell the truth? **(I doubt ...)** ....

6   Where is the nearest swimming pool? **(Could you tell me ...)** ....
....

7   Who left that message on our answerphone? **(She wondered ...)** ....
....

8   What time are they due to arrive? **(He wanted to know ...)** ....

Reported Commands/Requests/Suggestions

●   To report **commands, requests, suggestions** we use an introductory verb (**advise, ask, beg, offer, suggest** etc) (see pages 111,112) followed by a **to-infinitive**, an **-ing form** or a **that-clause** depending on the introductory verb.

"Be careful," he said to me.	➡ *He told me to **be careful**. (command)*
"Please don't talk," he said to me.	➡ *He asked me **not to talk**. (request)*
"Let's watch TV," he said.	➡ *He **suggested watching** TV. (suggestion)*
"You'd better go to the dentist," he said.	➡ *He **suggested that I (should)** go to the dentist. (suggestion/advice)*

7 Reported Speech

Turn the following sentences from Direct to Reported Speech.

1 "Don't run down the corridors, please," he said to us. ...*He asked us not to run down the corridors*....
2 "May I leave the room, please?" said the student. ....
3 "Let's turn on the television," said Paul. ....
4 "Soldiers! Stand to attention!" said the Major. ....
5 "Can you open the window?" she said to me. ....
6 "Shall we go ice-skating on Saturday?" said Miles. ....
7 "Don't touch the statue!" he said to us. ....
8 "Shall we go camping this summer?" said my brother. ....
9 "Let's have a picnic tomorrow," said John. ....
10 "You'd better go to bed now," he said to the children. ....
....

Modal Verbs in Reported Speech

● Some modal verbs change in Reported Speech when the reported sentence is out of date, as follows:
will/shall ➡ would, can ➡ could (present reference) / **would be able to** (future reference), **may ➡ might/could,**
shall ➡ should (asking for advice) / **would** (asking for information) / **offer** (expressing offers), **must ➡ must/had**
to (obligation) (* **must** remains the same when it expresses possibility or deduction), **needn't ➡ didn't need to /**
didn't have to (present reference) / **wouldn't have to** (future reference).

Direct Speech	Reported Speech
He said, "I'll phone you this evening."	➡ He said that he **would** phone me that evening.
He said, "I **can** speak French."	➡ He said (that) he **could** speak French. (fact)
He said, "I **can** join you soon."	➡ He said (that) he **would be able** to join us soon. (ability)
He said, "I **may** be late home."	➡ He said (that) he **might** be late home.
He said, "How **shall** I get there?"	➡ He asked how he **should** get there. (advice)
He said, "Where **shall** we go?"	➡ He asked where they **should** go. (information)
He said, "**Shall** I take you home?"	➡ He **offered** to take me home. (offer)
He said, "You **must** try harder."	➡ He said (that) I **had to** try harder. (obligation)
He said, "You **must** be joking."	➡ He said (that) I **must** be joking. (deduction)
He said, "You **should** take a holiday."	➡ He said (that) I **should** take a holiday.
He said, "She **had better** tidy her room."	➡ He said (that) she **had better** tidy her room.
He said, "She **needn't** know who he was."	➡ He said (that) she **didn't need to/have to** know who he was.
He said, "You **needn't** meet me tomorrow."	➡ He said (that) I **wouldn't have to** meet him the next day.

6 **Turn the following sentences into Reported Speech.**

1 He said, "Shall I carry your bags?" ...*He offered to carry my bags*....
2 He said, "She needn't see the report." ....
3 He said, "I'll pick you up at 4 o'clock." ....
4 He said, "You should get away for a while." ....
5 He said, "Kevin may need your help later." ....
6 He said, "You must control your feelings.". ....
7 He said, "You need to let me know tomorrow." ....
8 He said, "She had better not say that again." ....
9 He said, "We must be cousins." ....
10 He said, "I can run faster than you." ....
11 He said, "I can meet you next week." ....
12 He said, "Who shall I go to for help?" ....
13 He said, "Where shall we go to eat tonight?" ....
14 He said, "Shall I lend you the money?" ....

Special Introductory Verbs

Introductory verb	Direct Speech	Reported Speech
agree + to-inf	"Yes, I'll be happy to help you."	➡ He **agreed to help** me.
demand	"Tell the truth!"	➡ He **demanded to be told** the truth.
offer	"Would you like me to open the door?"	➡ He **offered to open** the door.
promise	"I'll definitely be here early."	➡ He **promised to be** there early.
refuse	"No, I won't lend you any money."	➡ He **refused to lend** me any money.
threaten	"Hand over your money or I'll shoot you."	➡ He **threatened to shoot** me if I didn't hand over my money.
claim	"I saw him steal the car."	➡ He **claimed to have seen** him steal the car.
advise + sb + to-inf	"You should see a doctor."	➡ He **advised me to see** a doctor.
allow	"You can borrow my car."	➡ He **allowed me to borrow** his car.
ask	"Please, turn the light off."	➡ He **asked me to turn** the light off.
beg	"Please, please stop shouting so loudly."	➡ He **begged me to stop** shouting so loudly.
command	"Leave the room!"	➡ He **commanded us to leave** the room.
encourage	"Go ahead, drive the car."	➡ He **encouraged me to drive** the car.
forbid	"You must not arrive late tonight."	➡ He **forbade me to arrive** late that night.
instruct	"Lift the receiver and wait for the dialling tone."	➡ He **instructed me to lift** the receiver and wait for the dialling tone.
invite sb	"Would you like to come out to dinner with me?"	➡ He **invited me to go** out to dinner with him.
order	"Close the door immediately."	➡ He **ordered me to close** the door immediately.
permit	"You may leave now."	➡ He **permitted/allowed me to leave** then.
remind	"Don't forget to water the plants."	➡ He **reminded me to water** the plants.
urge	"Try to be punctual."	➡ He **urged me to try** to be punctual.
warn	"Don't go near the edge of the cliff."	➡ He **warned me not to go** near the edge of the cliff.
want	"I'd like you to study harder."	➡ He **wanted me to study** harder.
accuse sb of + -ing form	"You stole my handbag!"	➡ She **accused me of stealing** her handbag.
apologise for	"I'm sorry I was rude to you."	➡ He **apologised for being** rude to me.
admit (to)	"Yes, I broke the window."	➡ He **admitted (to) breaking/having broken** the window.
boast about	"I'm more intelligent than you."	➡ He **boasted about being** more intelligent than me.
complain to sb about	"You always leave the door open."	➡ He **complained to me about my** always **leaving** the door open.
deny	"No, I didn't break the window."	➡ He **denied breaking/having broken** the window.
insist on	"You must take all the medicine."	➡ He **insisted on me/my taking** all the medicine.
suggest	"Let's go out for a walk."	➡ He **suggested going** out for a walk.
agree + that-clause	"Yes, it's a great idea."	➡ He **agreed that** it was a great idea.
boast	"I'm the best player of all."	➡ He **boasted that** he was the best player of all.
claim	"I know who stole your car."	➡ He **claimed that** he knew who had stolen my car.
complain	"You never help me."	➡ She **complained that** he never helped her.
deny	"I never touched the vase!"	➡ He **denied that** he had ever touched the vase.
exclaim	"It's a success!"	➡ He **exclaimed that** it was a success.
explain	"It's a difficult theory to follow."	➡ He **explained that** it was a difficult theory to follow.
inform sb	"Your application is under review."	➡ He **informed me that** my application was under review.
promise	"I won't forget again."	➡ He **promised that** he wouldn't forget again.
suggest	"You ought to help her out."	➡ He **suggested that** I help her out.
explain to sb + how	"That's how I crashed the car."	➡ He **explained to me how** he had crashed the car.

7 Reported Speech

Introductory verb	Direct Speech	Reported Speech
wonder where/what why/how + clause (when the subject of the introductory verb is **not the same** as the subject in the reported question)	He asked himself, "How can she do that?" ➡ He asked himself, "Where have they gone?" ➡ He asked himself, "Why is Tom so rude?" ➡ He asked himself, "What will they do?" ➡	He **wondered how** she could do that. He **wondered where** they had gone. He **wondered why** Tom was so rude. He **wondered what** they would do.
wonder + whether + to-inf or **clause**	He asked himself, "Shall I take the job?" ➡	He **wondered whether** to take/ he should take the job.
wonder where/what/ how + to-inf (when the subject of the infinitive is the **same** as the subject of the verb)	He asked himself, "What shall I do next?" ➡ He asked himself, "How can I break the news?" ➡	He **wondered what** to do next. He **wondered how** to break the news.

7 First write an appropriate introductory verb, then report the following sentences.

1 "You took my bag, didn't you?" ...accuse... – ...She accused me of taking her bag....
2 "I'll bring my homework tomorrow." .... – ....
3 "Get out of the room now!" .... – ....
4 "The train leaves at 6 o'clock." .... – ....
5 "Don't forget to make a dental appointment." .... – ....
6 "Please, please help me!" .... – ....
7 "You must give us a call when you get back!" .... – ....
8 "I won't help you." .... – ....
9 "Would you like to go out with us?" .... – ....
10 "If you do that again, I'll punish you." .... – ....
11 "I didn't break the vase!" .... – ....
12 "Will the rain ever stop?" .... – ....
13 "First turn this knob, then flick the switch." .... – ....
14 "Yes, you're right." .... – ....
15 "What about going for a walk?" .... – ....
16 "You should go on a diet." .... – ....
17 "You mustn't touch the camera." .... – ....
18 "Don't cross the road without looking both ways." .... – ....
19 "Would you like me to water your plants?" .... – ....
20 "Yes, it was me who broke the teapot." .... – ....
21 "It is a difficult situation, you see." .... – ....
22 "I met the Queen once, you know." .... – ....
23 "You always leave the bathroom in a mess!" .... – ....
24 "You may use the fax machine whenever you want." .... – ....
25 "You must stay until 5 o'clock every day!" .... – ....
26 "Give me the money!" .... – ....
27 "I crossed the Atlantic single-handed." .... – ....
28 "You may call me by my first name." .... – ....
29 "Please, empty all the ashtrays before you leave the room." .... – ....
30 "Cease fire!" .... – ....
31 "Go on, tell us what's on your mind." .... – ....
32 "I'd like you to cook dinner tonight." .... – ....
33 "I'm sorry I spoilt the surprise party." .... – ....
34 "Sure, I'd be glad to lend a hand." .... – ....
35 "I'll never let you down again." .... – ....

Reporting a dialogue or a conversation

● In conversations or dialogues we use a mixture of statements, commands and questions. When we report dialogues or conversations, we use: **and, as, adding that, and he/she added that, explaining that, because, but, since, so, and then he/she went on to say, while, then** etc or the introductory verb in the present participle form. Exclamations such as: **Oh!, Oh dear!, Well!** etc are omitted in Reported Speech.

Direct Speech		Reported Speech
"I was sorry to hear you haven't been well. I hope you're feeling better now," she said.	➡	*She said she was sorry to hear I hadn't been well **and added that** she hoped I was feeling better.*
"What a brilliant idea!" she exclaimed. "Why didn't I think of that?"	➡	*She exclaimed that it was a brilliant idea **and** wondered why she hadn't thought of it.*
"Can you make dinner tonight, Tom?" she said. "I'm working late."	➡	*She asked Tom if he could make dinner that night, **explaining that** she was working late.*

Exclamations - Yes/No short answers - Question tags

● **Exclamations** are replaced in Reported Speech with **exclaim, thank, wish, say, cry out in pain** etc, **give an exclamation of surprise/horror/disgust/delight** etc. The exclamation mark becomes a full stop. Exclamatory words such as **Oh!, Eek!, Wow**! etc are omitted in the reported sentence.

"Wow!" she said when she saw the huge cake. ➡ *She **cried out in surprise** when she saw the huge cake.*

● **Yes/No short answers** are expressed in Reported Speech with a **subject + appropriate auxiliary verb OR subject + appropriate introductory verb**. *"Can you help me?" she said. "No," he said.* ➡ *She asked him if he could help her but he said he **couldn't**. **OR** She asked him if he could help her but he **refused**.*

● **Question tags** are omitted in Reported Speech. We can use an appropriate introductory verb to retain their effect. *"They haven't made up their minds yet, have they?" she said.* ➡ *She **wondered** if they had already made up their minds.*

8 Rewrite the following conversations in Reported Speech.

A "Hello John. Have a seat, won't you?" Mr Williams said.
"Thank you, sir," John replied. "I'm sorry I'm a bit late, but the traffic was dreadful."
"Don't worry John, it's not important," Mr Williams said.
"You see, I finally made up my mind last night to give you Alan Tomkin's job, since he's retiring."
"That's excellent news Mr Williams, and I give you my word I'll do my best to do a good job," John replied.
"Why don't you take your new contract home tonight and study it, John?" Mr Williams said.
...Mr Williams greeted John, and invited him to sit down....

....
....
....
....

B "I've got a job interview today. Can you give me some advice?" said Graham. "Well," said Tracy, "You should dress smartly. You needn't wear a suit, but you had better wear a tie. You must arrive on time. And you ought to prepare some questions about the company." "Thanks," said Graham. "I'll let you know how I get on." "Yes, phone me tonight," Tracy replied.

....
....
....
....

7 Reported Speech

Punctuation in Direct Speech

- We capitalise the first word of the quoted sentence. The full stop, the question mark, the exclamation mark and the comma come inside the inverted commas. The comma comes outside the inverted commas only when **he said/asked** precedes the quoted sentence. *"She is working," he said. He said, "She is working." "She," he said, "is working."* We do not use a comma after the question mark. *"Can I leave now?" I asked.* **BUT** *I asked, "Can I leave now?"*
- When the subject is a pronoun, it comes before the reporting verb (**said, asked** etc), but when the subject is a noun, it often comes after **said, asked** etc at the end or in the middle of the quoted sentence. *"He crashed his car," she said. "He crashed his car," said Anna. "He," said Anna, "crashed his car."* **BUT** *She/Anna said, "He crashed his car."* (NOT: ~~Said Anna~~, *"He crashed his car."*)
- Each time the speaker changes, we normally start a new paragraph.

9 Turn the following into a conversation. Mind the punctuation.

The ballerina claimed that she couldn't perform that evening. The theatre manager demanded to know the reason but the ballerina refused to discuss it. The manager insisted that she must perform and reminded her that she had signed a contract. Then, he threatened not to pay her if she didn't dance. The ballerina exclaimed that this was a disgraceful way to treat a star and she reminded him how famous she was. Then, she warned him that she might never dance for the company again. The manager apologised for losing his temper, suggested that they should be reasonable about the matter and begged her not to let the public down. Then, he politely asked her why she couldn't perform and she explained that she had twisted her ankle.

...*"I can't perform this evening," said the ballerina....* ....
....
....
....
....

Subjunctive

- The bare infinitive form of the subjunctive is used after certain verbs and expressions to give emphasis. These are: **advise, ask, demand, insist, propose, recommend, request, suggest, it is essential, it is imperative, it is important, it is necessary, it is vital** followed by **(that) + subject**. In British English we normally use **should + simple form** instead of the bare infinitive form of the subjunctive. *It is essential (that) you **finish** this work today. (more usual) It is essential **that you should finish** this work today. (less usual)*

10 Give the correct form of the verbs in brackets. Some of the verbs are passive.

1 It is imperative that we ..*follow/should follow*... **(follow)** his orders to the last letter.
2 He insisted that he .... **(pay)** for the meal.
3 He proposed that women .... **(admit)** into the club.
4 It is important that you .... **(take)** these pills three times a day.
5 He demanded that no one else .... **(allow)** to see the contract.
6 She recommended that we .... **(stay)** at the other hotel.

11 Turn the following sentences into Direct Speech.

1 He denied spending the rent money. ...*"No, I didn't spend the rent money," he said....*
2 She exclaimed that it was a brilliant idea. ....
3 He explained to me how he had become a millionaire. ....
4 I offered to help her with her composition. ....
5 They permitted us to swim in their pool. ....

114

6 She insisted on his wearing a tuxedo at the wedding. ....

7 He wondered where to send his application. ....

8 She complained to me about my leaving the car unlocked. ....

9 They encouraged their son to take piano lessons. ....

10 He instructed me to unplug it first and then use a screwdriver. ....

....

12 Turn the following dialogue into Reported Speech.

John: "I feel really awful today, Mum."

Mum: "Why, what's the matter?"

John: "I've got a dreadful headache and I feel a bit dizzy."

Mum: "Oh dear, that sounds quite serious."

John: "I know. I wonder what's wrong with me. I've been feeling like this for a few days."

Mum: "Maybe you should go and see a doctor."

John: "Yes, I think so."

Mum: "I'll make you an appointment. And perhaps you should take the day off school."

John: "But Mum, I can't take the day off school just for a headache. I've got a test today."

...John said he felt really awful that day. ...

13 Turn the following into a conversation, taking care to use the correct punctuation.

A policewoman was questioning a possible witness about a bank robbery in North London yesterday. She wanted to know if the man had any information which would help the police. The witness claimed to have seen three men run out of the bank and get into a red van which was parked nearby. He insisted that one of the men had been carrying a large suitcase. The policewoman then asked the witness to describe the three men, but he admitted that he had not been able to get a good look at them. The policewoman suggested that he come to the police station to look at some photographs of possible suspects. The man agreed and promised that he would do whatever he could to help.

...A policewoman was questioning a possible witness about a bank robbery in North London yesterday. "Do you have any information...

14 Turn the following into Direct Speech.

Mr Granger said good morning to everyone and thanked them all for coming. He said that he expected that they were all wondering why he had called the meeting, and promised that he wouldn't keep them in suspense any longer. He explained that a large multinational company had offered to buy the factory for £10 million and he went on to invite people to give their views on whether or not they should sell. He warned them that it was a very important decision they had to make and urged them to think about the matter very carefully as everyone's future could depend on it.

15 Rewrite the following sentences in Reported Speech.

1 "Don't come home late," she said to me. "You've got to get up early tomorrow morning."

   ...She advised me not to come home late as I had to get up early the next morning....

2 "Can I borrow a cup of sugar?" she asked. "I've run out." ....

....

3 "Why are you always making fun of Jane?" she asked him. "She gets really upset." ....

....

4 "Would you like to come over for lunch on Sunday?" she asked. "We are having a barbecue." ....

....

5 "Are you staying in tonight?" Jim asked her, "Or aren't you?" ....

....

6 "No, I didn't take your ticket," he said, "but I know who did." ....

....

7 Reported Speech

7 "Betty can't come shopping with us," she said. "She's got a driving lesson." ....

8 "Okay, so I made a mistake," he said. "I'm sorry." ....

9 "Can you come home early?" she said to me. "I've got a surprise for you." ....

10 "Let's go for a picnic," he said. "It's such a lovely day." ....

11 "Why are you leaving now?" she asked. "The party's just beginning." ....

12 "I'm going to study hard," he said. "I want to pass this test." ....

13 "I really like the pink dress," she said to the sales assistant. "How much is it?" ....

14 "I saw Victoria in the supermarket," he said. "She didn't look very well." ....

15 "This is delicious," she said to him. "You should cook professionally." ....

16 "OK. I'll go to the cinema with you," she said, "but let's have dinner first." ....

17 "Tell me where you've been," he said, "and don't stay out late again." ....

18 "Come to dinner on Saturday," she said. "Don't forget, I live at 34 Green Street." ....

19 "You really should go to college," he said. "A secretarial course is always useful." ....

20 "Hurry up," she said, "the performance is starting in half an hour." ....

21 "If you don't cooperate, we'll fall behind schedule," he said. ....

22 "Do you want me to take you home after school?" he asked. "It's too far for you to walk." ....

16 Complete the sentences using the words in bold. Use two to five words.

1 "I got better marks in the test than you did," she said.
 about She ...*boasted about getting better marks*... in the test than I had.
2 "How about going to the Caribbean for our honeymoon?" she asked.
 suggested She .... to the Caribbean for their honeymoon.
3 "You must do your homework now," he said.
 on He .... my homework immediately.
4 "First you turn right and then left to get to the shop," he said.
 how He .... to get to the shop.
5 "No, I won't lie for you any more," she said to him.
 to She .... any more.
6 "Get this dog out of the house now!" he shouted at me.
 demanded He .... the dog out of the house immediately.
7 "You'd better not do that again or I'll lose my temper," he said to me.
 warned He .... that again or he'd lose his temper.
8 "Don't forget to move everything out of the hall," she said to us.
 reminded She .... everything out of the hall.
9 "You're right, he is a bit strange," she said.
 agreed She .... a bit strange.
10 "Shall I go tonight?" he asked himself.
 to He .... go that night.
11 "I think you should stay in bed and get plenty of rest," the doctor told her.
 she The doctor .... in bed and get plenty of rest.
12 "Will I see him again soon?" she asked herself.
 would She .... see him again soon.

116

13 "What a wonderful new outfit you're wearing!" she said.
exclaimed She .... a wonderful new outfit.
14 "You mustn't forget to buy a Father's Day card this year," she told me.
reminded She .... a Father's Day card that year.
15 "Nobody must find out where I'm hidden," he said.
found He said that it was vital .... where he was hidden.
16 "I'm the greatest footballer of all time," he said.
boasted He .... the greatest footballer of all time.
17 "I'll never forget the way we met," he said.
would He .... the way they had met.
18 "Tidy your room before you go out," she said to me.
on She .... my room before I went out.
19 "Let's go for a walk," she said to them.
go She .... for a walk.
20 "Do your shoelaces up or you'll fall over," she said.
me She .... my shoelaces, otherwise I'd fall over.
21 "I don't like this settlement," he said.
complained He .... like that settlement.
22 "Where's Sally going on holiday?" asked Jane.
was Jane .... on holiday.
23 "Don't touch that saucepan because it's hot," she said to me.
not She .... the saucepan because it was hot.
24 "I'm sorry I missed the appointment," he said.
apologised He .... the appointment.
25 "You need to leave now," he said to me.
necessary He told me that it was .... at once.
26 "Please, please don't go Suzie," she cried.
begged She .... go.
27 "You broke that window Tom," said Mr Smith.
of Mr Smith .... window.
28 "Oh, you look so beautiful," he said to her.
remarked He .... very beautiful.
29 "You needn't come tomorrow," said Grandma to me.
have Grandma said .... to go the next day.
30 "You shouldn't stay in the sun for longer than fifteen minutes," the doctor told us.
advised The doctor .... in the sun for longer than fifteen minutes.
31 "You must not enter the room without permission," he said to us.
to He .... the room without permission.
32 "Do try and practise a bit more," she said to us.
urged She .... a bit more.
33 "I would like you to be there by 6 o'clock," she said to them.
wanted She .... there by 6 o'clock.
34 "OK, I'll wait a little longer," she said.
to She .... a little longer.
35 "Of course I didn't take your wallet," she said.
denied She .... his wallet.
36 "Yes, I think it is the best option," she said.
that She .... best option.
37 "Leave this building immediately!" he said to us.
ordered He .... the building immediately.
38 "You mustn't get out of the car," my mother said to us.
forbade My mother .... of the car.
39 "Will I ever see them again?" he asked himself.
whether He .... ever see them again.
40 "You might book a room before you go," she said to us.
suggested She .... a room before we went.

7 Reported Speech

17 Use the words in capitals to form a word that fits in the space in the same line.

Reasons to Keep a Pet

Most animal **(0)** ...*lovers*... will tell you that there are many benefits to keeping a pet. As **(1)** .... have found, owning a pet can **(2)** .... improve your health, as pet owners are shown to have lower blood pressure and cholesterol levels than people who don't keep animals. | **LOVE** **RESEARCH** **SIGNIFY**

(3) .... in a recent survey admitted to being very **(4)** .... to their animals. Cats and dogs, in particular, are excellent **(5)** .... Although the world can sometimes be an **(6)** .... place, your pet is usually your friend for life. | **PARTICIPATE** **ATTACH** **COMPANY** **FRIEND**

Additionally, dog owners are less likely to feel **(7)** .... when walking, as there is less **(8)** .... of them being attacked. Walking with your pet also provides a **(9)** .... form of physical exercise. Children, too, can learn how to be caring adults by keeping a pet, and pets can decrease feelings of **(10)** .... and isolation. | **SECURE** **LIKELY** **VALUE** **LONELY**

Oral Development 11

In pairs, students look at the first picture and make up a short dialogue according to the situation given. Next, a pair of students act out the dialogue while the rest of the class takes notes. Then students report the conversation. Do the same with the other picture.

Yesterday, Nick and Rob, who are colleagues, spent their lunch hour together for the first time. What could they have been talking about?

Last week, Pamela ran into an old school friend, Louise, while shopping. They had coffee together. What could they have been saying?

Phrasal Verbs

keep at sth: continue working on sth
keep away (from): stay away
keep back: 1) stay back, 2) conceal
keep behind: make sb remain after others have left
keep sb/sth down: control
keep (oneself) from: 1) prevent from, 2) avoid
keep in with: remain friendly with
keep sb/sth off: (cause) to stay at a distance
keep on: continue
keep up with: to continue doing or stay at the same level with (sth)

....

let sth down: lengthen a garment
let sb down: disappoint
let sb off: not to punish
let on: reveal a secret
let out: make (a garment) looser, larger etc
let up: lessen, stop gradually

18 Fill in the correct particle(s).

1 She hired an assistant because she couldn't keep ...*up with*... the work.
2 The firefighter told us to keep .... from the burning building.
3 It's a good idea to keep .... John as he might be helpful to you later.
4 He's going to keep .... taking his driving test until he passes.
5 He put up a "No Trespassing" sign to keep walkers .... his land.
6 Tell me the whole story; don't keep anything ....
7 The judge let the boys .... with a warning.
8 When she put on weight, she had to let .... all her clothes.
9 It was raining hard earlier but it's letting .... now.
10 John didn't let .... that Jim had broken the window.
11 This skirt is rather short. You'd better let it ....
12 I thought I could trust Sam, but he let me ....

19 Look at Appendix 1, then fill in the correct preposition.

1 There was a long queue ...*at*... the bus stop.
2 We have to win this election .... all costs.
3 His gambling habit left him seriously .... debt.
4 She left the oven on all day .... accident.
5 Many Asian countries, India .... instance, use English as a second language.
6 My pen pal and I have a lot .... common.
7 The officer was .... charge of 20 men.
8 .... all accounts, he's a very capable diplomat.
9 .... the beginning of the play, the hero sees the heroine for the first time.
10 I thought he was honest .... the beginning, but I was wrong.
11 I don't like being taken .... granted!
12 By the end of the film, the viewers were .... tears.
13 Dr Milton discovered the vaccine .... chance.
14 Please don't change all your plans just .... my sake.
15 Read the text .... detail, then answer the questions.
16 The scandal has been .... the news for weeks now.
17 We can offer you a 10% discount if you pay .... cash.
18 Payment can be made .... cheque or with a credit card.
19 Martha was .... a loss to explain why she'd been sacked.
20 There's a beautiful cottage .... sale in our village.
21 You're .... a good mood today! Have you had some good news?
22 Your order will be sent .... post within 3 days.
23 There's a restaurant .... the top of the Eiffel Tower.
24 The books were piled one .... top of the other.
25 We regret that the lift is not .... use today.
26 I'm sorry. I took your jacket .... mistake this morning.
27 The judges announced their decision .... the end of the competition.
28 We were worried at first but, ... the end, everything went well.
29 Let's go out to dinner .... a change.
30 The offices are .... 77 Oxford St.
31 He lives .... the suburbs and commutes to the city every day.
32 The mirror lay .... pieces on the floor.

20 Complete the sentences using the words in bold. Use two to five words.

1 How long will it take you to build the shelves?
   building   When ...*will you finish building*... the shelves?
2 Perhaps she got caught in traffic.
   have   She .... in traffic.

3 The management won't let passengers smoke on the train.

are Passengers .... on the train.

4 "Why is he so secretive?" she asked herself.

was She .... so secretive.

5 People say he is very clever.

be He .... very clever.

6 She is proud of her beautiful house.

pride She .... beautiful house.

7 We couldn't sleep at night as the air conditioning was faulty.

difficult The faulty air conditioning .... to sleep at night.

8 "You've caused a lot of pain to my family," she said to him.

causing She .... a lot of pain to her family.

9 She is scared to be alone in the house at night.

afraid She .... in the house at night.

10 She won't tolerate his rudeness any longer.

put She won't .... any longer.

11 It's likely that they will go to the party.

are They .... the party.

12 You will be collected from your hotel at 8.00 by taxi.

call A taxi .... at your hotel at 8.00.

21 For questions 1 - 12, read the text below and think of the word which best fits each space. There's an example at the beginning (0).

World Population

As of 2003 **(0)** ...*the*... human population had reached 6.2 billion, and **(1)** .... the growth has slowed **(2)** .... in recent years, it will be many decades **(3)** .... it stops. The reason **(4)** .... this growth is causing so **(5)** .... concern is that we cannot keep up **(6)** .... the corresponding increase **(7)** .... demand for food, water, healthcare, jobs, education and housing. It also increases the likelihood of damage **(8)** .... the environment.

Much of the growth has been in the poorer countries of the world, but overpopulation is also a problem for some rich countries, including Britain. With a population of approximately 60 million, Britain has more than 233 inhabitants **(9)** .... square kilometre. Furthermore, it is estimated that the number of people in the country will have increased to 67.5 million by 2031, **(10)** .... the rate of growth slows down.

Populations not only increase because of higher birth rates and longer life expectancy, but also because of people moving from poor countries to rich countries. As a result of people living longer, **(11)** .... countries including Britain, have a high percentage of people over 65. This **(12)** .... a strain on demographic support ratios.

22 Fill in the following collocation grids.

	a bank	a purse	time	a house	a person	an office	a car	a shop
rob	✓							
burgle								
steal								

23 Complete the sentences using the words in bold. Use two to five words.

0 I had never met Karen's sister before.
   first   It ...*was the first time*... I had ever met Karen's sister.
1 "I'm sorry I was so rude yesterday," said Jack.
   for   Jack .... so rude the previous day.
2 John asked me how much I had paid for the painting.
   cost   John wanted to .... the painting.
3 "Why don't we visit a museum on Sunday?" said Pat to Joey.
   suggested   Pat .... a museum on Sunday.
4 She regrets buying a St Bernard puppy.
   wishes   She .... a St Bernard puppy.
5 Martin and his wife were in complete agreement about selling the house.
   completely   Martin and his wife .... other about selling the house.
6 Bobby's parents are incapable of controlling him.
   ability   Bobby's parents don't .... control him.
7 It isn't worth seeing that film if you've seen it before.
   point   There's .... that film if you've seen it before.
8 The plane was late arriving because of high winds.
   on   Due to high winds, the plane .... time.

24 Use the words in capitals to form a word that fits in the space in the same line.

Surfing in Hawaii

(0) ...*Evidence*... of surfing in Hawaii goes back to 1500 BC. Rock **EVIDENT**
drawings show stick figures on long boards, which offers **(1)** .... **PROVE**
that surfing has long been a part of Hawaiian culture and history. In
ancient times, it is believed that chiefs surfed to maintain their physical
(2) .... as well as for its entertainment value. **STRONG**

Should you be **(3)** .... to visit Hawaii, you too can learn this sport **FORTUNE**
of kings by taking an **(4)** .... course. It is unlikely that you will **INTRODUCE**
sustain any **(5)** ...., as you will be taught by experienced instructors **INJURE**
and the waves are only 2 feet high. 15-foot high waves such as were
featured in the film 'Point Break' are only for the entirely **(6)** ....! **FEAR**

In any case, most organised beaches offer **(7)** .... **SUPERVISE**
from lifeguards, but experienced surfers may prefer to go off on their own
to find more **(8)** .... beaches. Also, keep in mind that the size **SECLUDE**
of the wave goes with the size of your surfboard. Surfboards come in a
variety of **(9)** ...., so a short board, for example, would be **LONG**
(10) .... for a tall wave. **SUITABLE**

8 Conditionals/Wishes/Unreal Past

Conditionals

	If-clause (hypothesis)	Main clause (result clause)	Use
Type 1 **real present**	If + any present form (Present S., Present Cont. or Present Perfect)	Future/Imperative can/may/might/must/should + bare inf/Present Simple	true or likely to happen in the present or future
	*If the weather **is** nice, we **will go** on an excursion.* *If you **have done** your homework, you **can watch** TV.* *If you **have** a headache, **take** an aspirin.*		
Type 2 **unreal present**	If + Past Simple or Past Continuous	would/could/might + bare infinitive	untrue in the present; also used to give advice
	*If I **were** you, I **wouldn't speak** to him again. (advice)* *If he **didn't eat** so many sweets, he **wouldn't have** a problem with his teeth.* *(but he eats a lot of sweets - untrue in the present)*		
Type 3 **unreal past**	If + Past Perfect or Past Perfect Continuous	would/could/might + have + past participle	imaginary situation contrary to facts in the past; also used to express regrets or criticism
	*If she **had known** how to use the mixer, she **wouldn't have broken** it.*		

● When the if-clause precedes the result clause, we separate the two clauses with a comma. *If he had been more careful, he wouldn't have caused the accident.* **BUT** *He wouldn't have caused the accident if he had been more careful. (no comma)*

● Conditionals are usually introduced by **if**. Other expressions are: **unless**, (=if not), **providing**, **provided (that)**, **as long as**, **in case**, **on condition (that)**, **BUT for** + **-ing form/noun**, **otherwise**, **or else**, **what if**, **supposing**, **even if**, **only if**.
Unless you work more efficiently, you'll be fired.
I will do it only if you promise not to tell anyone.

● After **if** we normally use **were** instead of **was** for all persons in conditionals type 2 in formal English.
If I were/was you, I would tell her everything.

● We do not normally use **will**, **would** or **should** in if-clauses. *If you want this, you can have it.* (NOT: ~~if you will want.~~) However, **will**, **would** or **should** can be used in if-clauses to make a **request** or express **annoyance**, **doubt/uncertainty** or **insistence**. *If he should come, show him in. (doubt/uncertainty - I doubt that he will come ...) If you will/would be more patient, I'll be with you in a minute. (request - Will you please be more patient?)*

---

1   Put the verbs in brackets into the correct tense, then identify the types of conditionals.

1   If you ...*don't put up*... **(not/put up)** this shelf, you won't have anywhere to put your books. *(1st type)*
2   If he .... **(change)** jobs, he would be a lot happier. ....
3   If I were you, I .... **(tell)** her how you feel. ....
4   If you continue to shout so loudly, you .... **(wake up)** the baby. ....
5   Even if he .... **(ask)** them, they wouldn't have agreed to come. ....
6   Unless you .... **(feel)** any better, you can take the rest of the day off. ....
7   If she .... **(not/threaten)** him, he wouldn't have left. ....
8   I .... **(not/trust)** him if I were you. ....
9   If you're patient for a few minutes, I .... **(be able)** to finish this. ....
10   He .... **(not/go)** with her if he had known she would behave so irresponsibly. ....
11   I wouldn't have been able to do it unless she .... **(help)** me. ....
12   Sometimes if you .... **(take)** a chance, it pays off. ....

13 If he .... (**wake up**) earlier, he wouldn't have been late for work. ....
14 If they will go on making so much noise, I .... (**have to**) punish them. ....
15 If we .... (**intend**) to spend the day in London, we would have bought a day pass. ....
16 Keep your voice down in case he .... (**overhear**) us. ....
17 If she .... (**be**) more experienced, she would be more likely to get the job. ....
18 If the food .... (**not/be**) so bad, we wouldn't have complained. ....
19 Sales will increase provided that the advertising campaign .... (**be**) successful. ....
20 If you .... (**spend**) less on clothes, you would be able to save some money. ....

2 Rewrite the following as conditional sentences.

1 You need to go to Egypt to see the Sphinx.
If ...*you go to Egypt, you can see the Sphinx*....
2 John didn't leave early so he didn't get there on time.
If ....
3 She used factor 12 suntan lotion as she gets sunburnt easily.
If ....
4 The fax machine is broken so I'll have to send it by post.
If ....
5 Calling her might make her feel better.
If ....
6 There'll be an election if the president resigns.
Providing ....
7 More tickets need to be sold, otherwise the concert will be cancelled.
If ....
8 You'll have trouble selling your house if you're not prepared to accept a lower offer.
Unless ....
....
9 He cancelled his trip because he had run out of money.
If ....
10 Tom didn't wear a coat and caught a cold.
If ....
11 You need to study to pass this exam.
Unless ....
12 You really ought to go somewhere sunnier to get a suntan.
Unless ....

3 Complete the text by putting the verbs in brackets into the correct tense.

If I were world leader, I **1**) ...*would try*... (**try**) to stop the destruction of the earth and I **2**) .... (**make**) the world a better place for all people. If the world's problems had been tackled sooner, the quality of life **3**) .... (**improve**) long ago. First of all, I would try to bring about peace in the world. As long as there is fighting between nations, millions of people **4**) .... (**continue**) to suffer and die. If wars continue, children **5**) .... (**be left**) without parents and **6**) .... (**grow up**) in a world of misery and fear. But as long as people disagree over land and possessions, the fighting **7**) .... (**go on**). Therefore, I would ensure that all people were treated as equals and given the same opportunities in life. It would also help if all countries **8**) .... (**stop**) producing arms so there would no longer be the weapons with which to fight. In addition, I would introduce laws to reduce pollution. If pollution levels had been controlled earlier, life **9**) .... (**not/become**) so unbearable. If I **10**) .... (**have**) the power, I would ban all cars from city centres and increase public transport. If there were more trees, the air we breathe **11**) .... (**be**) cleaner. Unless measures are taken soon, it **12**) .... (**be**) too late both for ourselves and our children.

4 **Rephrase the following in as many ways as possible using the words from the list below.**

only if, otherwise, as long as, unless, providing,
on condition that, if

1 Should you go to Rome, you must see the Colosseum.
2 You can swim but there must be an adult with you.
3 Drive carefully so that you won't have an accident.
4 He will get a bonus if productivity increases.
5 I'll lend you the money, but you must pay me back soon.

Omission of "if"

If can be omitted in if-clauses. In this case **should**, **were** and **had** (Past Perfect) come before the subject.
If he should win the race, he'll be very happy. ➡ *Should he win the race, he'll be very happy.*
If I were you, I wouldn't tell him. ➡ *Were I you, I wouldn't tell him.*
If I had known the truth, I'd have called the police. ➡ *Had I known the truth, I'd have called the police.*

5 **Rewrite the following sentences omitting "if".**

1 If I were you, I would think twice before accepting his offer.
  ...Were I you, I would think twice before accepting his offer....
2 If you had brought more money with you, we could have gone on holiday.
  ....
3 If I were you, I'd leave an hour earlier to be sure of getting there on time.
  ....
4 If you get through to the theatre, could you reserve four tickets for tonight's performance?
  ....
5 If you had paid the telephone bill on time, your phone wouldn't have been cut off.
  ....

Mixed Conditionals

All types of conditionals can be mixed. Any tense combination is possible if the context permits it.

	If-clause	Main clause	
Type 2	If they **were working** all day, (They were working all day	they **will be** tired now. so they are tired now.)	**Type 1**
Type 2	If I **were** you, (You are not me If he **were** a better driver, (He is not a good driver	I **would have accepted** the job. so you didn't accept the job.) he **wouldn't have crashed** the car. so he crashed the car.)	**Type 3**
Type 3	If she **had finished** earlier, (She didn't finish earlier	she **would be going** to the party tonight. so she isn't going to the party.)	**Type 2**

6 **Rewrite the following as mixed conditional sentences as in the example.**

1 He is not an honest person so he didn't tell the truth.
  ...If he were an honest person, he would have told the truth....
2 They were awake all night so they are tired now.
  ....

3 You didn't tell me earlier so we are not going to the cinema tonight.

....

4 She didn't cancel the milk so the milkman keeps delivering it.

....

5 The ship left Plymouth yesterday so it will be in Spain now.

....

6 They were painting the house all day so they are covered in paint now.

....

7 She didn't do her homework so she's in trouble with her teacher.

....

8 She is so disorganised that she missed the deadline.

....

9 The children were playing in the garden all day so they are very dirty now.

....

10 He doesn't take his job seriously so he wasn't promoted.

....

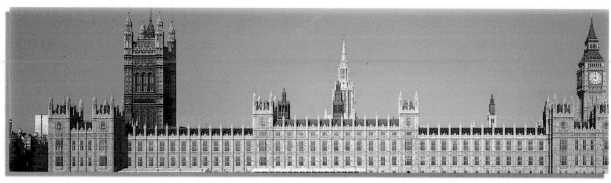

---

7   Complete the following sentences with an appropriate conditional clause.

1 Should you go to London, you ...*must visit the Houses of Parliament.*....
2 If he doesn't practise more, he ....
3 Unless you get permission, ...
4 Only if we ban the hunting of whales ....
5 If I could afford it, ...
6 If you had booked a table in the restaurant, ...
7 Should you meet George, ...
8 Were she in my shoes, ...
9 The fire wouldn't have started if ....
10 But for his money, she ....
11 Had you followed my advice, ...
12 Only if we stop cutting down trees ....
13 Were she more sincere, ...
14 If you had watered the plants, ...

---

8   Complete the sentences using the words in bold. Use two to five words.

1 I would have lent you my car but I didn't know you needed to borrow it.
   had   If ...*I had known you*.. needed to borrow my car, I would have lent it to you.
2 As long as you are very careful, you can use my CD player.
   provided   You can use my CD player .... very careful.
3 If there isn't an interpreter at the conference, she won't be able to understand the speakers.
   unless   She won't be able to understand the speakers .... at the conference.

4 He didn't get the job because he was late for the interview.
   would   If he hadn't been late for the interview, he .... job.
5 I only learnt to drive because you taught me.
   never   I .... drive if you hadn't taught me.
6 You'd better see a doctor.
   were   If .... see a doctor.
7 Tim will be able to operate the machine but somebody must show him how.
   only   Tim will be able to operate the machine .... how.
8 She didn't take an umbrella so she got completely soaked.
   have   If she had taken an umbrella, she .... soaked.
9 I will buy a new car but I must save enough money first.
   save   Provided .... first, I will buy a new car.
10 She broke her leg so she couldn't go skiing.
   broken   If .... leg, she could have gone skiing.
11 Kay can't be at home, otherwise she would have answered the phone.
   would   If Kay .... have answered the phone.
12 I would be grateful to receive any information you may have.
   could   I would be grateful .... any information you may have.
13 Karen can make the pie but she must have the recipe.
   long   Karen can make the pie .... the recipe.
14 If you see Miles, can you ask him to contact me immediately?
   see   Should .... ask him to contact me immediately?
15 Chris wants to phone his boss but he hasn't got the number.
   would   If Chris .... phone his boss.

Wishes		
	Form	**Use**
I wish (if only) (wish/regret about the present)	+ Past tense	wish/regret about a present situation we want to be different
*I wish we **were** in Paris now. (It's a pity we aren't.)*		
I wish (if only) (wish/regret about the present)	+ could + bare infinitive	wish/regret in the present concerning lack of ability
*I wish I **could** swim. (**BUT** I can't)*		
I wish (if only) (regret about the past)	+ Past Perfect	regret that something happened or didn't happen in the past
*I wish you **had told** me earlier. (**BUT** you didn't)*		
I wish (if only) (impossible wish for a future change)	+ subject + would + bare inf (**a. wish** and **would** should have a different subject. We never say: ~~I wish I would, He wishes he would etc~~ **b. wish** + inanimate subject + would is used to express the speaker's lack of hope or disappointment	wish for a future change unlikely to happen or wish to express dissatisfaction; polite request implying dissatisfaction or lack of hope

*I wish he **would** stop smoking. (**BUT** I don't think he will - wish for a future change unlikely to happen.)*
*I wish students **would pay** more attention. (dissatisfaction)*
*I wish the wind **would** stop blowing. (**BUT** I'm afraid it won't stop blowing - wish implying disappointment)*
*I wish you **would be** more careful. (Please, be more careful - request implying lack of hope)*

● After **I wish** we can use **were** instead of **was** in all persons. *I wish she **were/was** more patient.*

9   Put the verbs in brackets into the correct tense.

Dear Mum,

I feel really unhappy! I wish I **1)** ...*hadn't taken*... **(not/take)** this job. If only I **2)** .... **(give)** it more thought before I made the decision to come here. I wish the people here **3)** .... **(be)** more friendly - that would make it much better. If only I **4)** .... **(have)** longer breaks. Looking at a computer screen all day is tiring and sometimes I find myself wishing it **5)** .... **(explode)**! I wish my boss **6)** .... **(give)** me something different to do. I wish there **7)** .... **(be)** someone here I could talk to, but I haven't made any friends. If only I **8)** .... **(make)** some, but it's very difficult. I wish you **9)** .... **(live)** nearer to me! Please write. I miss you!

Love,

Jenny

10   Write sentences as in the example.

1   You felt sick and you missed your friend's birthday party.
     ...*I wish I hadn't felt sick. If I hadn't felt sick, I wouldn't have missed my friend's birthday party.*...

2   You got up late and you missed the train.
     ....

3   You weren't offered the job because you weren't qualified.
     ....

4   You're not a senior staff member so you can't use the car park.
     ....

5   You didn't go to the meeting so you didn't hear about the safety inspection.
     ....

6   You want to go away for the weekend but you've got lots of homework.
     ....

7   You want a pet but you're allergic to animals.
     ....

8   You damaged the video because you didn't know how to connect it.
     ....

9   You like chocolate but you're on a diet.
     ....

10   You enjoy playing tennis but you have twisted your ankle.
     ....

11   Complete the sentences using the words in bold. Use two to five words.

1   It's a pity I can't go to the beach today, but I have to stay at home and study.
    could   I wish ...*I could go to the beach*... today, but I have to stay at home and study.

2   If it weren't raining, we could go on a picnic.
    stop   I wish .... so we could go on a picnic.

3   It's a shame we didn't see the exhibition.
    had   We wish .... the exhibition.

4   George needs a new car but he can't afford to buy one.
    could   George wishes .... a new car.

5   It's a pity Jenny wasn't invited to the party.
    been   Jenny wishes .... to the party.

6 I've been offered a job in Paris, but I can't speak French.
speak   I wish .... because I've been offered a job in Paris.
7 George never arrives on time when we arrange to go out.
only   If .... on time when we arrange to go out.
8 I would really like to be lying on the beach now.
were   I .... on the beach now.

12 Put the verbs in brackets into the appropriate form.

Mary was telling Julie about her planned trip to a tropical island. It sounded wonderful. "If I were you, I **1)** ...*would be*... **(be)** so excited," Julie said. "I am," replied Mary," but I wish you **2)** .... **(come)** with me. We **3)** .... **(have)** such fun!" "I know. If only I **4)** .... **(know)** earlier, I **5)** .... **(not/spend)** all my money on redecorating the kitchen. Anyway, what clothes are you planning to take with you?" "Well, I'm hoping to buy some new ones. If you **6)** .... **(finish)** work early today, we **7)** .... **(go)** shopping in town." "If I **8)** .... **(be)** you, I'd make sure I took light clothes and lots of insect repellent. What **9)** .... **(you/do)** when you get there?" "Sunbathe, swim and go for long walks on the beach." "Make sure you **10)** .... **(send)** me a postcard and take lots of pictures." "Don't worry, I will."

13 Rewrite the letter using wishes or if-clauses as in the example.

Dear Christine,

I just had to drop you a line and let you know what a terrible day I've had today.

Well, first of all, I thought I would let the canaries out of their cage to fly around for a while. What a mistake! They flew straight out of the open window and I haven't seen them since!

Then, I decided to surprise my husband by putting up some new bookshelves in the lounge. Oh dear! I drilled a hole straight into the wiring in the wall and cut off the whole street's electricity supply. What a disaster! The neighbours are furious with me.

On top of that, when my husband came home from work, he tripped over the bucket I had left in the middle of the floor. Unfortunately, he hurt his ankle and he was angry with me. I shouldn't have left the bucket there.

Anyway, hopefully tomorrow will be better than today.

With love,
Elise

...I wish I hadn't had such a terrible day yesterday....

14 Complete the following sentences.

1 If only I had kept my appointment with the dentist yesterday, ...*I wouldn't have toothache now....*
2 I wish I had paid my electricity bill, ...
3 If I were Prime Minister, I ....
4 If it rains tomorrow, ...
5 Pete wishes he had worked harder at school, ...
6 Sarah will go to the party if ....
7 If only I had more money, ...
8 Liz wishes she had got up earlier, ...
9 If only Jo hadn't locked her keys in the car, ...
10 If John gets a promotion at work, ...
11 If the government bans smoking in public areas, ...
12 If only I hadn't shouted at Julie, ...
13 If Jenny had locked the front door, ...
14 If you are late for a job interview, ...
15 If you have a headache, ...

Conditionals / Wishes / Unreal Past 8

Unreal Past

The Simple Past can be used to talk about imaginary, unreal or improbable situations in the present and the Past Perfect can be used to talk about imaginary, unreal or improbable situations in the past. This is called Unreal Past. Unreal Past is used as follows:

Past Simple	Past Perfect
● **Conditionals Type 2** (unreal in the present) *If I **were** you, I wouldn't do that.*	● **Conditionals Type 3** (unreal in the past) *If he **had warned** me, this wouldn't have happened.*
● **wish** (present) *I wish she **were** more cooperative.*	● **wish** (past) *If only I **hadn't lost** all my money last night.*
● **I'd rather/sooner sb ...** (present) *I'd rather you **paid** me today.*	● **I'd rather/sooner sb ...** (past) *I'd rather you **had not told** everyone.*
● **Suppose/Supposing** *Suppose your father **caught** you smoking, what would you do?*	● **Suppose/Supposing** *Suppose he **had left** before the boss came, what would have happened?*
● **as if/as though** (untrue situation in the present) *She behaves as if she **were** the Queen.*	● **as if/as though** (untrue situation in the past) *Soon after being introduced, they were talking to each other as if they **had been** friends for years.*
● **it's (about/high) time ...** *It's time you **started** work.*	

would rather = I'd prefer

● when the subject of **would rather** is also the subject of the following verb

I'd rather + { **Present bare infinitive** (present/future reference) *I'd rather play tennis.*
 Perfect bare infinitive (past reference) *I'd rather not have gone out with him yesterday.*

● when the subject of **would rather** is different from the subject of the following verb

I'd rather sb + { **Past Simple** (present/future reference) *I'd rather you stopped smoking.*
 Past Perfect (past reference) *I'd rather you had mentioned that before.*

● **prefer + gerund/noun + to + gerund/noun** (general). *I prefer **(drinking) tea to (drinking) coffee.***
● **prefer + full infinitive + rather than + bare infinitive** (general preference)
*I prefer to drink coffee **rather than** (drink) tea.*
● **would prefer + full infinitive + rather than + bare infinitive** (specific preference)
*I'd prefer to live in London **rather than** (live in) Swansea.*
● **would rather + bare infinitive + than + bare infinitive** *I'd rather fly to Munich **than go** there by car.*

had better = should

● **I had better + present bare inf** (present/future reference)
*He **had better consult** a lawyer. (= He should consult a lawyer.)*
● **It would have been better if + Past Perfect** (past reference).
*It would have been better if you **hadn't talked** to James last night. (= You shouldn't have talked to James last night.)*

15   Put the verbs in brackets into the correct form.

1 Suppose they ...*had cancelled*... **(cancel)** the flight. How would you have got home?
2 We'd rather you .... **(take out)** separate holiday insurance.
3 I hate it when you speak to me as if I .... **(be)** a child.
4 She'd rather .... **(not/show)** him her passport.
5 It's high time he .... **(face)** up to his responsibilities.
6 If only I .... **(not/leave)** the window open!
7 If they .... **(go)** out less, they'd have more money.
8 Chris prefers .... **(work)** mornings rather than evenings.
9 Suppose Helen .... **(invite)** your ex-boyfriend, would you still go to the party?
10 I'd rather Sam .... **(not/play)** his music so loud.
11 Sylvia wishes she .... **(have)** long hair.
12 She had only lived there three months but she spoke the language as if she .... **(live)** there longer.
13 Tom's mother made him go to school although he would rather .... **(stay)** at home.
14 I feel a bit sick now. I wish I .... **(eat)** so much.
15 He much prefers .... **(listen)** to CDs to .... **(go)** to live concerts.
16 I'd prefer .... **(ride)** my bicycle to the shops rather than .... **(take)** the bus.
17 I'd rather .... **(live)** alone than .... **(share)** a flat with a stranger.
18 I prefer .... **(talk)** with friends rather than .... **(watch)** television.
19 If she .... **(work)** harder, she wouldn't have failed her exams.
20 You'd better .... **(go)** to bed as we have to be up early tomorrow.

16   Complete the sentences using the words in bold. Use two to five words.

1 Your mother's worried about you. You should phone her.
    better   You ...*had better phone*... your mother as she's worried about you.
2 Will you ever think about finding a flat of your own?
    time   It's .... about finding a flat of your own.
3 Look at how he lives - he thinks he's a millionaire.
    if   He lives .... a millionaire.
4 This summer, I would rather book a holiday in Monaco than Lyon.
    prefer   This summer, I .... a holiday in Monaco rather than Lyon.
5 Why didn't you tell me yourself that you were leaving?
    rather   I'd .... me yourself that you were leaving.
6 She wants to be more like her mother.
    wishes   She .... more like her mother.
7 I should have taken that job in Canada last year.
    only   If .... that job in Canada last year.
8 You should have checked the oil before you set out.
    better   It .... you had checked the oil before you set out.

17   Fill in the gaps with the appropriate auxiliary verb.

1 He hasn't got a yacht but he wishes he ...*had*... .
2 She can't afford a maid but she wishes she ....
3 I didn't pay attention in class but I wish I ....
4 He had his hair cut really short but now he wishes he ....
5 He's going to the dentist this afternoon but he wishes he ....
6 She made a terrible mistake but now she wishes she ....
7 They probably won't change their minds but I wish they ....
8 He always brings his dog to my house but I really wish he ....
9 I forgot to enclose the cheque but I wish I ....
10 He won't let me leave early but I wish he ....

Conditionals / Wishes / Unreal Past 8

18 Put the verbs in brackets into the correct form.

Dear Jenny,

Sorry I didn't answer your last letter. If I **1)** ...had realised... **(realised)** how serious the situation was, I would have written to you straightaway. You obviously need my advice. I only wish I **2)** .... **(be)** with you now to help you. I think it's about time you **3)** .... **(leave)** your job and **4)** .... **(start)** to look for a new one. If your boss **5)** .... **(insist)** on treating you so unfairly, then you have very little choice. You say that you'd rather **6)** .... **(have)** a job you hate than no job at all, but is that really true? If you **7)** .... **(be)** worried about money, don't be. You can come home and live with your father and me for a while. I'd rather you **8)** .... **(live)** nearer home anyway. Your old boss at the library, Mr Green, says you could have your old job back if you **9)** .... **(want)** it. You could have been Head Librarian by now if you **10)** .... **(not/leave)**! Anyway, I'll let you know if I **11)** .... **(hear)** about any other suitable jobs. Take care and let me know if you **12)** .... **(make)** any decisions.
Love,
Mum

19 Complete the sentences using the words in bold. Use two to five words.

1 I didn't pass my exams and now I can't go to university.
 wish I ...wish I had passed... my exams; then I could go to university.
2 I was about to buy the painting, when I realised it was a fake.
 if I would have bought the painting .... it was a fake.
3 I didn't see the TV programme because I didn't know it was on.
 known If .... the TV programme was on, I would have seen it.
4 I think you should go on holiday.
 were If ...., I would go on holiday.
5 You shouldn't have told Sally my secret.
 told I'd .... Sally my secret.
6 You'd think he was a politician.
 though He behaves .... a politician.
7 You should be in bed now. It's late.
 went It's .... to bed.
8 It would have been better if you had passed on the message.
 only If .... the message.
9 If the teacher asked you to answer that question, what would you say?
 asked Suppose .... to answer that question, what would you say?
10 It's a pity it's raining.
 stop I .... raining.
11 She couldn't tell you because she didn't know.
 would Had .... told you.
12 Why did I listen to John? He always tells lies.
 listened If .... to John. He always tells lies.
13 We should have left by now if we don't want to miss the bus.
 time It's .... if we don't want to miss the bus.
14 I would have liked you to have informed my parents about my change of plan.
 rather I .... my parents about my change of plan.
15 It would have been better if they had got the earlier train.
 only If .... the earlier train.
16 You ought to have set a wedding date by now.
 time It's .... a wedding date.

131

20 For questions 1 - 12, read the text below and think of the word which best fits each space. There's an example at the beginning (0).

Big Ben

Big Ben is **(0)** ...*in*... fact the bell which tolls on the hour in the clock tower of the Houses of Parliament and not the tower and clock, as is commonly **(1)** .... It is thought to **(2)** .... been named after Sir Benjamin Hall.

The bell was completed **(3)** .... 10th April, 1858. With a weight of more **(4)** .... 13 tons, it was the heaviest bell in Britain at that time. It **(5)** .... striking the time until 1859, but cracked later that year and **(6)** .... silent for the next three years. The crack can **(7)** .... seen even today. An electric motor is now used to wind the clock mechanism, and checks **(8)** .... Greenwich Observatory have rarely shown an error of more than one second. On some **(9)** ...., the clock has stopped accidentally, but seldom **(10)** .... to mechanical problems.

Radio made Big Ben a symbol, and on New Year's Eve in 1923 Big Ben **(11)** .... its first broadcast. It has been heard nightly **(12)** .... since.

Oral Development 12

Students look at the pictures below then, in turns, make sentences using conditionals or wishes to say what the man is thinking.

S1: I wish the wind would change direction.
S2: If the wind changes direction, we'll avoid the rocks.   etc

Phrasal Verbs

look after: take care of
look down on: despise (opp. look up to)
look for: search for
look forward to: anticipate
look into: investigate
look on: 1) be a spectator, 2) regard; consider
look out (for): watch out
look over: inspect carefully
look through: study carefully (sth written)
look up: 1) look for an address, name, etc in the relevant book or list, 2) visit sb after a lapse of time (specially sb living at some distance)

·······················

make for: move quickly towards
make up: 1) invent (story, poem etc), 2) make an amount complete, 3) compose, 4) reconcile, 5) prepare (by mixing)
make oneself up: put cosmetics on
make up for: compensate for
make out: 1) complete; fill in, 2) distinguish, 3) understand

21 **Fill in the correct particle(s).**

1 I've been looking ...*for*... my diamond ring everywhere.
2 The hotel manager will look .... your complaint.
3 I must look .... this essay before I hand it in tomorrow.
4 Now that he's rich, he looks .... all his friends who still work at the factory.
5 He looks .... his father who he considers to be a hero.
6 Look .... for sharks when you go swimming.
7 Look .... her phone number in the directory if you can't remember it.
8 John looks .... the children while Mary goes to work.
9 I'm sure he made the whole story ....
10 I'll make .... forgetting our anniversary.
11 We decided to make .... the nearest beach.
12 He made .... the cheque to me personally.
13 Your writing is so bad, I can't make .... what you've written.
14 She spends hours making herself .... every morning.

22 **Complete the sentences using the words in bold. Use two to five words.**

1 Although his mother warned him, the boy continued to play in the road.
   despite   The boy continued to play in the road ...*despite being/having been warned by*... his mother.
2 Their garden is much bigger than ours.
   nearly   Our garden is .... theirs.
3 He could read before he was three years old.
   able   He .... before he was three years old.
4 She hired a professional gardener to prune the trees.
   had   She .... a professional gardener.
5 I won't go with you unless you let me pay my own way.
   if   I won't go with you .... me pay my own way.
6 I regret ever telling her about my plans.
   wish   I .... her about my plans.
7 He can't tolerate his neighbours' behaviour much longer.
   put   He .... his neighbours' behaviour much longer.
8 She started to ride when she was ten years old.
   been   She .... she was ten years old.
9 "You really shouldn't have said that to her," he said to me.
   criticised   He .... that to her.
10 They hired him because of his excellent qualifications.
   due   They hired him .... had excellent qualifications.
11 He was late every day so he lost his job.
   result   He was late every day .... lost his job.
12 In general, I'd much rather walk than ride a bike.
   walking   In general, I .... a bike.
13 He hasn't signed the contract yet.
   still   The contract .... signed.

Consolidation 8

23 Look at Appendix 1, then fill in the missing preposition(s).

1 The contents of the parcel were broken ...*on*... arrival.
2 The situation is getting .... control; we must take action immediately.
3 The policeman took his family to the theatre as he was .... duty.
4 We heard about the plane crash .... the news.
5 He hasn't played tennis for a while, so he's .... practice.
6 The new safety measures are still .... discussion.
7 You're supposed to avoid eating sweets as you're .... a diet.
8 The balloon landed ..... a farm quite unexpectedly.
9 The parachutist landed .... a field.
10 You are .... arrest; you have the right to call your lawyer.
11 All medicines must be kept .... reach of children.
12 The factory is .... fire; vacate the area!
13 My favourite china teapot smashed .... pieces on the floor.
14 Someone planted a bomb .... a platform in Victoria Station.
15 Typewriters are going .... use as they're being replaced by computers.
16 The politician would only agree to speak to me .... the record.
17 Let's go .... a cruise around the Mediterranean.
18 Drinking alcohol is .... the law in many countries.
19 I'm sure the bus will arrive .... long.
20 This must be posted .... delay!
21 I was .... the impression he was abroad.
22 He doesn't like to carry cash, so he buys everything .... credit.
23 This newspaper is two weeks .... date!
24 I'm writing .... regard to your recent application.
25 .... our surprise, he won the competition.
26 They could recite the entire play .... memory.
27 Hurry up, please. We're a bit .... schedule.
28 ...... second thoughts, I'd rather not go out tonight.

24 Put the verbs in brackets into the correct tense.

If you 1) ...*want*... (want) to see the highest waterfall in the world, you have to go to Venezuela. There, you 2) .... (find) the Angel Falls - a spectacular sight. We 3) .... (go) there last year, and we were very impressed. We 4) .... (walk) in the countryside for about an hour when, suddenly, we 5) .... (hear) the sound of water. As we 6) .... (approach) the waterfall, we 7) .... (not/can) believe how loud the water was. It was the first time we 8) .... (ever/see) a waterfall and if we had known how amazing it was, we 9) .... (take) a video camera with us. We hope we 10) .... (return) one day to see this wonder of nature again.

25 Fill in the correct form of the infinitive or the -ing form.

In the past decade, academics have been involved in 1) ...*investigating*... (investigate) differences between men and women. Researchers have been especially interested in 2) .... (discover) what women can 3) .... (do) better than men. As far as language is concerned, studies show that girls begin 4) .... (talk) before boys and are capable of 5) .... (produce) more varied and sophisticated sentences. In addition to 6) .... (have) a better command of the language, women also appear 7) .... (have) better social skills and are more likely 8) .... (be) complimentary than men. Another area that has been investigated is how men and women lead. Women try 9) .... (share) power and make their employees 10) .... (feel) more worthwhile. Men, on the other hand, like 11) .... (demonstrate) their authority more formally and seem 12) .... (care) more about hierarchy. However, it is worth 13) .... (remember) that study results reflect averages, and there will always be exceptions.

134

26 For questions 1 - 12, read the text below and decide which answer (A, B, C or D) best fits each space.

Diamonds are Forever

It has been **(0)** ...*B*... practice in recent years for a man to buy his fiancée a diamond to **(1)** .... their engagement. Diamond rings have been bought by the aristocracy since the beginning of the century, but until the 1950s they were considered an expensive and **(2)** .... accessory for a simple wedding.

However, it was around this time that De Beers, the **(3)** .... producers of diamonds in the world, decided that they needed to **(4)** .... their market. As a result, they launched an advertising campaign which was **(5)** .... at couples with a slightly smaller budget. It was one of the most successful campaigns in the company's **(6)** .... For this campaign, the advertisers wanted to sell the idea that, although diamonds are a(n) **(7)** .... luxury, they are also the symbol of everlasting love. Thus a diamond engagement ring was supposed to signify the husband's life-long **(8)** .... to his wife.

The idea was expressed in the **(9)** .... which was first conceived by De Beers' advertisers: 'Diamonds are Forever'. This **(10)** .... to be highly profitable because the public bought the idea and consequently bought diamond rings by the **(11)** .... De Beers, who now have almost total **(12)** .... of diamond production worldwide, have never looked back.

0	**A** usual	**B** common	**C** average	**D** regular
1	**A** prove	**B** notice	**C** show	**D** mark
2	**A** unwanted	**B** unnecessary	**C** invaluable	**D** needless
3	**A** greatest	**B** biggest	**C** strongest	**D** largest
4	**A** stretch	**B** grow	**C** continue	**D** expand
5	**A** aimed	**B** pointed	**C** guided	**D** intended
6	**A** history	**B** past	**C** story	**D** record
7	**A** overpriced	**B** costly	**C** expensive	**D** dear
8	**A** devotion	**B** trust	**C** relationship	**D** faith
9	**A** word	**B** phrase	**C** part	**D** remark
10	**A** turned	**B** proved	**C** ended	**D** confirmed
11	**A** numbers	**B** millions	**C** thousands	**D** tons
12	**A** force	**B** power	**C** control	**D** strength

27   **Complete the sentences using the words in bold. Use two to five words.**

0   I had never met Fiona's parents before.
    first   It ...*was the first time*... I had ever met Fiona's parents.
1   "Don't blame me if you are late for your class," Maggie said.
    her   Maggie said that it .... if I was late for my class.
2   At weekends, I prefer watching television to playing computer games.
    rather   At weekends, I'd .... computer games.
3   I wrote down his address in my notebook.
    note   I .... his address in my notebook.
4   He had no one who could help him.
    turn   He .... for help.
5   Mr Peters got very rich after winning the football pools.
    made   Mr Peters .... won the football pools.
6   You can always depend upon Luke to help you in a crisis.
    down   Luke will .... in a crisis.
7   They were unable to think of a better solution.
    come   They .... a better solution.
8   Sheila last contacted us about a week ago.
    heard   We .... Sheila for about a week.

28   **For questions 1 - 10, read the text below. Use the word given in capitals at the end of each line to form a word that fits in the space in the same line.**

A really **(0)** ...*comforting*... thing when you're alone abroad and   **COMFORT**
surrounded by **(1)** .... is to receive a letter from a friend or   **STRANGE**
(2) .... from home. It's always interesting to know what people   **RELATE**
are up to.

But in responding, the hardest thing is to summarise a whole new way of
life, not to mention new friends and unfamiliar **(3)** .... Those   **SURROUND**
receiving your letters can never have a full **(4)** .... of your new   **UNDERSTAND**
job and your **(5)** .... routine; but you can make the picture   **DAY**
clearer by providing a **(6)** .... of these.   **DESCRIBE**

It is often thought to be easier nowadays to **(7)** .... send an   **SIMPLE**
email, but letters in **(8)** .... are more pleasurable to receive as   **COMPARE**
they have a more personal feel about them.

Letters from foreign parts also carry **(9)** .... postmarks which   **EXCITE**
an **(10)** .... stamp collector will be able to add to his collection.   **ENTHUSE**

Part 1

For questions 1 - 12, read the text below and decide which answer (A, B, C or D) best fits each gap. There is an example at the beginning (0).

Diaries

A diary is a daily (0) ...B... of events, thoughts and feelings (1) ..... either for the writer's own personal satisfaction or for later use. Most diarists neither (2) ..... nor necessarily want anyone else to read what they have written, so, on the whole (3) ..... they and perhaps their relatives and (4) ..... friends ever see their writings. On the other (5) ....., some people do write with the (6) ..... of informing and entertaining the public, although often diaries are only (7) ..... and published after the author's death.

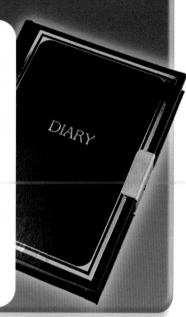

One example of a diarist who never thought his diary would be (8) ..... by the public was Samuel Pepys, who lived in the 17th century. His diary is the most impressive in the English language, recording some of the (9) ..... events in English history, yet it is also the story of a very lovable man. Another example is that of Anne Frank, a young Jewish girl who was in (10) ..... from the Nazis in Amsterdam during the Second World War. It is a unique and moving (11) ..... of this time in her life and shows the (12) ..... courage she had.

0	A memo	(B) record	C file	D list
1	A possessed	B held	C kept	D preserved
2	A predict	B anticipate	C wait	D expect
3	A merely	B simply	C only	D barely
4	A deep	B close	C near	D tight
5	A hand	B side	C place	D position
6	A reason	B target	C intention	D function
7	A uncovered	B invented	C located	D discovered
8	A seen	B revealed	C shown	D noticed
9	A largest	B biggest	C strongest	D greatest
10	A secret	B hiding	C disguise	D cover
11	A version	B report	C account	D statement
12	A unthinkable	B wonderful	C incredible	D special

For questions 13 - 24, read the text below and think of the word which best fits each gap. Use only one word in each gap. There is an example at the beginning (0).

Buying a New Bike

Until recently, few people went cycling, but **(0)** ...*over*... the last few years, more bikes have **(13)** .... sold in Britain than cars. Now approximately two million **(14)** .... bought each year, the majority of them are mountain bikes.

There are over 500 different models to choose **(15)** ...., and the prices vary enormously. The cheapest can be bought for under £200, **(16)** .... you will need over £4,000 for a bike at the top end of the range. The reason **(17)** .... this difference is the quality of the frame. Cheap bikes are not recommended for anything more than occasional use **(18)** .... they may not have been assembled properly and therefore are not safe to ride. Furthermore, they may get easily damaged because they are often not very **(19)** .... made. The more expensive models are much lighter because they are made **(20)** .... metals like aluminium.

When buying a new bike, it is best to go to a specialist bike shop **(21)** .... than a toy shop or garage. One reason for this is that a specialist will make **(22)** .... that the bike fits you properly, as a bike which is the wrong size can be dangerous and can cause backache.

To reduce the risk of injury, cyclists are advised to wear a helmet. **(23)** .... bikes travel at slower speeds than motorbikes, you can still suffer serious injuries to the head **(24)** .... you fall off.

Part 3

For questions 25 - 34, read the text below. Use the word given in capitals at the end of some of the lines to form a word that fits in the gap in the same line. There is an example at the beginning (0).

Dolphins

Humans are harming dolphins at an (0) ...*alarming*... rate. Long fishing nets known as 'Walls of Death' are mainly to blame. Since their (25) .... in the 1960s, millions of dolphins, whales and seals have been (26) .... caught up in them and killed.

ALARM

INTRODUCE
ACCIDENT

The nets are used by fishermen operating (27) .... who want to increase the size of their catch. They are dropped into the sea at night where they catch anything that is (28) .... enough to get in their way. This is a very (29) .... method of fishing, as many fish are lost or injured when the nets are hauled in. As the nets are almost (30) ...., the dolphins have (31) .... in seeing them and so are lured to their death.

LEGAL

FORTUNE
ECONOMIC

VISIBLE
DIFFICULT

Fortunately, there are now a number of charities who are working to raise (32) .... of this issue. Their work is helping the (33) .... of dolphins, so hopefully this (34) .... may soon be stopped.

AWARE
CONSERVE
DESTROY

Part **4**

For questions 35 - 42, complete the second sentence so that it has a similar meaning to the first sentence, using the word given. Do not change the word given. You must use between two and five words including the word given. There is an example at the beginning (0).

0 They worked hard on the project.
effort
They ...*put a lot of effort*... into the project.

35 The new musical failed to impress the critics.
succeed
The new musical .... the critics.

36 It's a good idea to keep your savings in the bank.
should
Your savings .... in the bank.

37 "I am on a diet so I shouldn't eat fast food," Stella said.
better
"I am on a diet, so I .... fast food," Stella said.

38 The two sisters look the same to me.
tell
I .... between the two sisters.

39 I had never redecorated a house before.
first
It .... I had ever redecorated a house.

40 She described the event to the police in detail.
description
She gave .... the event.

41 People say a strange creature lives in Loch Ness.
said
A strange creature .... in Loch Ness.

42 He went to drama school in order to become an actor.
aim
He went to drama school .... an actor.

1 I'll have James .... these figures.
   A to checking   **C** check
   B to check   **D** checking

2 She threatened .... the meeting.
   A to leave   **C** to leaving
   B leave   **D** leaving

3 He was made .... a fine.
   A pay   **C** to pay
   B paying   **D** to paying

4 We'd rather go camping than .... in a hotel.
   A staying   **C** to stay
   B stay   **D** to staying

5 If you had looked harder, you .... him at the station.
   A will see   **C** see
   B would see   **D** would have seen

6 It's time I .... my summer holiday.
   A will organise   **C** have organised
   B organise   **D** organised

7 Unless she .... in the next ten minutes, we will have to go without her.
   A phones   **C** will have phoned
   B phoned   **D** will phone

8 .... I look after the children for you?
   A Will   **C** Would
   B Ought   **D** Shall

9 I don't know when we ...... house.
   A will move   **C** move
   B had moved   **D** have moved

10 .... I've read the book three times, I still don't understand it.
   A Nevertheless   **C** However
   B Despite   **D** Although

11 I wish he .... give up his idea of becoming a rock star.
   A will   **C** had
   B would   **D** can

12 I prefer classical music .... popular music.
   A rather   **C** to
   B than   **D** from

13 Peter denied .... anything to do with the missing money.
   A having   **C** to have
   B have   **D** to have had

14 My luggage is twice as .... as yours.
   A heaviest   **C** more heavy
   B heavier   **D** heavy

15 I .... her to phone the office for me.
   A had   **C** got
   B made   **D** insisted

16 They .... him of lying in court.
   A denied   **C** charged
   B accused   **D** insisted

17 She gave me a .... belt for my birthday.
   A wonderful blue leather
   B leather blue wonderful
   C blue leather wonderful
   D leather wonderful blue

18 If I were a magician, I .... a peaceful world.
   A would have created **C** create
   B will create   **D** would create

19 I wish I .... better in last week's test.
   A had done   **C** did
   B would do   **D** will do

20 He .... a scholarship last month.
   A was offered   **C** has been offered
   B is offered   **D** will be offered

21 Can't you do this .... quicker?
   A even   **C** much
   B any   **D** very

22 The teacher .... us to stand up.
   A spoke   **C** talked
   B said   **D** asked

23 She insisted on .... for everything.
   A to pay   **C** to paying
   B paying   **D** pay

24 She .... the silverware polished yesterday.
   A will have   **C** is having
   B had   **D** has

Revision 2

B Fill in the gaps with the correct form of the verb in brackets.

Many people wish they **1)** .... **(have)** a job that paid as well as Harold's, so if they heard him complain about it the way he does, they probably **2)** .... **(not/have)** much sympathy for him. "If only I **3)** .... **(run)** my own business," he says, "I **4)** .... **(be)** much happier. I wish the bank **5)** .... **(give)** me a loan when I asked for one last year. If they had done so, I **6)** .... **(be able to)** start up my own company there and then." But, as everyone knows, if you **7)** .... **(work)** for yourself, you **8)** .... **(have to)** work very hard indeed, and Harold certainly isn't that dedicated.

C Put the verbs in brackets into the correct form.

I wish I **1)** .... **(can)** play a musical instrument. If I **2)** .... **(have)** the choice, I **3)** .... **(be)** a pianist, and play in a jazz band. If only my parents **4)** .... **(make)** me take lessons when I was a child! When I asked my mother about this, she said: "We **5)** .... **(buy)** you a piano if you **6)** .... **(ask)** us, but you never mentioned it." How I wish I **7)** .... **(say)** something! Still, I suppose if I start saving up now, I **8)** .... **(be able to)** buy myself one in a couple of years.

D Complete the sentences using the words in bold. Use two to five words.

1 The steak was so tough that we couldn't eat it.
   such   It .... that we couldn't eat it.
2 You'd better not be late again.
   were   If I .... be late again.
3 "OK, I'll prepare lunch now," he said.
   to   He .... at once.
4 Emily and Kim have the same number of pencils.
   as   Emily .... Kim.
5 Julie is not as artistic as her mother.
   less   Julie .... her mother.
6 You must fasten your seatbelts securely before takeoff.
   fastened   Seatbelts .... before takeoff.
7 "Don't touch the iron; it's hot," he said.
   warned   He .... the iron because it was hot.
8 I haven't had a chocolate bar for two months.
   time   The .... a chocolate bar was two months ago.
9 The builders will have finished the repairs by Thursday.
   been   The repairs .... by Thursday.
10 As people get older, they become more forgetful.
   the   The .... forgetful they become.
11 I ate more than was necessary last night.
   need   I .... so much last night.
12 As long as you impress the interviewer, you may be offered the job.
   provided   You may be offered the job .... the interviewer.
13 That's the field we play football in.
   where   That's .... football.
14 Someone stole my bike last night.
   had   I .... last night.
15 Matthew is less friendly than Thomas.
   so   Matthew isn't .... Thomas.
16 You should have called them last night.
   better   It .... you had called them last night.

17 This is Sarah and she works for the BBC.
who This is Sarah .... the BBC.
18 Why did you insist that we should appoint Mr Vermont chairman?
make Why .... Mr Vermont chairman?
19 She doesn't know much about sport but she acts like an expert.
though She acts .... an expert on sport.
20 "Don't forget to reserve the tickets," she said to him.
reminded She .... the tickets.

E Fill in the blanks with the correct particle(s).

1 The manager will look .... your complaint.
2 She is a good friend; she never lets me ....
3 I can't make .... his handwriting.
4 My boss and I get .... really well.
5 She made .... a story to tell her children.
6 You shouldn't look .... poor people.
7 It took him three weeks to get .... the flu.
8 I was held .... for two hours by heavy traffic.

F Fill in the blanks with the correct preposition(s).

1 He paid for his shopping .... cash.
2 His lack of punctuality resulted .... his dismissal from work.
3 He was unaware .... the consequences.
4 Chris is very determined to succeed .... his profession.
5 Which one of the twins are you referring ....?
6 The relationship .... my father and me isn't good.
7 I found this silver brooch .... chance.
8 Keep the food .... reach of the dog or he'll eat it.

G Use the words in capitals to form a word that fits in the space in the same line.

Esperanto

Have you ever thought the world should speak one language? While it would be **(0)** ...*impossible*... for people to forget their own languages, a common one could be used for travel and business, for example. Late in the 19th century, a clever Polish doctor called Zamenhof had the idea that an **(1)** .... language was needed, and, in 1887, he invented Esperanto.

In his hometown, people spoke four different languages, but the four groups often had **(2)** .... Zamenhof immediately reached the **(3)** .... that this was because they were **(4)** .... to communicate well with each other. This inspired him to create an easy **(5)** .... second language which everyone could learn. When Esperanto made its first **(6)** .... in 1887, it became popular **(7)** ...., and by the turn of the century, it was already **(8)** .... spoken outside Poland.

1987 saw the **(9)** .... of 100 years of Esperanto, and today it continues to be spoken by millions of people, who find it the most **(10)** .... way to communicate with people outside their own country.

POSSIBLE
NATIONAL
ARGUE
CONCLUDE
ABLE
LOGIC
APPEAR
IMMEDIATE
WIDE
CELEBRATE
EFFECT

9 Nouns / Articles

Nouns

- Nouns are: **abstract** (invasion, visit etc), **concrete** (invader, visitor etc), **proper** (David, Madrid, Japan etc), **collective** (audience, family, government etc) and **common** (book, sofa etc).

The Plural of Nouns

Nouns are made plural by adding:

- **-s** to the noun. (book - books etc)

- **-es** to nouns ending in **-s, -ss, -x, -ch, -sh**. (bus - bus**es**, class - class**es**, fox - fox**es**, church - church**es**, rash - rash**es** etc)

- **-ies** to nouns ending in **consonant + y**. (body - bod**ies**, party - part**ies** etc)

- **-s** to nouns ending in **vowel + y**. (boy - boy**s**, play - play**s** etc)

- **-es** to nouns ending in **-o** (potato - potato**es**)

- **-s** to nouns ending in: **vowel + o** (video - video**s**), **double o** (taboo - tabo**os**), **abbreviations** (photograph/photo - photo**s**), **musical instruments** (cello - cello**s**) and **proper nouns** (Navajo - Navajo**s**). Some nouns ending in **-o** can take either **-es** or **-s**. These are: buffaloes/buffalos, mosquitoes/mosquitos, volcanoes/volcanos, zeroes/zeros, tornadoes/tornados etc

- **-ves** to some nouns ending in **-f/-fe**. (scarf - scar**ves**) (**BUT** chiefs, roofs, cliffs, safes etc)

- Some nouns of Greek or Latin origin form their plural by adding Greek or Latin suffixes. (basis - **bases**, crisis - **crises**, terminus - **termini**, criterion - **criteria**, medium - **media** etc)

Compound nouns form their plural by adding **-s/-es**:

- to the second noun if the compound consists of two nouns. (corkscrew - corkscrew**s**)

- to the noun if the compound consists of an adjective and a noun. (steering wheel - steering wheel**s**)

- to the first noun if the compound consists of two nouns connected with a preposition or to the noun if the compound has only one noun. (doctor of philosophy - doctor**s** of philosophy, hanger-on - hanger**s**-on)

- at the end of the compound if this is not made up of any nouns. (runaway - runaway**s**)

Irregular Plurals: man - **men**, woman - **women**, foot - **feet**, tooth - **teeth**, louse - **lice**, mouse - **mice**, child - **children**, goose - **geese**, sheep - **sheep**, deer - **deer**, fish - **fish**, trout - **trout**, ox - **oxen**, salmon - **salmon**, spacecraft - **spacecraft**, aircraft - **aircraft**, means - **means**, species - **species**, hovercraft - **hovercraft**

1 Write the plural of the following words.

1	potato	...potatoes...	11	zoo	....
2	house	....	12	fishing rod	....
3	photo	....	13	fox	....
4	dessert spoon	....	14	child	....
5	fish	....	15	trout	....
6	video	....	16	louse	....
7	lorry	....	17	teacher	....
8	toy	....	18	baby	....
9	calf	....	19	workman	....
10	wolf	....	20	ship	....

21	boyfriend	....
22	mother-in-law	....
23	stepmother	....
24	type	....
25	stereo	....
26	mosquito	....
27	superstar	....
28	story	....
29	flyover	....
30	bunch	....

Countable - Uncountable Nouns

Nouns can be **countable** (those that can be counted) *1 egg, 2 eggs etc* or **uncountable** (those that can't be counted) *bread, wood* etc. Uncountable nouns take a singular verb and are not used with **a/an**. **Some**, **any**, **no**, **much** etc can be used with them. *Luggage is obtained from the Luggage Reclaim Area. Can I have some bread, please?* **BUT** a relief, a pity, a shame, a wonder, a knowledge (of sth), a help. *What a relief! What a pity! What a shame!*

Uncountable nouns are:

● **Mass nouns** (fluids, solids, gases, particles): *beer, blood, bread, butter, air, oxygen, corn, flour etc.*
● **Subjects of study:** *history, literature, maths, physics, accountancy, chemistry, economics etc*
● **Languages:** *Spanish, French, Japanese, Portuguese, Italian, Chinese etc*
● **Games:** *baseball, billiards, football, golf, darts, rugby, cricket, cycling etc*
● **Diseases:** *flu, pneumonia, measles, mumps, chickenpox, tuberculosis etc*
● **Natural phenomena:** *darkness, fog, gravity, hail, snow, sunlight, shade etc*
● **Some nouns:** *accommodation, advice, anger, applause, assistance, behaviour, business, chaos, countryside, courage, dirt, education, evidence, homework, housework, information, intelligence, knowledge, luck, music, news, peace, progress, seaside, shopping, traffic, trouble, truth, wealth, work etc*
● **Collective nouns:** *baggage, crockery, cutlery, furniture, jewellery, luggage, machinery, money, rubbish, stationery etc*
Note: With expressions of duration, distance or money meaning "a whole amount" we use a singular verb. *Two months was too long to spend in hospital.*

Many uncountable nouns can be made countable.

a **piece** of paper/cake/information/advice/furniture; a **glass/bottle** of water/beer/wine; a **jar** of jam; a **rasher** of bacon; a **pint** of beer; a **box/sheet** of paper; a **packet** of tea; a **slice/loaf** of bread; a **pot** of yoghurt; a **pot/cup** of tea; a **kilo/pound** of meat; a **tube** of toothpaste; a **bar** of chocolate/soap; a **bit/piece** of chalk; an ice **cube**; a **lump** of sugar; a **bag** of flour; a **pair** of trousers; a **game** of soccer; a(n) **item/piece** of news; a **drop/can** of oil; a **can** of Coke; a **carton** of milk; a **block** of wood; a **flash/bolt** of lightning; a **clap/peal** of thunder etc

Plural Nouns

● objects consisting of two parts: **garments** (trousers, pyjamas etc), **instruments** (binoculars, compasses etc), **tools** (scissors, pliers etc)
● arms, ashes, barracks, clothes, congratulations, earnings, (good) looks, outskirts, people, police, premises, riches, stairs, surroundings, wages etc. *The police are looking for the bank robbers.*
Group nouns (army, audience, class, club, committee, company, council, crew, crowd, headquarters, family, jury, government, press, public, staff, team etc) can take either a singular or a plural verb depending on whether we see the group as a whole or as individuals. *(the staff as a group)* **The staff were given** a bonus at Christmas. *(each member of the staff separately as individuals)* **The staff is required** to fill out a medical form.

Note how certain nouns can be used in the singular and plural with a different meaning.

Singular	Plural
*Give me a **glass** of water, please.*	*I've been wearing **glasses** since I was 8 years old.*
*Has she always had short **hair**?*	*There are so many **hairs** in the sink!*
*How would you rate this on a **scale** of 1 to 10?*	*Can you put that fish on the **scales** for me please?*
*In Japan it is not a **custom** to kiss your friends.*	*Our bags were thoroughly searched at **customs**.*
*Have you got any lined **paper** I could use?*	*He showed his **papers** to the customs officer.*
*She's wearing a ring made of **wood**.*	*John loves his Sunday afternoon walk in the **woods**.*
*I can't talk now; I have a lot of **work** to do.*	*A lot of Dali's **works** are on display in this museum.*
*We had at least 200 **people** at our wedding.*	*The **peoples** of Europe are hoping for change.*
*The **rain** is falling really heavily now.*	*The villagers are hoping for the **rains** to come soon.*
*You need **experience** for this job.*	*I had a lot of interesting **experiences** visiting Asia.*
*We used a **compass** to find our direction.*	*Use your **compasses** to draw some circles.*

9 Nouns / Articles

2 Underline the correct verb form.

1 Mathematics **is/are** my favourite subject.
2 Wood **come/comes** from trees.
3 The news **was/were** interesting this evening.
4 Her advice **was/were** useful.
5 Your furniture **is/are** so tasteful.
6 Tennis **is/are** a game played by 2 or 4 people.
7 Butter **contain/contains** a lot of fat.
8 The scissors **cut/cuts** really well.
9 Your hair **is/are** so shiny.
10 Japanese **is/are** difficult to learn.

11 Most people **is/are** worried about the future.
12 Children usually **like/likes** sweet things.
13 This company **has/have** six branches.
14 That jewellery really **suit/suits** you.
15 Water **is/are** necessary for survival.
16 My luggage **was/were** lost by the airline.
17 Measles **is/are** infectious.
18 This machinery **is/are** very noisy.
19 £300 **is/are** too much to spend on that dress.
20 Your scales **is/are** not very accurate.

3 Write the correct form of the verbs in brackets.

1 Hardwork ...*is*... **(be)** the key to success.
2 20 years .... **(be)** a long time to spend in prison for theft.
3 The staircase .... **(be)** too steep for my grandmother to climb.
4 Cathay Pacific .... **(be)** an Asian airline.
5 The people of Africa .... **(believe)** in various religions.
6 Flu .... **(make)** you feel miserable.
7 A loaf of bread .... **(cost)** more now than it did ten years ago.
8 I think olive oil ....**(add)** a lot of flavour to cooking.
9 The committee .... **(meet)** every Wednesday in the boardroom.
10 It is said that lightning never .... **(strike)** in the same place twice.
11 My favourite pyjamas .... **(be)** the ones with red and white stripes.
12 All the members of staff .... **(get)** together in the staff room.
13 Some people think French .... **(sound)** so romantic.
14 There .... **(be)** too much sugar in my tea.
15 Physics .... **(involve)** a lot of theoretical study.
16 Gravity .... **(pull)** things towards the centre of the Earth.
17 Good looks .... **(be)** all you need to be a model.
18 A crew of over five people .... **(work)** in most commercial aeroplanes.
19 Decorating a house .... **(be)** a lot of trouble.
20 Your trousers .... **(go)** nicely with this blue top.

4 Finish the sentences without changing the meaning of the first sentence.

1 She has got scruffy hair. Her hair ...*is scruffy*....
2 You need some teaching experience before we employ you. Some ....
....
3 He was given some very useful information. Some ....
4 He bought a new suit for the wedding. A new suit ....
5 An alarm protects this shop from burglaries. This shop ....
6 People use sand to make glass. Sand ....
7 I like playing darts more than any other game. Darts ....
8 Nowadays men and women wear trousers. Trousers ....
9 You are not allowed to park here. Parking ....
10 You need binoculars to see that far. Binoculars ....
11 Models always wear smart clothes. Smart clothes ....
12 This greengrocer's always has fresh vegetables. The vegetables ....
13 The government is passing new laws. New laws ....
14 I found physics very difficult at school. Physics ....
15 The man found the advice very useful. The advice ....

146

Word Formation

- To describe people we add **-ar, -er, -or, -ee** to the end of verbs, or **-ist, -ian** to the end of nouns or verbs making any necessary spelling changes. *employ - employee, lie - liar, drive - driver, act - actor, art - artist , music - musician*

Nouns can be formed from verbs

-age *(drain - drainage)*, **-al** *(propose - proposal)*, **-ance** *(hinder - hindrance)*, **-ation** *(investigate - investigation)*, **-ence** *(refer - reference)*, **-ion** *(protect - protection)*, **-ment** *(employ - employment)*, **-sion** *(decide - decision)*, **-sis** *(analyse - analysis)*, **-tion** *(repeat - repetition)*, **-y** *(injure - injury)*

Nouns can be formed from adjectives

-ance *(arrogant - arrogance)*, **-cy** *(fluent - fluency)*, **-ence** *(patient - patience)*, **-ion** *(desperate - desperation)*, **-iness** *(lonely - loneliness)*, **-ity** *(familiar - familiarity)*, **-ment** *(content - contentment)*, **-ty** *(anxious - anxiety)*, **-y** *(honest - honesty)*

5   Use the words in capitals to form a word that fits in the space in the same line.

Career Choices

Choosing the right career to suit your **(0)** ...*personality*... and one that lives up to your **(1)** ...., can be rather difficult. There is a **(2)** .... amount of factors you need to take into account, including the **(3)** .... of the job.
First of all, you need to know what **(4)** .... are necessary before you apply. It would be unwise, for example, to apply for a job for which you are **(5)** ....
If you are really **(6)** .... you should think about your career prospects and whether there are any opportunities for **(7)** ....
On the other hand, you may be looking for a job with less **(8)** .... and shorter **(9)** .... hours.
Finally, ask yourself if your choice of career will be **(10)** .... enough to keep you interested for your whole life.

PERSON
EXPECT
CONSIDER
REQUIRE
QUALIFY
EXPERIENCE
AMBITION
PROMOTE
RESPONSIBLE
WORK
SATISFY

6   Complete the sentences using the words in bold. Use two to five words.

0   I had never been to London before.
    first   It ...*was the first time*... I had ever been to London.
1   The prime minister wouldn't say anything about the new tax law.
    make   The prime minister refused .... on the new tax law.
2   "Shall I take the kitten home?" he asked himself.
    whether   He .... take the kitten home.
3   It's not worth talking to him.
    point   There .... to him.
4   I don't recommend eating at this restaurant.
    advisable   It's .... at this restaurant.
5   Don't forget to sign the application form before you post it.
    has   The application form .... before you post it.
6   This particular mobile phone is very popular.
    demand   There .... this particular mobile phone.
7   I promised I would find time to reply to all my emails.
    word   I .... I would find time to reply to all my emails.
8   My parents don't want me to play outside in the cold weather.
    object   My parents .... outside in the cold weather.

Nouns / Articles

7 For questions 1 - 10, read the text below. Use the word given in capitals at the end of each line to form a word that fits in the space in the same line.

Beethoven's Deafness

Ludwig van Beethoven is remembered as one of the greatest **(0)** ...*composers*... of all time. His talent and his music have been the **(1)** .... for many other composers too. Beethoven was also an **(2)** ...., talented pianist who had a highly regarded reputation as a **(3)** ...., early in life.

He began to lose his hearing in his late twenties but only **(4)** ...., at first. In spite of this, he continued to create **(5)** .... masterpieces throughout his life. Even when his **(6)** .... was almost total, he still managed to compose brilliantly. Beethoven was eager to make a living without the **(7)** .... on the church or the crown. He did this by selling his **(8)** .... to publishers and by attracting a number of **(9)** ...., patrons who were willing to provide him with **(10)** .... support.

COMPOSE
INSPIRE
ORDINARY
MUSIC
GRADUAL
REMARK
DEAF

DEPEND
COMPOSE
WEALTH
FINANCE

Indefinite article (A/An) / Definite article (The)

● **A/An** is used with singular countable nouns to talk about indefinite things. *There's **a man** standing at the door. (indefinite)* We can use **some** in the affirmative with plural countable nouns or uncountable nouns and **any** in questions and negations. *There are **some people** at the bus stop. Give me **some milk** please. **Are there any cups** in the cupboard? There **isn't any sugar** left.*

● A/An can also be used meaning "per" *(He goes to the gym twice **a/per** week)* or with money *(**a/one** pound)*, fractions *(**a/one** quarter)*, weight/measures *(**a/one** metre)*, whole numbers *(**a/one** thousand)*, price/weight *(£2 **a** kilo)*, frequency/time *(three times **a** week)*, distance/fuel *(60 miles **a** gallon)*, distance/speed *(60 km **an** hour)*, and illnesses *(**a** fever, **a** cold, **(a)** toothache, **(a)** backache)*.

● **The** is used with singular and plural nouns, countable and uncountable ones, to talk about something specific or when the noun is mentioned for a second time. *Can I try on **the** blue dress, please? (**Which dress? The blue one; specific**) There was a rat in the kitchen. I killed **the** rat with my boot.*

● **A/An** or **the** is used before singular countable nouns to refer to a group of people, animals or things. *A/The dolphin lives in the sea. (**We mean all dolphins**).* **A/An** or **the** is never used before a noun in the plural when it represents a group.
Dolphins are intelligent animals. (NOT: ~~The dolphins~~ *are intelligent animals*)

8 Fill in **a, an, the, any** or **some** **where necessary.**

1 I need ...*a*... car and I know .... kind of car I want. It must do 160 kilometres .... hour and also do 17 kilometres .... litre.

2 "Have you got .... money? I had .... this morning, but I did .... shopping, and .... fruit was so expensive! 50p .... kg for .... apples! It's .... disgrace!"

3 .... everyone knows .... lion is .... king of .... jungle but is .... shark .... king of .... sea? I can't think of .... fish which will eat .... shark!

4 .... man came to .... door this morning and asked to see the water meter. I asked him if .... price of .... water was going up and he said it would increase by 10p .... cubic metre.

5 "How much is .... dress material in .... window?" "£5 .... metre, madam." "Do you have any in .... blue?" "Yes, there's .... blue material in .... stockroom."

6 Let me give you .... advice. If you need .... help with .... work I've given you, go to .... person who runs your department.

148

Word Formation

The is used before	The is omitted before

The is used before

- nouns which are unique. *the Earth, the Colosseum*

- names of cinemas *(The Plaza)*, hotels *(The Savoy)*, theatres *(The Palladium)*, museums *(The Prado)*, newspapers/magazines *(The Independent)* **BUT** *(Time)*, ships *(The Cutty Sark)*, institutions *(The British Council)*, galleries *(The Tate Gallery)*

- names of rivers *(the Nile)*, seas *(the Black Sea)*, groups of islands/states *(the Shetland Isles, the USA)* mountain ranges *(the Himalayas)*, deserts *(the Sahara desert)*, oceans *(the Atlantic)*, canals *(the Manchester Canal)* and names or nouns with "of". *(the Valley of the Kings, the Garden of Gethsemane)* **Note:** *the equator, the Arctic/Antarctica, the South of France, the South/West/North/East*

- musical instruments, dances. *the piano, the samba*

- names of families *(the Hunters)*, nationalities ending in -sh, -ch or -ese *(the English, the Dutch, the Japanese etc)*. Other plural nationalities are used with or without the. *(the North Americans, the Austrians etc)*

- titles *(the Patriarch, the Duchess of Windsor, the King)*. **BUT** "The" is omitted before titles with proper names. *King Carlos*

- adjectives used as plural nouns *(the young, the unemployed, the homeless, the blind etc)* and the superlative degree of adjectives/adverbs. *He's the **most** friendly boy in the group.*

- **Note:** "most" used as a determiner followed by a noun, does not take "the". *Most people like swimming.* **BUT** *Of all European countries, Greece has **the most ancient** monuments.*

- the words: beach, cinema, city, coast, country(side), earth, ground, jungle, radio, pub, sea(side), sky, station, shop, theatre, village, weather, world etc but not before "man". *She went to **the library** to return some books.* **Note:** "the" is optional with seasons. *(the) summer*

- morning, afternoon, evening, night. *I'll be home late in **the** evening.* **BUT** *at night, at noon, at mid-night, by day/night, at 4 o'clock etc*

- historical references/events. *the Russian Revolution, the Renaissance, the Cold War* **(BUT** *World War II)*

- only, last, first (used as adjectives). *He was **the first** person to arrive.*

The is omitted before

- proper nouns. *I'll see **Ann** tomorrow.*

- names of sports, games, activities, days, months, holidays, colours, drinks, meals and languages (not followed by the word "language"). *He plays football well. He likes red. We speak German.* **BUT** *The ancient Greek language is hardly used now.*

- names of countries *(England)*, **(BUT** *the Argentine, the Netherlands, (the) Sudan, the Hague, the Vatican City)*, cities *(London)*, streets *(Carnaby Street)*, **(BUT** *the High Street, the Strand, the Mall, the A11, the M4 motorway)*, squares *(Trafalgar Square)*, bridges *(Tower Bridge)* **(BUT** *the Bridge of Sighs, the Forth Bridge, the Severn Bridge, the Golden Gate Bridge)*, parks *(Central Park)*, stations *(Euston Station)*, individual mountains *(Kilimanjaro)*, islands *(Sicily)*, lakes *(Lake Victoria)*, continents *(Africa)*

- possessive adjectives. *That isn't your pen.*

- two-word names whose first word is the name of a person or place. *John F. Kennedy Airport, Windsor Castle* **BUT** *The White House, (because the first word "White" is not the name of a person or place)*

- pubs, restaurants, shops, banks and hotels which have the name of their founder and end in -s or -'s. *Woolworth's, Lloyds Bank, Tom's Bar* **BUT** *the Red Lion (pub) (because "Red Lion" is not the name of a person or place)*

- bed, church, college, court, hospital, prison, school, university, when we refer to the purpose for which they exist. *John went to hospital. (He is a patient.)* **BUT** *His mother went to **the** hospital to see him last week. (She went to the hospital as a visitor.)* Work (= place of work) never takes "the". *She is at **work**.*

- the words home, Father/Mother when we talk about our own home/parents. *Father is at home.*

- means of transport: by bus/by car/by train/by plane etc but: in the car, on the bus/train etc. *She travelled by **bus**.* **BUT** *She caught **the** 5 o'clock bus.*

- We say: flu/the flu, measles/the measles, mumps/the mumps **BUT** *He's got malaria.*

9 Nouns / Articles

Fill in the where necessary.

1 Shall we have ..—.. lunch at .... home or go to ....
Royal Oak and Castle?

2 .... Prince Philip visited .... Royal Albert Hall today.

3 .... Pete's Bar is situated in .... Terminal 1 at
.... Heathrow Airport.

4 .... Browns were .... first to leave .... party at
.... midnight.

5 We landed at .... Charles de Gaulle airport in .... Paris and were met by .... ambassador in person.

6 Tim's gone to .... hospital to pick up .... results of .... tests .... Mum had last week.

7 .... most world maps are out of date now, due to .... political events which have taken place recently.

8 .... Chicago Bulls, from .... USA are one of .... best-known basketball teams.

9 When .... Berlin Wall was pulled down, it was a great moment in .... history.

10 Lots of people go for .... exotic holidays in .... Asia, but you must take care not to catch .... malaria.

11 We decided to go to .... island of Sicily last summer, and we've decided to go to an island again this
year; either to .... Rhodes or .... Canaries.

12 In .... Jerusalem we visited .... Dome of the Rock, ... Church of the Holy Sepulchre and
saw the site of .... Solomon's Temple.

13 Lots of people are without jobs in .... city, so .... government has decided to give ....
unemployed special benefits.

14 Tarzan, ... Lord of .... Jungle, had a friend called .... Cheetah.

15 Many people go trekking in .... mountains like .... Alps or .... Himalayas.

16 .... English spend their holidays in hot countries because they enjoy going to .... beach.

17 .... royal yacht sailed across .... Indian Ocean.

18 You'll find my house if you walk along .... Green Street and turn right into .... High Street.

19 Many of .... England's young men died in .... First World War.

20 .... Vatican City is one of .... most beautiful places in .... Rome.

21 .... people from .... Brazil dance .... samba really well.

22 We went to .... pub rather than .... cinema because .... Father wanted to.

Fill in the where necessary.

Dear George,

I've just returned from 1) ..—.. America after spending 2) ....
summer working with children at a camp for 3) .... blind. I
travelled to 4) .... States by 5) .... aeroplane and while I was
on 6) .... plane I met some other people going to work at the
camp. There were 7) .... Germans and Italians and also some
people from 8) .... Netherlands. However, it was 9) ....
French who were 10) .... most noticeable nationality as there
were so many of them. Once I arrived, 11) .... most of my time
was spent arranging activities such as 12) .... music, sports and
crafts. The children learned to play 13) .... guitar, to practise
14) .... swimming and even to speak 15) .... French. After
the camp was over, I spent some time travelling. My favourite sights
were 16) .... Grand Canyon and 17) .... Lake Michigan. I
also visited 18) .... Empire State Building and I loved 19) ....
Disneyland. I had a great time, and I hope to be able to do 20) ....
same thing next summer after I've finished 21) .... university.
Best wishes,
Alex

11 Fill in a/an or the where necessary.

1 ...*The*... Tower of London is on .... north side of .... Thames.
2 He has visited a number of places including .... USA, ... Middle East and .... Asia.
3 .... University of Cambridge is one of .... most famous in .... United Kingdom if not in .... Europe.
4 He took .... job with .... government because he's interested in .... politics.
5 New Year celebrations are held in .... Trafalgar Square in .... London and in .... Times Square in .... New York.
6 .... month I spent in .... France was one of .... best times in my life.
7 After six months in .... hospital, my grandmother is coming .... home.
8 .... Sunset Boulevard is .... most famous street in .... Hollywood.
9 .... millionaire purchased .... mansion as .... gift for his wife's birthday.
10 .... Nile flows from near .... Lake Victoria to .... Mediterranean.
11 She goes to .... church every Sunday, and also goes to .... church every Friday to help with the cleaning.
12 My perfect day in London would include shopping at .... Harrods, eating at .... Pierrot's and going to .... opera at .... Covent Garden.
13 .... Mount Everest is in .... Himalayas.
14 .... Falklands are islands in .... South of .... Atlantic Ocean.
15 He came into .... antique gold watch when his grandfather passed away.
16 When I visit .... Netherlands, I always stay at .... Park Hotel in .... Amsterdam.
17 Tom teaches at .... university near his home.
18 .... van crashed into .... back of my car in .... Green Street yesterday.
19 Of .... Seven Wonders of the World, I've only visited .... Pyramids.
20 After .... Prime Minister visited .... prison, he promised to improve conditions in .... prisons.
21 We heard .... lovely sermon at .... church in .... Lord Street .... last night.
22 She caught .... cold because she didn't come in from .... rain.

A couple of, several, a few, many, a (large/great/good) number of, both are followed by a countable noun. (Too) much, a little, a great/good deal of, a large/small amount/quantity of are followed by an uncountable noun. A lot of, lots of, hardly any, some, no, plenty of are followed by a countable or uncountable noun.

12 Underline the expressions which can be used with nouns as in the example.

1 The teacher gave us **several, a lot of, many, too much, a few** homework to do.
2 You've got **some, a lot of, both, plenty of, many** beautiful furniture.
3 Can you lend me **a few, some, a lot of, a couple of, a little** money?
4 Jane likes **both, a couple of, too much, a little, some** your paintings.
5 Have you had **a lot of, plenty of, both, a little, too much** letters from Suzie?
6 Everyone can do with **some, a little, both, a good deal of, several** peace and quiet at times.
7 There are **a little, a number of, several, a small amount of, no** Asian people living in our street.
8 There are **much, no, a small amount of, hardly any, lots of** people in the shop.
9 He spent **a couple of, much, lots of, a good deal of, a few** time reorganising his files.
10 The children ate **a good deal of, too much, a few, a good number of, a little** food at the party.

13 Complete the sentences using the words in bold. Use two to five words.

0 You shouldn't miss the opportunity to go shopping in London.
advantage   You should ...*take advantage of*... the opportunity to go shopping in London.
1 You shouldn't take any notice of what Peter says.
pay   Don't .... what Peter says.
2 He failed to persuade the court he was innocent.
succeed   He .... the court he was innocent.
3 You can always rely on her in a crisis.
down   She will .... in a crisis.
4 The film was so boring that I fell asleep.
bored   I .... the film that I fell asleep.
5 I advise you to book a table at the restaurant.
idea   It would .... to book a table at the restaurant.
6 Mary regrets inviting James to her party.
wishes   Mary .... James to her party.
7 What made the boss decide to cancel the meeting.?
reason   What was .... the meeting?
8 It is probable our team will lose this match.
likely   Our team .... this match.

Oral Development 13

Look at the following list and say each item using "the" where necessary.

Pyramids, Tahiti, Parthenon, Eiffel Tower, Mount Rushmore, Bangkok, Taj Mahal, Dome of the Rock, Suez Canal, Charing Cross, Sultan of Brunei, oriental music, Louvre, Heathrow Airport, Hong Kong, Leaning Tower of Pisa, Mount Vesuvius, Hanging Gardens of Babylon, River Thames, Cosmopolitan, Paris, Netherlands, Jamaica, Oslo, Unicef, Prince of Wales, Lake Constance, Rocky Mountains, United Nations, Crete, Lake Geneva, Fifth Avenue, Spanish language, English Channel, Pacific, Carlton Hotel, Marks and Spencer, Holy Land, Queen Sofia, Argentine, Ionian Islands

S1: The Pyramids
S2: Tahiti etc

Phrasal Verbs

put aside: save (usu money)
put away: put in the usual place
put down: 1) suppress by force, 2) write down; make a note, 3) attribute to, 4) criticize
put forward: propose
put off: postpone
put on: 1) switch on, 2) increase (weight), 3) pretend to be/have
put out: 1) extinguish, 2) cause inconvenience
put through: connect by phone
put up: 1) offer hospitality, 2) erect, 3) raise prices
put up with: tolerate

....

run across: meet or find by chance
run after: chase
run away with: steal
run down: 1) (of a battery) lose power, 2) (passive) be exhausted, 3) knock down, 4) speak badly of sb
run into: 1) meet unexpectedly, 2) collide with
run out of: come to an end
run over: read through quickly; review
run up against: face; encounter
run through: examine quickly; rehearse

---

14   Fill in the correct particle(s).

1 Please put ...*out*... your cigarettes before takeoff.
2 The hotel receptionist put me .... to room 617.
3 We put .... our wedding for another two months.
4 She has some money put .... for her old age.
5 She puts .... all her thoughts in a diary every night.
6 I'll accept a lift if it doesn't put you .... too much.
7 I can't put .... his rude behaviour any more.
8 He always puts his wife .... by insulting her in public.
9 Could you put .... the air conditioning? It's hot in here.
10 They have run .... money for the political campaign.
11 He ran .... his notes before entering the exam room.
12 The plans for the new road ran .... a lot of local opposition.
13 She feels run .... after working so hard recently.
14 The thief ran .... all the money from the bank.
15 He ran .... his ex-wife in the supermarket.
16 Our car was badly damaged when a van ran .... it.

---

15   Complete the sentences using the words in bold. Use two to five words.

1 I had difficulty in completing the course.
   complete   I found ...*it difficult to complete*... the course.
2 We were delayed at the airport for three hours.
   held   We .... airport for three hours.
3 I wish I had stayed at home instead of going to Ann's.
   rather   I'd .... than gone to Ann's.
4 Doctors say smoking damages people's health.
   said   Smoking .... people's health.
5 I'm sorry I missed your party.
   wish   I .... your party.
6 They couldn't go on holiday because their car had broken down.
   prevented   They .... on holiday because their car had broken down.
7 Have you decided about taking the job?
   mind   Have you .... taking the job?
8 Weight is measured on scales.
   used   Scales .... weight.
9 My aunt made me my wedding dress.
   had   I .... by my aunt.
10 The grandparents took care of the child.
   looked   The child .... the grandparents.
11 Lisa types quicker than Michelle.
   type   Michelle .... as Lisa.
12 "I didn't steal Mark's wallet," Ted said.
   stolen   Ted .... Mark's wallet.

Prepositions of Time

AT	IN	ON
at 9.30	in the	on Thursday
at Christmas/Easter	morning/evening/afternoon/night	on Easter Sunday etc
at noon/night/midnight	in the Easter/Christmas holiday(s)	on Christmas Day
at lunch/dinner/breakfast (time)	in October (months)	on Friday night
at that time	in (the) winter (seasons)	on January 18th
at the moment	in 1995 (years)	on a winter afternoon
at the weekend (on the weekend:	in the 20th century	on that day
Am. English)	in two hours (two hours from now)	

16 Look at the table above, then fill in the correct prepositions.

HEALTH & FITNESS CLUB

You'll arrive at the health farm **1)** ...on... Thursday, that's **2)** .... June 15th. You should try to arrive **3)** .... the morning if you can. **4)** .... the first day, we won't be doing a lot, just resting, so you can go and lie by the pool if you like. You'll be expected to get up early **5)** .... Friday morning **6)** .... about 7 o'clock. Your day's programme will be given to you **7)** .... breakfast. **8)** .... the summer, we have a lot more guests and so **9)** .... that time, you'll be assigned to your different groups. Lunch will be served **10)** .... noon, and, **11)** .... lunch, you'll be given an opportunity to meet the other trainers. There'll be a rest period **12)** .... the afternoon followed by a swim and sauna for those who are interested. We like to have a bit of a dance **13)** .... Friday night, so bring your party clothes! We will be conducting a period of meditation and relaxation **14)** .... the weekend, but all the trainers will be around to keep you busy. Don't forget that we are also running a second session **15)** .... August and another one **16)** .... Christmas for those who are interested.

17 Think of the word which best fits each space. Write only one word in each space.

Italy

Italy is a fascinating country, a wonderland of **(0)** ...both... man-made and natural beauty. No **(1)** .... where you go in this small but varied country, you **(2)** .... find something to interest and delight you. The big cities such **(3)** .... Milan, Rome and Naples are filled **(4)** .... ancient monuments, beautiful palaces and some of the best examples of modern architecture in the world, while **(5)** .... cities such as Pisa are worth visiting for famous sights like the Leaning Tower, as **(6)** .... as their churches, parks and surrounding countryside. Because Italy is a long and narrow country, the climate **(7)** .... north to south varies a lot. **(8)** .... in the north it is cold with mountains and lakes, in the **(9)** .... it is a paradise with lots of sunshine, warm seas and sandy beaches. And, **(10)** .... course, everywhere you go, **(11)** .... is the delicious food, which is just **(12)** .... good a reason for visiting Italy as seeing the sights.

18   Complete the sentences using the words in bold. Use two to five words.

0   John was sitting by himself in the café.
     own   John was sitting ...*on his own*... in the café.
1   Apart from Kelly, nobody liked my idea.
     one   Kelly .... liked my idea.
2   Our teacher has postponed our field trip for a week.
     off   Our field trip .... our teacher for a week.
3   "What did the mugger look like?" the policeman asked me.
     give   The policeman asked me .... of the mugger.
4   There's no point in waiting for Tim any longer.
     waste   Waiting for Tim any longer .... time.
5   Looking after the dog is your responsibility.
     responsible   You .... looking after the dog.
6   I don't feel like going out tonight.
     mood   I'm .... going out tonight.
7   Susan has a full-time job and also plays tennis three times a week.
     as   Susan has a full-time job .... tennis three times a week.
8   There is very little petrol left in the car.
     run   The car .... petrol.

19   Use the words in capitals to form a word that fits in the space in the same line.

Snoring

In Britain alone, over 3 million people snore **(0)** ...*loudly*... enough to disrupt   **LOUD**
their partner's sleep. In some cases, snoring makes **(1)** ....   **BREATHE**
difficult, causing oxygen **(2)** .... to the brain and heart and   **DEPRIVE**
thus waking the person up suddenly. It is known to ruin the lives of many
people who are **(3)** .... to sleep properly.   **ABLE**

Although some people decide to have an **(4)** .... for snoring,   **OPERATE**
there are less drastic **(5)** .... to the problem, as people can treat   **SOLVE**
themselves at home. They can limit the number of **(6)** ....   **ALCOHOL**
drinks they have at bedtime, as these cause a **(7)** ....   **RELAX**
of the muscles, which can lead to snoring. A **(8)** ....   **REDUCE**
in smoking, or quitting altogether, may also help, since smoking can make
it difficult to breathe. Taking an allergy test is also a good idea.

If an allergy is causing **(9)** .... in your nose, it could   **CONGEST**
(10) .... result in snoring.   **POSSIBLE**

10 Emphatic Structures / Inversion

Emphatic Structures

We use emphatic structures to emphasise a particular part of a sentence.

- **it is/was (not) + subject/object + that/who(m)** (statements/negations)
  It was Mary that/who called you. It was the manager that/who(m) I wrote to.
  It was the radio that broke down. (only "that" can be used because the subject is not a person)
  It wasn't me that/who called the police. It isn't the TV that needs to be repaired.

- **is/was it + subject/object + that/who(m)** (questions)
  Is it Jim that/whom you are going to meet? Was it his bicycle that got stolen last night?

- **that is/was + question word** (statements)
  That's what he did to save the boy.

- **is/was that + question word or question word + is/was it + that** (questions)
  Was that why they moved house? Why is it that you are always late for work?

- **question word + subject + verb + is/was**
  What he needs is a long holiday.

- To express **admiration, anger, concern** etc we use question words with **ever**.
  Whatever are you talking about?

- **do/does/did + bare infinitive** is used in the Present Simple, Past Simple or Imperative to give emphasis.
  I do promise to keep your secret. Do have some more coffee. He did buy the diamond ring.

1 Rewrite the sentences as in the example.

1 **Ann** decorated the pumpkin.
   ...*It was Ann who/that decorated the pumpkin*....
2 The children need **somewhere to play**. ....
3 Did **you** give him that horrible pair of trousers? ....
   ....
4 **What** do you mean by talking to me like that? ....
   ....
5 You should **concentrate more while you're driving**. ....
   ....
6 I telephoned our cousins. ....
7 **Where** are you going to be at Easter? ....
   ....
8 You need **a nice cup of tea**. ....
9 **When** did you get home? ....
10 **Why** did you borrow money from Al? ....

2 Complete the sentences using the words in bold. Use two to five words.

1 You weren't paying attention when the accident happened.
   that   It ...*was you that wasn't*.... paying attention when the accident happened.
2 The doctor promised that I would be out of bed in a couple of days.
   did   The .... would be out of bed in a couple of days.
3 Alexander Fleming discovered penicillin.
   was   It .... discovered penicillin.
4 Did you meet Marlon Brando in Hollywood?
   met   Was .... Marlon Brando in Hollywood?
5 The committee doesn't want to accept any new members to the club.
   is   What the .... to accept any new members to the club.

6 He said he was coming with us.
say   He .... with us.
7 Did you go to the Rivera Club last night?
it   Was .... you went to last night?

Inversion

We can invert the subject and the auxiliary verb in the sentence to give emphasis. This happens:

● after certain expressions placed at the beginning of a sentence.
Barely, Hardly (ever) ... when, In no way, In/Under no circumstances, Little, Never (before), Nor/Neither, No sooner ... than, Not even once, Not only ... but also, Not since, Not till/until, Nowhere, Only by, Only in this way, On no account, On no occasion, Only then, Rarely, Scarcely (ever) ... when, Seldom. *Little did he say about his accident. Rarely does he visit us.*
Note that when **only after, only by, only if, only when, not since, not till/until** are put at the beginning of a sentence, we use inversion in the main clause.
Only when you see him will you realise how much he has suffered.

● after **so, such, to such a degree** (in result clauses) placed at the beginning of a sentence.
So hard does he work that he will soon be promoted.

● in conditionals when **should, were, had** (Past Perfect) are placed at the beginning of the sentence. Note that "if" is omitted.
Should you go out, leave the key under the mat. *(If you should go out ... - Type 1)*
Were I you, I would apologise. *(If I were you ... - Type 2)*
Had he been invited, he would have come. *(If he had been invited ... - Type 3)*

● after **so, neither/nor, as** to express agreement.
"I enjoy romance films." "So do I." ("So" is used to agree with an affirmative statement.)
"Tim didn't come." "Neither/Nor did Ann." ("Neither/Nor" are used to agree with a negative statement.)
Her students loved her, as did her colleagues.

In the following structures we invert the subject and the main verb.

● after **adverbs of place**. *There goes the bus!* (**BUT** *There it goes!*) *Here is your pen!* (**BUT** *Here it is!*)

● in **Direct Speech** when the reporting verb comes after the quote and the subject is a noun.
"What a nice dress!" said Susan. (**BUT** *"What a nice dress!" she said.*)

3 Complete the sentences using the words in bold. Use two to five words.

1 We can go on with the plan only if you agree.
can   Only if ...*you agree can we go*... on with the plan.
2 Edna won't leave the house under any circumstances.
will   Under .... leave the house.
3 If the river rises any higher, the town will be flooded.
rise   Should ...., the town will be flooded.
4 If you'd paid on time, you wouldn't have been cut off.
paid   Had ...., you wouldn't have been cut off.
5 He had just recovered from flu when he caught a bad cold.
sooner   No .... from flu than he caught a bad cold.
6 He took such a long holiday that he forgot how to do his job.
did   Such a long holiday .... that he forgot how to do his job.
7 They managed to get our attention only by shouting and waving their arms.
manage   Only by shouting and waving their arms .... to get our attention.
8 He only asks for help when he is really desperate.
ask   Only when he is really desperate .... for help.

10 Emphatic Structures / Inversion

9 If I see him, I'll give him your message.
  should   I'll give him your message .... him.
10 Tom never seems worried about his future.
  seem   Never .... worried about his future.
11 I've never had such fun anywhere else.
  else   Nowhere .... such fun.
12 Lynn didn't realise that her mother was so worried about her.
  realise   Little .... that her mother was so worried about her.
13 The army marched forward into battle.
  marched   Forward .... into battle.
14 Her parents and her friends warned her not to go alone.
  as   Her parents warned her not to go alone, ... friends.
15 She sang so well that she was offered a record deal.
  sing   So .... that she was offered a record deal.
16 Unemployment hasn't been at such a high level at any time since the 1930's.
  been   Not since the 1930's .... at such a high level.
17 I only watch television if I don't have anything else to do.
  do   Only when I have nothing else to do .... television.
18 She'd barely finished drying her hair when her first guests arrived.
  had   Barely .... drying her hair when her first guests arrived.
19 He didn't thank me once for feeding his cat.
  once   Not .... me for feeding his cat.
20 If there had been a phone nearby, he would have called an ambulance.
  there   Had .... nearby, he would have called an ambulance.
21 The door to the basement isn't to be left open on any account.
  account   On .... to the basement to be left open.
22 We won't tell anybody the good news until we're certain it's true.
  will   Not until we're certain it's true .... anybody the good news.
23 He felt so unwell that he had to cancel their date.
  did   So .... that he had to cancel their date.
24 Bob forgot his mother's birthday and his sister's too.
  did   Bob didn't remember his mother's birthday; .... his sister's.
25 He was so anxious that he kept biting his nails.
  his   Such .... he kept biting his nails.
26 Brown bread is healthier and tastier than white bread.
  only   Not .... than white bread, but it's healthier too!
27 I didn't expect that they would throw a surprise party for my birthday.
  expect   Little .... they would throw a surprise party for my birthday.
28 It isn't often that temperatures in Spain fall below 0˚C.
  fall   Seldom .... below 0˚C in Spain.
29 If I were you, I'd accept the offer.
  you   Were .... accept the offer.
30 This is the only way the Prime Minister can win the election.
  this   Only .... the Prime Minister win the election.

4   Rewrite the sentences using so or such at the beginning of the sentence.

1 As the exams were difficult, many students complained.
  So ...*difficult were the exams that many students complained*....
2 His dream was so strange that his psychiatrist wrote about it in a medical journal.
  So ....
3 The explorers took such a long time to find the tomb that they had nearly run out of supplies.
  Such ....
4 Many people think she's English because she speaks the language so fluently.
  So ....

158

5 She is so ignorant that she has never heard of Shakespeare.
Such ....
6 He was so surprised that he nearly fell off his chair.
Such ....
7 The dancer moved so gracefully that he appeared to be skating.
So ....

5 Fill in so, neither/nor **and the appropriate verb.**

1 "I don't feel like staying in today."
"...*Neither do I...* . Let's go to the beach instead."
2 "I really like our new teacher."
"........................ . She's really patient, isn't she?"
3 "I can't decide what to buy Chris for his birthday."
"........................ . What can you give a man who has everything?"
4 "I should really start doing some kind of exercise."
"........................ . I've put on a lot of weight."
5 "I'd really love to go out tonight."
"........................ . Let's go to the new Italian place round the corner."
6 "I can't stand this heat any more."
"........................ . Let's get in the car and go for a drive."
7 "I had the time of my life at the party last night."
"........................ . I'll never forget you dancing the tango with old Mrs Marple."
8 "I've spent lots of money on clothes this month."
"........................ . There's hardly any space left in my wardrobe."
9 "I won't be surprised if they don't turn up this evening."
"........................ . They've been known to let people down in the past."
10 "We're thinking of going to Ibiza this summer."
"........................ . We've heard it's a great holiday resort."

6 Complete the sentences using the words in bold. Use two to five words.

1 He broke his leg during the summer holidays.
that   It was during ...*the summer holidays that*... he broke his leg.
2 He didn't realise a surprise party awaited him.
know   Little .... a surprise party awaited him.
3 Why did you leave work early today?
that   Why was .... early today?
4 It was impossible for us to have a day off work.
could   On no account .... a day off work.
5 You had to be lucky to discover gold in those days.
could   Only if you .... discover gold in those days.
6 Hillary and Tenzing were the first climbers to reach the summit of Mount Everest.
who   It was .... reached the summit of Mount Everest.
7 The courier met him at the station.
who   It was .... him at the station.
8 You should never park on double yellow lines.
circumstances Under .... on double yellow lines.
9 He seldom tells us what he's really thinking.
tell   Seldom .... he's really thinking.
10 You won't be given the job if you don't make a good impression.
will   Only by .... you be given the job.

7 Use the words in capitals to form a word that fits in the space in the same line.

Cloud Formation

A lot of **(0)** ...*poetry*... has been written about clouds, which many of us will remember from our **(1)** .... But how many of us know the **(2)** .... reason why clouds are formed? **(3)** ...., clouds form when rising air cools and the **(4)** .... in it forms into droplets. But what makes the air rise in the first place? There are three main reasons. The **(5)** .... of the sun heats the air and makes it lighter, so it goes upwards. Also the air goes up in order to pass over **(6)** .... kinds of land, for example, mountains. A third reason is weather fronts, which result in a **(7)** .... of cold and warm air. The warm air always ends up on top. In all three cases, as the air rises it cools, the water it contains is condensed and the result is the familiar **(8)** .... of rain.

As for the shapes of clouds, there are two **(9)** .... types; stratus clouds and cumulus clouds and **(10)** .... weather conditions can be predicted, depending on the type of clouds we see.

POET
CHILD
SCIENCE
BASIC
MOIST
WARM

VARY

COMBINE

OCCUR

CHARACTER
DIFFER

Oral Development 14

Look at the pictures below, then talk about them using emphatic structures or inversion.

It was Kirkpatrick who started the fight. Not only was he rude to the referee, but he also punched him on the nose.   etc

Phrasal Verbs

see about: deal with; make arrangements for (= see to)
see sb off: go with sb to their point of departure
see sb out: accompany sb to the door/exit of a house/building
see over: inspect (a house, flat etc)
see through sb/sth: not be deceived by sb/sth
see sb through: support sb until the end of a difficult time
see to: 1) make arrangements, 2) attend to sth

·······················

set about: 1) begin to do, 2) attack
set aside: save for a special purpose
set back: 1) delay progress of sth, 2) delay an event till a later date, 3) cost (slang)
set out: 1) begin a journey, 2) start a course of action with a clear aim in mind
set in: start and seem likely to continue
set on: (cause to) attack
set up: 1) start a business, 2) build; erect, 3) establish

8 **Fill in the correct particle(s).**

1 Don't do the washing up now, I'll see ...*to*... it later.
2 Let's make an appointment to see .... the property with the surveyor.
3 He thinks he's clever, but I can see .... his tricks.
4 You look after the children and I'll see .... the tickets.
5 We'll all come to the station to see you ....
6 He sets .... a little money every month.
7 As soon as the last guest had gone, he set .... cleaning the flat.
8 When he finished university, he set .... his own computer company.
9 He set .... to become a millionaire before he was thirty.
10 We'll need winter coats now that the cold weather has set ....
11 That leather jacket set me .... £300.
12 The sound equipment has been set .... ready for the concert.
13 The storm did a lot of damage and set construction .... by a week.
14 The gang of hooligans set .... him with sticks.
15 She set .... a committee to oppose the plans for the new building.

9 **Look at Appendix 1, then fill in the correct preposition.**

1 She was expelled ...*from*... school when they caught her taking some test papers.
2 He forgave me .... arriving late for his performance.
3 Don't worry – you'll be safe .... those men here. They won't find you.
4 I replied .... the invitation for the party.
5 It's so typical .... him to be late for an appointment.
6 Mozart was a genius .... composing operas.
7 The train to Liverpool departs .... platform 7 at 10.30.
8 He was ashamed .... the way he had treated his friend.
9 In this city, you have to beware .... the busy roads as they're very dangerous.
10 This new hairdryer does not comply .... British safety standards.
11 The boy was named .... his grandfather.
12 Joan is frightened .... spiders.
13 The barrister was very happy .... the jury's verdict.
14 All the tax is included .... the price written on the item.
15 If the boat was going to sink, there would be a great need .... lifejackets.
16 If you persist .... calling me such horrible names, I'm going to tell the teacher.
17 Jimmy agreed .... his fiancée where they should get married.
18 I was shocked .... the price they charged.
19 Don't forget to thank your grandmother .... your present.
20 The hijackers surrendered .... the police.
21 It's about time you stopped relying .... your parents.

10 *Fill in the following collocation grid.*

	the bus	one's temper	weight	a film	money	a target	one's mind	the train
lose								
miss	✓							

Consolidation 10

11 Complete the sentences using the words in bold. Use two to five words.

1 She said she was sorry for ruining my dress.
   ruined   She ...*apologised for having ruined*... my dress.

2 You'd better reconsider his offer.
   were   If .... reconsider his offer.

3 The house she lives in is just round the corner.
   where   The .... just round the corner.

4 "Why don't you try on the blue dress?" she said to me.
   that   She .... the blue dress.

5 I'd prefer him to be back before 11 o'clock.
   rather   I .... before 11 o'clock.

6 Sheila doesn't agree with John's way of thinking.
   approve   Sheila .... way of thinking.

7 He would never have read the book if you hadn't suggested it.
   for   But ...., he would never have read the book.

8 They are building me a new shed.
   having   I .... built.

9 Katie will move to London, but she must find a job first.
   finds   Only if Katie .... move to London.

10 She left the house early because she was afraid the traffic might be bad.
   case   She left the house early .... bad.

11 He didn't find time to phone her until midnight.
   round   He didn't .... until midnight.

12 I wish I had curly hair like yours.
   rather   I .... like yours.

12 Fill in the gaps with the correct form of the verb in brackets.

Mrs Pickles **1)** ...*has been living*... (**live**) in her two-storey house for over five years. She **2)** .... (**do**) most of the housework herself but, once a month, she **3)** .... (**clean/ upstairs windows**) by a professional window cleaner called Fred. At the end of each month, Fred calls round **4)** .... (**collect**) his money. One day, Mrs Pickles **5)** .... (**ask**) Fred an unusual question. **6)** "........................ (**you/use**) the bathroom last time you were here?" Fred blushed. He **7)** .... (**use**) Mrs Pickles' upstairs bathroom because he **8)** .... (**not/ want**) to wait until he got home. "Yes I did, Mrs Pickles ... I'm sorry." "Don't worry," she laughed. "I don't mind you **9)** .... (**use**) my bathroom. But if you **10)** .... (**need**) to use it again, **11)** .... (**you/try**) to remember to unlock the bathroom door before you **12)** .... (**climb**) back out of the window?"

13 For questions 1 - 12, read the text below and decide which word A, B, C or D best fits each space.

Stress

Stress is important. We all need a certain **(0)** ...*C*... of it in order to **(1)** .... fulfilling lives. However, if we have too much of it, it can have the opposite **(2)** .... Some people can tolerate greater **(3)** .... of stress than others, but most of us will **(4)** .... at some time in our lives. It is **(5)** .... a good idea to learn a few stress management techniques. Identifying the **(6)** .... of the problem we have, so that we can **(7)** .... it more effectively, is one of the first **(8)** .... towards reducing stress. The second is talking to a person you can trust, who will listen and, if necessary, **(9)** .... you some positive advice. Not only are smoking and drinking harmful to our health, they actually increase stress **(10)** .... than reduce it. Take up walking instead, which is not only healthy but it helps you think more **(11)** .... too. Unnecessary noise should be avoided as much as possible, however, laughter is one of the best ways to **(12)** .... yourself feel considerably better.

0	A number	B bulk	C amount	D load
1	A guide	B lead	C conduct	D direct
2	A influence	B solution	C answer	D effect
3	A levels	B degrees	C grades	D layers
4	A endure	B suffer	C tolerate	D torture
5	A therefore	B so	C however	D nevertheless
6	A purpose	B occurrence	C cause	D reason
7	A answer	B treat	C do	D cope
8	A movements	B means	C ways	D steps
9	A give	B show	C supply	D hand
10	A more	B rather	C as	D quite
11	A clearly	B well	C skilfully	D cleanly
12	A succeed	B have	C do	D make

14 Think of the word which best fits each space. Write only one word in each space.

The Wright Brothers' First Flight

The Wright brothers **(0)** ...*started*... flying in 1902. Their first flight was in a glider, which they designed to test the stability of its wings. Once they **(1)** .... satisfied that they could fly in the air steadily, without the fear **(2)** .... falling straight down, they began working on their design for the first aeroplane, **(3)** .... would be propelled by a motor. They wrote to several carmakers, asking **(4)** .... they could build a motor for them, but most either did not reply **(5)** .... said they were too busy. Finally, they decided to build the motor **(6)** .... The major problem they faced was how to make the motor powerful **(7)** .... to propel the aeroplane without being too heavy. They soon realised that they would need to make the aeroplane bigger, **(8)** .... than make the motor smaller. After months of planning, they were ready to build the first prototype. It was a funny looking machine **(9)** .... four wings and no seat for the pilot. The two brothers were very **(10)** .... of their invention but could not decide **(11)** .... would be the one to fly it. They tossed a coin and Wilbur won. The world's first ever aeroplane **(12)** .... off and flew into the air, making history.

15 For questions 1 - 10, read the text below. Use the word given in capitals at the end of each line to form a word that fits in the space in the same line.

Depression

Throughout the course of our lives, we all experience episodes of **(0)** ...*unhappiness*..., sadness, or grief. Often, when a loved one dies, or we suffer a **(1)** .... tragedy or difficulty such as losing a job, we may feel depressed. Most of us are able to cope with these and other types of **(2)** .... events.

HAPPY
PERSON

STRESS

Over a period of days or weeks, the **(3)** .... of us are able to return to our normal daily **(4)** .... But when these feelings of sadness turn to feelings of **(5)** .... and include a loss of appetite, low self-esteem and sleep problems, then we may have clinical depression. This condition is not just sadness or 'the blues', as it is sometimes **(6)** .... to. It is an illness that can challenge your **(7)** .... to perform even routine tasks. It represents a burden for both the sufferer and his family. It can be mixed up with other **(8)** .... problems such as anxiety and stress.

MAJOR
ACT

HOPE

REFER
ABLE

PSYCHOLOGY

However, doctors can now treat this kind of depression **(9)** ...., so no time should be lost in seeking help.

EFFECT

If you are worried or **(10)** .... if these symptoms sound familiar, call your doctor.

PARTICULAR

Part **1**

For questions 1 - 12, read the text below and decide which answer (A, B, C or D) best fits each gap. There is an example at the beginning (0).

Why are broken **mirrors** believed to be **unlucky?**

Breaking a mirror is said to **(0)** ...*C*... seven years' bad luck. Although most people may **(1)** .... that they are not superstitious, they would nonetheless be a little **(2)** .... if they did break a mirror. This age-old superstition is possible to have come from the **(3)** .... belief that when a person **(4)** .... at their reflection, they were seeing their own soul. If that reflection was broken, then the soul would be **(5)** .... The seven-year **(6)** .... probably arises from another ancient belief, that the body replaced itself every seven years. After this time had **(7)** ...., the soul would then be renewed. Superstitions surrounding mirrors don't **(8)** .... there. Break one in Yorkshire, and you'll **(9)** .... your best friend. In America, it's not bad luck to break one on **(10)** .... If you do it accidentally, simply **(11)** .... out a dollar bill and give it to someone to break the bad luck in half. In many countries, it's a **(12)** .... custom to cover any mirrors in the house with a cloth when someone has died.

	A	B	C	D
0	carry	fetch	Ⓒ bring	take
1	tell	claim	persist	object
2	disturbed	uneasy	uncomfortable	troubled
3	ancient	old	aged	antique
4	looked	saw	watched	observed
5	disappeared	ruined	exploded	destroyed
6	period	time	distance	date
7	left	spent	passed	been
8	end	complete	go	begin
9	overlook	misplace	miss	lose
10	purpose	accident	reason	chance
11	remove	have	take	bring
12	common	standard	plain	familiar

For questions 13 - 24, read the text below and think of the word which best fits each gap. Use only one word in each gap. There is an example at the beginning (0).

The Brain

Contrary to popular belief, it is not true **(0)** ...*that*... we use only 10 percent of our brain power; it is **(13)** .... of the myths of modern times. The brain controls all of our bodily functions as **(14)** .... as carrying out the most complicated processes **(15)** .... thought and imagination.

There must therefore, be some spare capacity built into the system because brain cells – unlike most of the body's other cells – are not **(16)** .... to divide and therefore are incapable **(17)** .... replacing themselves **(18)** .... they die.

It is possible to increase the abilities of our brain. We do **(19)** .... when we learn to read, for example. Current research shows that the learning process creates new connections with brain cells **(20)** .... increases our mental powers.

But scientists are unable to say exactly how **(21)** .... of the brain we don't use. Despite a lot of research, the brain is still the **(22)** .... mysterious organ in the body and it will be many years **(23)** .... enough information can be gathered to explain all **(24)** ....

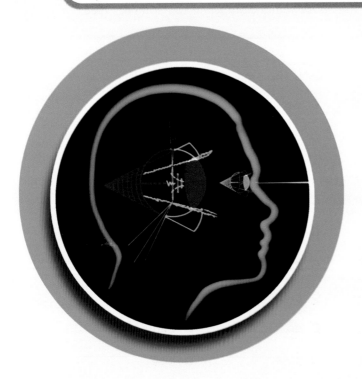

Part 3

For questions 25 - 34, read the text below. Use the word given in capitals at the end of some of the lines to form a word that fits in the gap in the same line. There is an example at the beginning (0).

Burglars

The **(0)** ...*majority*... of burglaries occur when people go on holiday. **(25)** .... guests often take advantage of an empty house. However, there are a number of safety measures you can take.	**MAJOR** **INVITED**
It is **(26)** .... to cancel any doorstep deliveries. If burglars see a pile of newspapers or other items outside awaiting, **(27)** ...., they will realise the **(28)** .... are away.	**ADVISE** **COLLECT** **OCCUPY**
Move **(29)** .... items like TVs away from windows where they can be seen by potential intruders. There is no point in putting **(30)** .... in their way.	**VALUE** **TEMPT**
Put all expensive items of **(31)** .... in storage. This could be a safe in a bank or a special post office box. If **(32)** .... are left at home, there is every **(33)** .... they will be found. Burglars know all the typical places to look.	**JEWEL** **POSSESS** **LIKELY**
Finally, don't forget to ask a neighbour to keep a **(34)** .... eye on your home while you are away.	**WATCH**

Part **4**

For questions 35 - 42, complete the second sentence so that it has a similar meaning to the first sentence, using the word given. Do not change the word given. You must use between two and five words including the word given. There is an example at the beginning (0).

0 They worked hard on the project.
effort
They ...*put a lot of effort*... into the project.

35 Has Martin decided to move house?
mind
Has Martin .... to move house?

36 We really must go home now.
time
It's .... now.

37 She intends to go back to college in September.
intention
It .... back to college in September.

38 All this exercise has exhausted me.
worn
I .... all this exercise.

39 "You had better leave your passport at reception!" said the group leader.
advised
The group leader .... passport at reception.

40 Shall I carry your shopping for you?
to
Would .... your shopping?

41 With the exception of Ann every actor was included in the play.
except
The play .... Ann.

42 Sue definitely won't be first in the class.
chance
Sue has .... first in the class.

Determiners / Pronouns 11

Determiners are: indefinite article (a/an), definite article (the), demonstratives (this - these/that - those), possessive adjectives (my, your, his etc), quantifiers (some, any, every, no, both, each, either, neither, enough, several, all, most etc) and numbers (one, two etc).

Demonstratives (this - these / that - those)

This/These are used	That/Those are used
● for people or things near us. *This box is yours.* ● for present/future situations. *I'm going out with Ted this week.* ● when the speaker is in or near the place he/she is referring to. *This house was built in 1856. (The speaker is near or in the house.)* ● to introduce people or to identify ourselves on the phone. *"Ann, this is Jane."*	● for people or things not near us. *That boy over there is my son.* ● for past situations. *That day was the worst of his life.* ● to refer back to something mentioned before. *"We're moving to York." "That's fantastic!"* ● when speaking on the phone to ask who the other person is. *"Hello? This is Alan Smith. Who's that, please?"*

Note: This/These - That/Those are not always followed by nouns. *This is all I can do to help you.*

1 Fill in: this, that, these **or** those.

1 "I'll never forget my holiday in Moscow. ...*That*... was the holiday of a lifetime!"
2 "What are you doing .... Thursday?" "Well, I have to go to work as usual."
3 "Didn't you just love .... striped trousers in the shop we just passed?"
4 Mmm! .... is the best soup I've ever tasted!
5 "Do you see .... girl over there? She's my cousin's girlfriend."
6 "Hello, ... is Mrs Cook. Can I speak to Mr Brown please?"
7 "I can't go out in .... dress. It's much too tight."
8 "I've been accepted by my first choice of university." "Congratulations. .... is fantastic!"
9 "................ were the days when we used to sing and dance every night."
10 Don't you think .... new electronic diaries that we saw in the shop are really clever?
11 "................ belonged to my grandmother," said Tim as he slipped the diamond ring onto Ann's finger.
12 "Don't you think .... trousers suit me?"
13 "................ biscuits are delicious. Did you make them yourself?"
14 "................ records you threw out were my original hits from the sixties!"
15 Aren't .... boys over there your students?
16 "................ lamp needs repairing." "................ is what I was trying to tell you."

2 Fill in: this, that, these **or** those.

"What did you think of **1)** ...*that*... dress Priscilla was wearing last night?" "Oh, it was awful, wasn't it? — And **2)** .... earrings!" "Ugh! Her sense of style is even worse **3)** .... days than it was when she was at school." "I wonder what outrageous outfit she'll be wearing to the Windsor's cocktail party **4)** .... evening." "**5)** .... is something that we'll just have to wait and see."

169

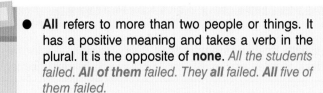

- **All** refers to more than two people or things. It has a positive meaning and takes a verb in the plural. It is the opposite of **none**. *All the students failed.* *All of them failed.* *They all failed.* *All five of them failed.*
  All + that-clause (= the only thing) takes a singular verb. *All that he said was not to worry.*

- **Both** refers to two people or things. It has a positive meaning and takes a verb in the plural. It is the opposite of **neither/not either**. *Pam and Ann are singers.* *Both Pam and Ann are singers.* *They are both singers.* *Both of them are singers.* *Both girls are singers.*

- **Whole** (= complete) is used with countable nouns. We always use **a, the, this, my** etc + **whole + countable**. *the whole day = all day*

- **Either** (= any one of two) / **Neither** (= not one and not the other) refer to two people or things and are used before singular countable nouns. *Neither girl enjoys horror films.* **Neither of/Either of** take a verb either in the singular or plural. *Neither of them is/are French.*

- **None** refers to more than two people or things. It has a negative meaning and isn't followed by a noun. *"Are there any mistakes?" "No, none."* **None of** is used before nouns or object pronouns followed by a verb either in the singular or plural. It is the opposite of **all**. *None of the three girls/them know(s) how to do it.* **Note: no + noun.** *There's no room for you.*

- **Every** is used with singular countable nouns. It refers to a group of people or things and means "all", "everyone", "everything" etc. *He goes to the gym every day.*

- **Each** is used with singular countable nouns. It means "one by one", considered individually. *Each member of the team was given a medal.* Note that **every one** and **each one** have **of** constructions. *Every one of/Each one of the players is to be given a bonus.*

- **One/Ones** are used to avoid repetition of a countable noun. *"Which dress do you like?" "This one."*

---

3   Underline the correct item.

1 **Both**/**Neither** Mozart and Beethoven were great composers.
2 **Neither**/**Either** Sam or David will clean the garage.
3 I finished the **all**/**whole** exercise in five minutes.
4 I've kept in touch with **all**/**every** my old school friends.
5 **Neither**/**Either** of the girls passed the exam. They both failed.
6 Victor goes to the same restaurant **every**/**all** day.
7 **None**/**Each** of the people he contacted were interested.
8 We have to pay our telephone bill **each**/**every** three months.
9 You'll get fat if you eat **all**/**none** those biscuits.
10 **Either**/**Both** Tom and Lynn had a good time.
11 She spent the **whole**/**all** afternoon lying on the beach.
12 **Each**/**All** of the candidates will be interviewed individually.
13 **None of**/**Every** the students believed that the exam results would be released so early.
14 I don't like **either**/**neither** of these coats. I'll look for one somewhere else.
15 You'd better read through the **all**/**whole** contract before you sign it.
16 You're going to have to look through **each**/**both** one of these files separately.
17 There's a leak in **both**/**each** the hot water tank and the cold water tank.
18 **Neither**/**Either** of the DVDs you bought is the one I really wanted.
19 **None**/**All** of the girls were ready for the dance on time. They got there late.
20 "Do you like these boots?" "No, I prefer these **one**/**ones**."
21 **Each**/**All** one of the candidates was given a questionnaire before the interview.
22 Fiona and I went to the opera. We **both**/**all** enjoyed it very much.
23 There's **no**/**none** space for a washing machine in my kitchen.
24 **All**/**Every** that she wants is another baby. She simply adores big families.
25 I go swimming nearly **either**/**every** day.
26 My drama group put on a play but **none**/**all** of us were pleased with the performance.

Mozart

Beethoven

4 Fill in: all, both, whole, either, neither, none, every, each or one(s).

1 ...*None*... of the toxic waste has been cleared up by the company.
2 He's studying .... politics and modern languages at university.
3 "I think these are the .... you like."
4 They spent the .... day packing for their holiday.
5 She spends .... her time studying for her exams.
6 In .... game there is an element of risk.
7 John and Fiona had a lot of work yesterday. .... of them went out.
8 "Do you like this skirt?" "I think that .... is more flattering."
9 The members of the club were .... given copies of the regulations.
10 Both of these dictionaries are excellent - .... one of them will help you in your studies.

- **Both ... and ... + plural verb**. *Both Ann and Liz are vegetarians.*
- **Neither ... nor ... / Either ... or ... / Not only ... but also ... + singular** or **plural verb** depending on the subject which follows nor, or, but also. *Neither Bill nor John is willing to help. Not only Sue but also her family are going to the wedding.*

5 Rewrite the sentences using both ... and, neither ... nor, either ... or, not only ... but also.

1 Kay is a doctor and so is Niall. ...*Both Kay and Niall are doctors*....
2 Karen will pick you up from the station or else Miles will. ....
3 John hasn't been to Germany and his brother hasn't either. ....
4 Jo and Jim speak French. ....
5 Paul doesn't like going to the cinema. Tim doesn't either. ....
6 James likes going fishing; so does Kate. ....
....
7 This winter Liz is going skiing; so are her parents. ....
....
8 Tim will fix your car or else John will. ....
9 Pete and Nicki prepared the dinner. ....
10 Jane is going on a picnic this Sunday and so are her schoolmates. ....
....

6 Complete the sentences using the words in bold. Use two to five words.

1 My aunt lives on a farm and so does my cousin.
  and Both my ...*aunt and cousin live*... on a farm.
2 Danny can speak Chinese and so can his brother.
  but Not .... brother can speak Chinese.
3 Gordon is a journalist; his wife is too.
  are Both .... journalists.
4 The exhibition will be opened by the mayor or the Queen.
  or Either the .... open the exhibition.
5 Not only Patricia but also her husband want to emigrate.
  and Both .... to emigrate.
6 She doesn't enjoy sleeping in a tent and nor does her sister.
  nor Neither .... sleeping in a tent.
7 Bob is about to leave; Helen is about to leave too.
  also Not only .... about to leave.
8 My father didn't go to university and neither did my mother.
  nor Neither my .... to university.
9 You can ask John or Tom to help you prune the trees.
  either You can .... to help you prune the trees.

11 Determiners / Pronouns

A lot of - many - much

	countables	uncountables	
Positive	a lot (of)/lots of/ many (formal)	a lot (of)/lots of/ much (formal)	*There are **a lot of** animals in the zoo.* *There is **a lot of** sugar in my coffee.*
Interrogative	many	much	*Are there **many** books in the library?* *Did you have **much** time to read any of them?*
Negative	many	much	*There aren't **many** cakes left.* *I won't make any more as I don't have **much** flour left.*
	a few (= some)/ very few (= not many, not enough)	a little (= some)/ very little (= not much, not enough)	***A few** students passed the test.* ***Very few** prisoners escape from prison.* ***A little** salt gives flavour to food.*

- **A lot (of)/Lots of** + countable/uncountable nouns are normally used in positive sentences. *A lot of people attended the ceremony. She's got **lots of** furniture.* **A lot of** can also be used in questions and negations in informal English. *Was there **a lot of** disagreement over the proposal?*

- **Many** + **countables** / **much** + **uncountables** are normally used in questions or negations. *Are there **many** cakes? There isn't **much** Coke.* **Many** and **much** are often used in positive sentences after **too**, **so**, **how** or in formal English. *She didn't realise **how much** money she had spent. You should slow down; you're doing **too much**.*

- **A few** (= some, a small number) + **countables** **a little** (= some, a small amount of) + **uncountables** have a positive meaning. *I have **a little** money left so I'll buy **a few** sweets.*

- **Few** (= not many, almost none) + **countables** / **Little** (= not much, almost none) + **uncountables** have a negative meaning and are rather formal English. **Very few/very little, only a few/only a little** are more usual. ***Few** English people speak a second language. I've had **very little** success with my job applications. He had **only a few** problems in the exam even though he had done **only a little** work for it.*

Note: most, all, some, any, many, a few, several, both, one, two, much, (a) little are followed by **of** when a noun follows, preceded by possessives or words such as: this, that, these, those, the or a. *How **much** of the money I gave you did you spend? I liked **two of** her books, but I was bored by the others. So **many of** my friends are away that I've got no one to talk to.*

---

7   **Fill in:** a lot (of), much **or** many.

1 It takes ...*a lot of*... patience to bring up children.
2 There can't be .... people who haven't seen Jurassic Park.
3 She doesn't have .... time to herself these days.
4 Why haven't you washed the dishes? You didn't have .... else to do.
5 He's very popular. He always has .... people at his house.
6 We don't get on very well as we haven't got .... in common.
7 Will there be .... guests at the wedding?
8 You need .... courage to be a firefighter.
9 Have .... new people joined the club this year?
10 There are too .... mistakes in your composition.
11 There's still .... food left over from the party last night.
12 I hope we didn't make .... noise when we came in late last night.
13 She's eaten too .... sweets, so she doesn't feel well.
14 There's .... poverty in some African countries.
15 She must have .... money to afford such expensive clothes.

8   Underline the correct item.

1 Very **few**/much/little people can guess what the future will be like.
2 There are **little**/**too many**/**much** cars on the roads.
3 There's **a little**/**a few**/**much** light coming in through that window.
4 We've had **much**/**very little**/**a lot of** problems with the car.
5 Did you learn **many**/**much**/**a few** English on your summer course?
6 He was late because he had **little**/**few**/**a lot of** work to do.
7 I'm afraid I haven't got **much**/**many**/**a little** information about that matter.
8 Only **a few**/**a lot of**/**a little** people knew it was my birthday.
9 There are **a little**/**much**/**a few** sandwiches left on the table.
10 John's schoolwork leaves **lots of**/**many**/**few** room for improvement.
11 Did you spend **many**/**a few**/**much** money on this blouse?
12 There are only **a little**/**a few**/**a lot of** days left before the holiday.
13 I don't like **many**/**much**/**little** of Woody Allen's films.
14 Sally ate too **many**/**much**/**little** cake and now she feels sick.
15 There are **a lot**/**a little**/**a few** flowers in the garden.
16 I have only **a little**/**a few**/**a lot of** books but I'd like to have more.

Some - Any - No				
	Adjectives	**Pronouns**	**Adverbs**	
		people	things	places
Positive	some any	someone/somebody anyone/anybody	something anything	somewhere anywhere
Interrogative	any	anyone/anybody	anything	anywhere
Negative	no/not any	no one/not anyone nobody/not anybody	nothing not anything	nowhere not anywhere
Positive/Negative/ Interrogative	every	everybody (all people) everyone	everything (all things)	everywhere (in all places)

● **Some** is used before countable or uncountable nouns. *I'll buy **some** apples. He gave me **some** money.*
● **Some** and **its compounds** (somebody, something etc) are normally used in positive sentences. They are also used in questions when we want to make an offer, a request or when we expect a positive answer. *There's **someone** at the door. (= positive) Would you like **something** to eat? (= offer) Could I have **something** to drink? (= request) Is there **someone** waiting for me? (= I expect there is)* **BUT** *Is there **anyone** waiting for me? (= I'm asking in general)*
● **Any** is used before countable or uncountable nouns. Is there any sugar? **Any** and **its compounds** (anyone, anything etc) are normally used in questions. *Is there **anyone** here?* They are also used in positive sentences meaning "It doesn't matter how/what/which/when/who/where". *You can go **anywhere** you want.* **Any** and **its compounds** can be used after if in a positive sentence. *If **anything** is broken, I will hold you responsible.*
● **No/not any** are used before countable and uncountable nouns. **No/not any** and **their compounds** (no one/not anyone, nothing/not anything etc) are used in negations. *I know **no one** at this party. I don't know **anyone** at this party.* **Any** and **its compounds** are used with negative words (hardly, never, without, seldom, rarely etc). *I never go **anywhere** alone at night.* (NOT: *I never go nowhere alone at night.*)
● **Every** is used before singular countable nouns. **Every** and **its compounds** take a verb in singular. ***Every** worker in the factory **has** been well trained. (= all the workers) We've bought **everything** we need. (= all the things)*

9 Underline the correct item.

1 He didn't say **anything**/**nothing** to the police.
2 **No one**/**Anyone** was at home when I called.
3 There was hardly **no one**/**anyone** at the party.
4 I need **any**/**some** more milk for this cake.
5 I can't find my sister **anywhere**/**nowhere**.
6 Are you going **nowhere**/**anywhere** for your holiday?
7 John goes to sleep at 11.00 pm **any**/**every** evening.
8 Call round **any**/**some** time you like.
9 He needs **any**/**some** time to work out the answer.
10 **Anybody**/**Nobody** told me you were leaving.
11 **Anybody**/**Everybody** congratulated us.
12 She goes to school **every**/**some** day.
13 Is there **everything**/**anything** good on at the cinema?
14 Will you give them **nothing**/**some** homework tonight?
15 I think there's **anything**/**something** wrong with my car.
16 Sally isn't going **anywhere**/**nowhere** this weekend.
17 He doesn't want **anything**/**nothing** in particular for his birthday.
18 Shall I go and buy **some**/**anything** cheese?
19 There is **nowhere**/**everywhere** in the world I'd like to visit more than Egypt.
20 I didn't buy **some**/**any** milk.

10 Fill in: some, any, no, every **or their compounds.**

1 ...*Everyone*... knows that the sky is blue, but few people know why.
2 If you have .... questions, I'll be in my office.
3 .... wanted to miss the match, so .... arrived early.
4 The teacher asked if .... knew the answer to her question.
5 Would you like .... cheese or maybe .... sweet?
6 Have you seen Jim ....? I've been looking .... for him.
7 If you have .... spare time, there's .... I want to talk to you about.
8 .... is looking for John, but .... has seen him since this morning.
9 I've never been .... without finding .... interesting to see.
10 If .... is going to the supermarket could they get me .... milk?
11 Don't speak to me. There is .... you can say to me that will make .... difference to how I feel.
12 We never go .... for our holidays. Why don't we go .... this year?
13 Jerry is very tidy; he won't tolerate .... being out of place.
14 "I'll get you .... coffee." "Have you got .... cold - .... milk perhaps?"

● **Ever** can be added to certain **question words** to mean **"any"**. These words are: whoever (anyone who), whatever (anything that), whichever (any of), whenever (any time that), wherever (any place that), however (in any way that). *You can come **whenever** you like. (= any time that you like)*

11 Fill in: whoever, whatever, whichever, whenever, wherever **or** however.

1 I'm not sure how to advise you. I suggest you do ...*whatever*... you think best.
2 .... mum decides to put the washing out, it always starts raining.
3 My pen is missing! .... has borrowed it kindly return it, immediately.
4 "Welcome! Come in and sit down .... you can find an empty seat."
5 Red and green both look good on you. .... colour you choose, I'm sure it will suit you.
6 The interview is informal, so you can dress .... you want.
7 You know where to find me - come round .... you want, and we'll talk over your problem.
8 .... wins the elections is sure to be the best candidate.
9 You must get some advice about the career you wish to follow so that .... one you choose, you won't regret it.
10 There are two different routes from here to Manchester. Why not take .... is the shortest to save time?

Else

- **Else** (= more; different) is followed by a singular verb and can be used with the **indefinite pronouns** and adverbs **everyone, something, nobody, anywhere** etc. *You'd better ask Joanne. **Nobody else knows** better than her.* It can also be used with **who, what, where** and **how** to refer to people, things, places etc. ***What else** can be done to prevent crime?*
- **Else** forms its possessive case with **'s**. *Don't use my pen. Take **someone else's**.*
- **Or else** means "otherwise". *Get an umbrella **or else** you'll get wet.*

12 Complete the sentences using "else" structures.

1 You must study for the test *...or else...* you won't do well.
2 We always go to this restaurant. Can't we go ....?
3 She wasn't in the bank when they robbed it; you'd better ask ....
4 You have to speak to Mary; .... can make such an important decision.
5 I've only bought two tickets for the concert, as I wasn't sure if .... would want to go.
6 .... can cook as well as my mother.
7 When he was moving, he brought the big things in a van and .... in his car.
8 We always watch the football; can't we watch .... for a change?
9 Sandra and Cilla will be there, but I don't have a clue if .... is coming.
10 The waiter asked if we wanted to order ....

"Other" structures

- **the other(s)** = the rest. *These books are Tom's; **the others** are mine.*
- **others** = several more apart from those already mentioned. *People have different opinions when it comes to vegetarianism; some believe it's unhealthy and unnatural not to eat meat while **others** believe it is much better for our health.*
- **each other** = one another. *Good friends always help **each other** out.*
- **every other** = alternate. *I go jogging **every other** day.*
- **the other day** = a few days ago. *I bumped into George **the other day**; he looked well.*
- **the other one(s)** = not this/these but something else. *No, not that shirt. I want **the other one**; the black one please. These shoes are too small - can I try **the other ones**, please?*
- **another** = one more apart from those already mentioned. *Can you give me **another** cup of coffee?* **Another** can also be used with expressions of distance, money and time. *It'll cost **another** £5 to get it.*

13 Fill in: another, (the) other(s), each other, every other.

1 They went skiing *...the other...* day. It was fun.
2 Only four people turned up at the party. All .... guests had to go somewhere else.
3 This shirt doesn't fit me — can I try .... one on, please?
4 In .... four years, Tom will have qualified as a doctor.
5 Those magazines belong to Jim, ... belong to me.
6 There were only enough seats for 20 passengers on the bus — .... had to stand.
7 Some commuters believe it's economical to cycle to work while .... prefer to use a car-sharing scheme.
8 No, we're not close to our destination yet - we have .... six miles to go.
9 Even though they see .... every day, they still want to spend more time together.
10 Kate is very keen on playing the piano - she has lessons .... day and, in between, she practises at home.

11 Determiners / Pronouns

In Other Words

- Tom, Steve and Paul don't like tennis.
  None of them like/likes tennis.
- Ann is a typist. Mary is a typist, too.
  Both Ann and Mary are typists.
- Sally, Sue and Pam enjoy swimming.
  All three of them enjoy swimming.

- There isn't anything in the garden.
  There is nothing in the garden.
- No one will make me stay.
  There isn't anyone that/who will make me stay.
- Lynn doesn't like yogurt. Fiona doesn't like
  yogurt either. Neither of them likes yogurt.
  Neither Lynn nor Fiona likes yogurt.

14 Complete the sentences using the words in bold. Use two to five words.

1 No one knows the answer to my question.
   anyone   There ...*isn't anyone who knows*... the answer to my question.
2 There isn't anything I can do to help.
   is   There .... do to help.
3 Bob lives in Rome. John lives in Rome, too.
   live   Both .... in Rome.
4 Pete, Robert and Bill cook delicious meals.
   them   All .... delicious meals.
5 Mr Green can't drive. Mr Smythe can't drive either.
   can   Neither Mr Green .... drive.
6 The boys all dislike brussel sprouts.
   likes   None .... brussel sprouts.
7 These computers are not difficult to operate.
   of   None .... difficult to operate.
8 There wasn't anything he could do to avoid crashing.
   nothing   There .... to avoid crashing.
9 Five is an odd number. Seven is an odd number, too.
   are   Both .... odd numbers.
10 No one in the jury believed the witness.
   anyone   There .... jury that believed the witness.

Oral Development 15

Use both, all, neither **and** none **to compare the three women.**   *All three of them look happy.*

Lynn

25, single, two brothers, no sisters, likes cinema, didn't go to university, works in a company

Sarah

25, single, no brothers, no sisters, likes cinema, went to university, is self-employed

Pamela

33, single, two brothers, no sisters, likes cinema, went to university, works in a company

Pronouns

Personal pronouns		Possessive adjectives	Possessive pronouns	Reflexive-Emphatic pronouns
before verbs as subjects	after verbs as objects	followed by nouns	not followed by nouns	
I	me	my	mine	myself
you	you	your	yours	yourself
he	him	his	his	himself
she	her	her	hers	herself
it	it	its	---	itself
we	us	our	ours	ourselves
you	you	your	yours	yourselves
they	them	their	theirs	themselves

Note: We use **the** instead of a possessive adjective with parts of the body after prepositions. Verbs used in this pattern include: bite, hit, kiss, pat, punch, slap, sting, touch etc. *She slapped the boy on the face.* **(**NOT: ~~on his face~~**)**
Own + possessive adjective is used to emphasise the fact that something belongs to one person and no one else. *She's got her **own** car.* or *She's got a car **of her own**.*

15 Fill in the correct pronouns or possessives.

Dear Jean,
1) ...*We*...'re really enjoying 2) .... on holiday in Clacton and have found something different to do every day. 3) .... 'll never guess what happened to 4) .... last night. Fred and 5) .... went to see a comedy show. Stan Blair was the star attraction. Have 6) .... heard of 7) ....? He is a young, up-and-coming comedian who is just starting to make a name for 8) .... At the end of 9) .... act, he asked if anyone in the audience was celebrating 10) .... birthday that night. To 11) .... embarrassment, Fred shouted out that it was 12) ....! I was invited onto the stage and Stan presented 13) .... with a bunch of flowers. After the show, he met Fred and 14) .... in the bar for a drink and introduced 15) .... to the other members of the cast and they all signed 16) .... names on the back of one of 17) .... programmes. I haven't enjoyed 18) .... so much in ages. We both agreed that Stan had definitely made 19) .... holiday. Hope 20) .... was just as memorable.
Love,
Stella

16 Fill in the gaps with the or a possessive adjective.

1 He was crying because a wasp had stung him on ...*the*... nose.
2 She patted him lightly on .... shoulder to get .... attention.
3 He hugged .... son and said, "I'm proud of you."
4 The little boy kissed .... sister on .... cheek.
5 The boxer punched his opponent on .... nose.
6 She stroked .... hair and told him not to worry.
7 A falling brick nearly hit me on .... head.

11 Determiners / Pronouns

Reflexive - Emphatic Pronouns (myself - yourself etc)

- **Reflexive pronouns** are used after certain verbs (**behave, burn, cut, enjoy, hurt, kill, look at** etc) when the subject and the object of the verb are the same. *Did you cut* **yourself**? They can also be used after **be, feel, look, seem** to describe emotions or states. *She hasn't been* **herself** *recently.* Reflexive pronouns can be used after prepositions but not after prepositions of place. *She is very pleased with* **herself**. **BUT** *She looked behind her.* (NOT: ~~behind herself~~)
  Certain verbs (**wash, shave, dress, undress, meet, rest, relax, stand up, get up, sit down, wake up** etc) do not normally take a reflexive pronoun. *She woke up and dressed.* (NOT: ~~She woke up herself and dressed herself.~~) **Wash** or **dress** can be used with a reflexive pronoun to talk about young children or animals. *The little girl is* **washing herself**.
- **Emphatic pronouns** have the same form as reflexive pronouns but a different meaning. They give emphasis to the noun, or the fact that a certain person performs an action. *She* **herself** *organised the feast.* They can also mean "without help". *He painted the house* **himself**. *(without help)*
- Note these idioms: **Enjoy yourselves!** (= Have a good time!) **Behave yourself!** (= Be good!) **He likes being by himself.** (= He likes being alone.) **He lives by himself.** (= He lives on his own.) **By myself, by yourself, by himself** etc (= on my own, on your own, on his own etc) **Help yourself to tea.** (= You're welcome to take some tea if you want some.) **Do it yourself.** (= Do it without being helped.) **Make yourself at home!** (= Feel comfortable.) **Make yourself heard.** (= Speak loudly enough to be heard by others.) **Make yourself understood.** (= Make your meaning clear.)

Note: each other means "one another". Compare: *Tom and Bill are brothers who have been brought up to look after* **each other**. *Tom and Bill are very independent for their ages and they are extremely capable of looking after* **themselves**.

---

17 Fill in the pronouns then identify them: reflexive or emphatic.

1 The Chinese girl decorated the pumpkin ...*herself*... . *(emphatic)*
2 The winner looked very proud of ....
3 She brought up her children by ....
4 The couple wrote to .... when they had to spend time apart.
5 The children enjoyed .... when they visited Disneyland.
6 Ann was afraid of spiders, so she didn't go into the room by ....
7 Instead of hiring a catering company for the party, she decided to do all the cooking ....
8 The boy was asked to behave .... at the wedding.
9 He shouted loudly above the noise to make .... heard.
10 Cats are very clean animals: they are always washing ....
11 Doctors advise us that we have to exercise regularly in order to keep .... healthy.
12 The weather is affecting me at the moment - I don't feel .... at all!
13 He's very vain and loves looking at .... in the mirror.

18 Fill in with: of one's own, on one's own or one's own in the correct form.

1 He left ...*his own*.. family to go and live abroad.
2 I would like to have a room ....
3 She couldn't lift the table .... so she asked her husband to help her.
4 Let me handle this matter .... will you?
5 They had .... house designed by a top architect.
6 He's about to set up .... business and has asked me to help organise it.
7 He enjoys spending time ....
8 I'd really like a car ...., so I don't have to rely on my friends all the time.
9 "Is this .... motorbike, young man?" the policeman asked.
10 Although she can afford domestic help, she insists on doing the housework ....

Possessive case

's / s' (people or animals)	of (inanimate things)
● singular noun + **'s** *the cat's claws, the boy's hats* ● regular plural noun + **'** *the tourists' passports* ● irregular plural noun not ending in s + **'s** *the men's room, the children's playroom* ● compound noun + **'s** *his mother-in-law's car* ● **'s** after the last of two or more names to show common possession *Ann and Sally's flat (They share the same flat)* **BUT** *Ann's and Sally's flats (each one has got a flat)*	● **of** + inanimate thing/abstract noun *the door **of** the house, the beauty **of** the view* ● **of** + possessive case/pronouns when there is a determiner (this, any etc) before the nouns *Look at this painting of Picasso's. (one of Picasso's paintings), a dress of hers (one **of** her dresses)* ● **of** + **people** (in longer phrases) *That's the brother **of** one of my friends.* ● **'s/of** to talk about places or organisations *London's attractions/the attractions **of** London*

Note: phrases of place + 's *(at the butcher's)* **time/distance expression + 's/'** *(last week's news, three days' visit)*

19 Rewrite the following using the correct possessive form.

1 the butterflies - the wings *...the butterflies' wings...*
2 the students - the books ....
3 drive - three hours ....
4 the department store - the staff ....
5 living - the cost ....
6 some friends - my brother ....
7 bread - the price ....
8 the baby - the pram ....
9 John and Paul - the wives ....
10 the men - the changing rooms ....
11 the sea - the waves ....
12 Athens - Acropolis ....
13 Lucy and Emily - the mother ....
14 the house - my father's closest friend ....
15 the president - the decision ....
16 my physics professor - the report ....
17 the park - the playground ....
18 the Smiths - the car ....
19 my mother-in-law - the garden ....

20 Complete the following sentences using the words in bold. Use two to five words.

1 In England, Elizabeth II is the Queen.
   of   Elizabeth II *...is the Queen of...* England.
2 The gallery has just bought a painting by Monet.
   one   The gallery has just bought .... paintings.
3 I saw a play by Shakespeare at The Globe.
   plays   I saw .... at The Globe.
4 It takes half an hour to walk into town.
   is   It .... into town.
5 This necklace belonged to my mother-in-law.
   was   This .... necklace.
6 In France, the president is elected every five years.
   of   The .... every five years.

11 Determiners / Pronouns

There - It

- **There + be:** used for something mentioned for the first time or to say that someone or something exists. *There are some letters for you on your desk.*
- **Personal pronoun + be/other verb:** used to give more details about something or someone already mentioned. *There's someone at the door. He wants to see you.*
- **It + be:** used for identification. *There's someone outside. It's your landlord.*
- **It + be ... to-inf/that-clause** is used to begin a sentence. *It's nice to be with you. It's a pity that he didn't come.*
- It is also used for distance, temperature, time expressions, weather and in the following expressions: It seems that, It appears that, It looks like, It is said that, It doesn't matter etc. *It's freezing today, isn't it? It appears that he's been promoted; he's just bought a new car. It seems that there is a problem with the machine.* (**BUT** *we also say*): **There seems to be** *a problem with the machine.* **It looks like** *it's going to rain.*

21 Fill in: there or it.

1 ...*It*...'s very cold today; .... has been snowing all night.
2 ....'s a policeman at the door; .... seems that the neighbour has complained about the noise.
3 ....'s a holiday tomorrow, so no one has to go to work.
4 Let's go by taxi to the cinema; ....'s much too far to walk.
5 ....'s a letter on the doorstep; ....'s for you.
6 This report you've shown me is confusing - .... appears to be a mistake in it.
7 .... are many changes to be made to this report, but .... shouldn't take us too long.
8 .... is my privilege to introduce our distinguished guest speaker.
9 .... 's nothing much on TV tonight - ....'s a pity we don't have a DVD player.
10 .... is a shame you weren't able to come to the party. .... were lots of people there.

22 Complete the sentences using the words in bold. Use two to five words.

1 Everyone thanked me except Paul.
   person   The only ...*person who didn't thank*... me was Paul.
2 She said: "I dislike French films and so does Jim."
   neither   She said that .... French films.
3 If you decorate the house on your own, it will be cheaper.
   yourself   If you ...., it will be cheaper.
4 I take twenty minutes to drive to work every morning.
   drive   It's .... to my work every morning.
5 Try to watch your behaviour at the wedding reception.
   yourself   Try .... at the wedding reception.
6 I don't like being alone in the house at night.
   by   I don't like .... in the house at night.
7 There are only a few people who can speak Welsh.
   not   There .... can speak Welsh.
8 She left the shop with another person's bag by mistake.
   someone   She left the shop .... by mistake.
9 We spent all afternoon cleaning the living room.
   whole   We spent .... the living room.
10 We don't know much about supernatural phenomena.
   knowledge   We have .... about supernatural phenomena.
11 She passed the written exam and the oral exam as well.
   both   She passed .... exams.

12 She sat alone waiting for her friends to turn up.
own She sat .... her friends to turn up.
13 Nobody can find the solution to the problem.
anybody There .... can find the solution to the problem.
14 He has been everywhere except Australia.
country The .... been to is Australia.
15 In Australia the first inhabitants were the Aborigines.
of The .... were the Aborigines.
16 "You can call me whenever you want," he said.
time He said I .... that I wanted.
17 She told the children to go and play in another place.
else "Go ....," she told the children.
18 There aren't many chefs who can make Creme Bavaroise well.
few There are .... Creme Bavaroise well.
19 She invited both her relatives and her colleagues to the engagement party.
only She invited .... also her colleagues to the engagement party.
20 He has been to everything except the orchestra.
thing The .... been to is the orchestra.
21 We haven't had any luck finding a flat.
no We have .... finding a flat.
22 It takes three hours to climb to the top of the hill.
is It .... to the top of the hill.

23 Use the words in capitals to form a word that fits in the space in the same line.

Volunteering

You've seen news reports about people who need (0) ...*assistance*... | **ASSIST**
after a (1) .... disaster. Maybe you've walked past | **NATURE**
(2) .... people. Or, perhaps, you've watched TV programmes | **HOME**
about how lonely and (3) .... older people can get. | **ISOLATE**
So what can you do about any of those things? If you can't afford to make
a (4) ...., you can give some of your time and volunteer. | **DONATE**
Volunteering helps you feel you make a (5) .... – that you do | **DIFFER**
have the power to change things for the (6) .... It also | **GOOD**
provides you with a sense of (7) ...., as people depend on you | **RESPONSIBLE**
to survive. It's also a great way to learn new skills and develop a new
(8) .... of people and their needs — people with | **UNDERSTAND**
(9) ...., people in financial distress, sick kids, or the | **ABLE**
(10) .... | **ELDER**

Consolidation 11

Phrasal Verbs

stand by: 1) remain loyal esp in a difficult situation, 2) watch passively, 3) be ready for action
stand for: 1) represent, 2) (usu in questions and negations) tolerate; put up with
stand in for: replace sb temporarily
stand out: be very noticeable, prominent
stand up for: support; defend
stand up to: resist; stay in good condition

....

be taken aback: be strongly surprised
take after: look like
take sth back: admit that one was wrong in what one said
take down: 1) lengthen a garment (let down), 2) separate into pieces in order to repair or remove, 3) write down
take in: 1) give accommodation, 2) deceive
take for: identify sb or sth wrongly
take off: 1) remove clothes, 2) copy sb's speech or manners esp for fun; imitate
take on: 1) undertake responsibility, 2) employ
take sb out: take sb to the theatre etc
take over: take control or responsibility
take to: like
take up: begin to do sth as a hobby

24 **Fill in the correct particle(s).**

1 More and more people are beginning to stand ...*up for*... their rights.
2 She's so tall, she stands .... in any crowd.
3 The initials EU stand .... European Union.
4 Although he's in prison, his wife is standing .... him.
5 The star of the show was ill, so someone had to stand .... her.
6 We're not going to stand .... this injustice any longer.
7 I was taken .... by his offensive manner.
8 He wanted an energetic hobby, so he took .... water skiing.
9 I'm sorry, I take .... what I said. You're not lazy and selfish.
10 My mother takes .... foreign students to make extra money.
11 The vice president took .... the company when the president retired.
12 I took you .... your brother from a distance. You look so alike.
13 She takes .... her mother; they have the same eyes.
14 He was talking too fast and we didn't manage to take .... the whole lecture.
15 They're taking .... extra staff at the car factory.

25 **Think of the word which best fits each space. Write only one word in each space.**

Disneyland *Resort Paris*

Disneyland Resort Paris is a holiday and recreation **(0)** ...*resort*... in Marne-la-Vallée, 31 kilometres east **(1)** .... Paris, France. The complex features two theme parks, an entertainment district and seven resort hotels. Operating **(2)** .... April 12, 1992, it was the second Disney resort to open **(3)** .... the United States (following Tokyo Disney Resort). With 12.8 million visitors in 2006, it is **(4)** .... of Europe's leading tourist destinations. It was not so successful at **(5)** ...., as there were quite a few problems during the period when it was being built. A **(6)** .... of prominent people voiced their opposition and protested **(7)** .... the park, claiming it would damage the environment. This delayed construction for several years. More problems arose **(8)** ...., when the resort opened. The park's income was much **(9)** .... than expected and the park management needed to attract **(10)** .... people. The name of the park was changed **(11)** .... Euro Disney Resort to Disneyland Paris and eventually the park started making a **(12)** .... The park's latest attraction, Walt Disney Studios Park, opened its doors on March 16, 2002.

26 Complete the sentences using the words in bold. Use two to five words.

1 "You broke the television!" she said to me.
of She ...*accused me of breaking*... the television.
2 Is it necessary to write this report today?
have Does this report .... today?
3 I can't meet you at the airport.
impossible It's .... you at the airport.
4 You'd better hurry or else you won't be home on time.
will If .... home on time.
5 He always locks the windows so that he won't be burgled at night.
fear He always locks the windows .... at night.
6 There was only a little food left after the party.
any There .... after the party.
7 He didn't call me; he didn't send me a letter either.
did He neither called me .... a letter.
8 I didn't have a chance to say goodbye.
opportunity I had .... goodbye.
9 He found success after facing many difficulties.
against He .... before he found success.
10 She lost her passport at the airport.
got Her .... at the airport.
11 He can't make people understand him when he speaks French.
himself He .... when he speaks French.
12 Sally is coming to the party and Pam is coming too.
also Not only Sally, ... to the party.

27 Fill in the correct form of the verbs in brackets.

Jason's uncle, who was a sailor, **1)** ...*had been travelling*... (**travel**) around the world for years. On his return, he **2)** .... (**come**) to the house with presents for everyone. To Jason, he gave an old lamp which he **3)** .... (**buy**) in Saudi Arabia. Jason tried **4)** .... (**hide**) his disappointment at such a dirty old gift, but thanked his uncle for **5)** .... (**bring**) it anyway. When his uncle **6)** .... (**go**), Jason's mother wanted **7)** .... (**take**) the lamp to an antique shop and **8)** .... (**it/clean**). "That's OK," said Jason. "I **9)** .... (**do**) it myself." So he took it away and started **10)** .... (**polish**) it. As he **11)** .... (**rub**) away the dirt some smoke **12)** .... (**come**) out of it and, out of the smoke, appeared a large, rather frightening man. "Who are you?" **13)** .... (**cry**) Jason. "I am the Genie of the Lamp," the man **14)** .... (**reply**). "You can have three wishes. But be careful! If you **15)** .... (**wish**) well, you **16)** .... (**reward**), but if you **17)** .... (**wish**) badly, you **18)** .... (**bring**) disaster on yourself and your family." Jason thought for a while and said, "I wish everyone in the world **19)** .... (**have**) enough food." "Good boy," said the Genie. "And I wish the peoples of the world **20)** .... (**stop**) fighting each other," he said. "One more." Now Jason thought really hard. "My mum **21)** .... (**work**) a lot recently and she's really tired all the time. If she **22)** .... (**have**) a car, she **23)** .... (**not/be**) so tired." So he wished for a car. "You **24)** .... (**choose**) well," said the Genie and disappeared. Jason **25)** .... (**not/tell**) his mum about what **26)** .... (**happen**), but the next day a letter arrived for her saying: "You **27)** .... (**win**) the first prize in our car competition. A brand new Mercedes **28)** .... (**deliver**) to your home within the next few days."

183

Consolidation

28 **Fill in the correct prepositions of place or movement.**

between, down, on top of, over, in/inside, above, in front of, past, up, among, next to/by/beside, from ... to, through, under, below, behind, along, opposite, at, round/around, near, outside, on, against, onto, out of, across, to/towards/in the direction of, into

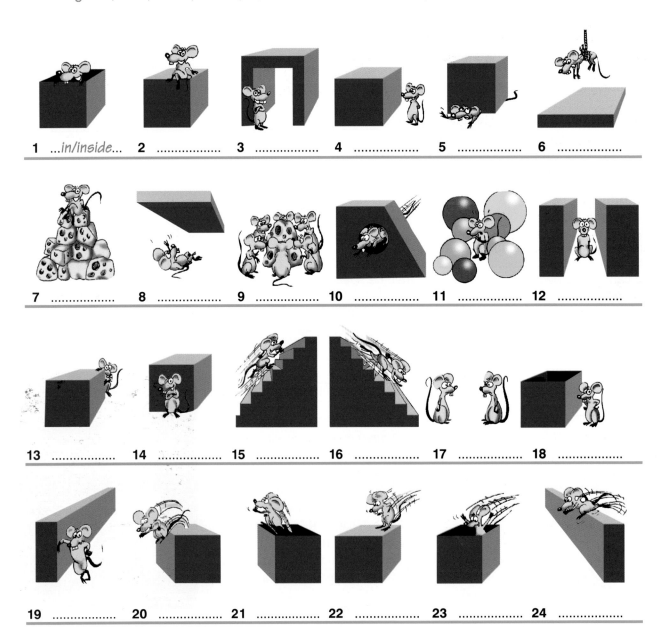

1 ...in/inside... 2 .... 3 .... 4 .... 5 .... 6 ....

7 .... 8 .... 9 .... 10 .... 11 .... 12 ....

13 .... 14 .... 15 .... 16 .... 17 .... 18 ....

19 .... 20 .... 21 .... 22 .... 23 .... 24 ....

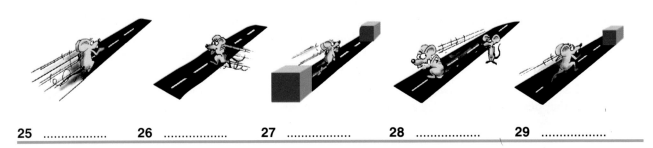

25 .... 26 .... 27 .... 28 .... 29 ....

184

For questions 1 - 12, read the text below and decide which answer (A, B, C or D) best fits each space.

The Dangers of the Sun

Holiday beaches are like huge barbecues where people **(0)** ...C... like burgers on a grill. They are keen to soak up the sun, but often they do not **(1)** .... the dangers that this can involve.

This does not mean that we should avoid the sun altogether. On the **(2)** ...., doctors agree that sunshine in limited amounts is actually good for you. However, by following some simple advice, holidaymakers can **(3)** .... a perfect tan while avoiding such dangers as sunburn and even cancer.

The sun is at its **(4)** .... between 11 am and 3 pm, so it is **(5)** .... to stay in the shade during these hours. Babies should be kept out of **(6)** .... sun at all times, as they are particularly sensitive, and children **(7)** .... wear sun block and a hat. It is also important to reapply sun cream regularly, **(8)** .... after swimming.

The eyes also need protection from the sun. We should not think of sunglasses as just a **(9)** .... accessory. They **(10)** .... vital protection from the sun's rays. Never wear sunglasses with cheap lenses; they do more **(11)** .... than good, so the extra money spent on a more expensive pair is well worth it.

Summer is a great season. By being **(12)** ...., we can enjoy the sun without unpleasant consequences.

0	**A** sit	**B** stand	**C** lie	**D** stretch
1	**A** realise	**B** think	**C** conceive	**D** aware
2	**A** opposite	**B** contrary	**C** other	**D** contrast
3	**A** manage	**B** succeed	**C** do	**D** achieve
4	**A** strongest	**B** hardest	**C** greatest	**D** deepest
5	**A** recommended	**B** warned	**C** demanded	**D** ordered
6	**A** straight	**B** open	**C** direct	**D** clear
7	**A** ought	**B** might	**C** may	**D** should
8	**A** only	**B** especially	**C** largely	**D** uniquely
9	**A** trend	**B** fashion	**C** style	**D** mode
10	**A** provide	**B** give	**C** supply	**D** add
11	**A** bad	**B** harm	**C** damage	**D** injury
12	**A** senseless	**B** sensitive	**C** sensible	**D** logical

12 Questions / Short Answers

To form **Yes/No questions** (questions which ask for "Yes" or "No" in the answer) we put the auxiliary or modal verb (be, have, can etc) before the subject. *He is watching TV.* ➡ ***Is he*** *watching TV?* With all other verbs we form Yes/No questions with **Do/Does** (Present Simple) or **Did** (Past Simple) *He likes pizza.* ➡ ***Does he*** *like pizza?* ***Did you go*** *to the library?* Yes/No questions are asked with a rising intonation. *Do you enjoy cartoons?* ↗

Wh-questions begin with a question word (**who, what, where, why, when, whose, which, how** etc) *"How old is he?"* When there is a preposition, it usually goes at the end of the question. In formal English it can be put before the question word. ***Who*** *was he accused by? (more usual)* ***By whom*** *was he accused? (formal English)* Questions are used to ask for information or permission. They are also used to make suggestions, requests, offers or invitations. ***How*** *far is the station? (information),* ***May*** *I go out? (permission),* ***Shall we*** *play tennis? (suggestion),* ***Could you*** *help me with the dishes? (request),* ***Would you like*** *some more coffee? (offer),* ***Would you like to*** *come to the beach with me? (invitation)*

1 Form questions, then identify the speech situation.

1 (you look after/the baby tonight?) ...*Could you look after the baby tonight? (request)*...
2 (we go/the cinema this weekend?) ....
3 (How old/be Mary on her birthday?) ....
4 (I get/you another cup of coffee?) ....
5 (you like/come to my party on Saturday?) ....
6 (What time/the next bus leave?) ....
7 (I use/the phone?) ....
8 (we buy/Joan a book for Christmas?) ....
9 (you/give me a lift to the station?) ....
10 (you see/Mick at school yesterday?) ....

We normally use the following question words to ask about:

people	things/animals	place	time	quantity	manner	reason
Who Whose (possession) Which (of) What	What Which (of)	Where	How long How often What time When	How many How much	How	Why

● **Which** is used when there is a **limited choice**. *"Which is your favourite film star - Meryl Streep or Glenn Close?"* It can also be used with the **comparative** and **superlative**. *"Which is more comfortable, a bicycle or a motorcycle?" "Which is the quickest route to Birmingham?"*

● **What** is used when there is an **unlimited choice**. *"What kind of music do you like?"* It can also be used in the following patterns: **What ... look like?** (asking for a description of physical appearance), **What ... for?, What colour?, What size?, What kind/sort?, What time?, What is he like?** (asking for a description of character), **What is it used for?** etc *"What colour are his eyes?" "What is your new teacher like?" "He's friendly and patient." "What does Ann look like?" "She's slim with a fair complexion."*

● **What** and **which** are sometimes both possible. *Which/What fruit does he like eating?*

2 **Fill in:** who, whose, which, what, where, how long, how often, what time, when, how many, how much, how **or** why.

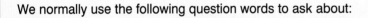

1 "...*Who*...starred in the film "The Godfather?" "Al Pacino."
2 "............................... calories do you consume every day?" "About 1,800."
3 "............................... of these skirts do you prefer, the blue or the pink?" "The blue one."

186

4 "................................ do you go to the gym?" "About once a week."
5 "................................ sugar do you take in your coffee?" "One spoonful."
6 "................................ are we going to the restaurant?" "At 6 o'clock."
7 "................................ did it take you to write your essay?" "About five hours."
8 "................................ are you crying?" "I've hurt my arm."
9 "................................ does your sister get back from Portugal?" "Next Wednesday."
10 "................................ is your favourite colour?" "Purple."
11 "................................ are you going on holiday this year?" "South Africa."
12 "................................ pen is this? I found it on the floor." "It's mine."
13 "................................ do you leave home in the morning?" "About 8 o'clock."
14 "................................ did you manage to break your arm?" "I fell off my bicycle."
15 "................................ is the new restaurant like?" "It's extremely elegant."
16 "................................ are the children up to?" "I don't know."
17 "................................ is the fastest way to get to Paris from here?" "By plane."
18 "................................ didn't you call me earlier?" "I was busy."
19 "................................ is your favourite subject at school?" "Latin."
20 "................................ money have you got left?" "None."

3 Ask questions where the word/phrase in bold is the answer.

1 Pete works for **British Telecom**.
...*Who does Pete work for?*...
2 Sara owns **two** cars. ....
3 She's **tall and fair**. ....
4 It's **nearly seven o'clock**. ....
5 I have French lessons **twice a week**. ....
....
6 I went to **Hawaii** on holiday. ....
....
7 There are **six students** in my class. ....
....

8 She's **very shy and quiet**. ....
9 I wasn't at work today **because I was ill**. ....
....
10 **David's** car was stolen. ....
11 **Shakespeare** wrote "King Lear". ....
....
12 We've lived here **for ten years**. ....
13 My new car cost **£10,000**. ....
....
14 Kay's gone out **shopping**. ....

Subject/Object Questions

If **who**, **which** or **what** are the subject of the question, the word order is the same as in statements (**subject questions**). If they are the object of the question, the verb is in question form (**object questions**).

subject		object
Greg	hit	David.

subject		object
David	hit	**Paul.**

Who hit David? (NOT: ~~Who did hit David?~~)   **Who did** David **hit**?

4 Write questions for the sentences below. The words in bold should be the answer.

1 **Tom** broke the window. ...*Who broke the window?*...
2 Jill invited **Paul** to the party. ....
....
3 Lions live in **Africa**. ....
4 **Anthony** arrived late. ....
5 Peter opened the **door**. ....
6 Kate gave the letter **to Julie**. ....
....
7 **Jenny** forgot to do her homework. ....
....

8 He likes **basketball**. ....
9 **Hugh** was rude to Jill. ....
10 **Jo** lost her purse. ....
11 **Professor Evans** gave the lecture. ....
....
12 **Jane** lost the keys to her car. ....
....
13 **Phil** borrowed your car. ....
14 Sue dropped **her glasses**. ....
15 **Tracy** loves ice cream. ....

187

Negative Questions

● **Negative questions** are formed with not but there is a difference in word order for the short and full form.
auxiliary + n't + subject + verb (short form) *Hasn't she called you yet?* *(everyday speech)*
auxiliary + subject + not + verb (full form) *Has she not called you yet?* *(used for emphasis)*

● Negative questions are used to express: **surprise** (***Didn't you*** *know she was my Mum?*), **annoyance or sarcasm** (***Can't you*** *be more patient?*), **a wish to persuade someone** (***Won't you*** *tell me who you went out with?*) and **expectation of a "Yes" - answer** (*Don't you know she got promoted?*)

5 In the following dialogues, make negative questions using the words given and decide if the expected response would be Yes or No, as in the example.

1 A: You're still in your pyjamas. ...*Aren't you supposed to be getting ready?*... **(supposed to/get ready)**
   B: ...*No,*... I've still got plenty of time.
2 A: Your mother is shouting for you. ....? **(hear her)**
   B: ...., but I want to play basketball a little longer.
3 A: You've been learning German for years. ....? **(speak yet)**
   B: ....,, but I'm too shy to try in front of strangers.
4 A: What a lovely hairdo! ....? **(tell me who does it for you)**
   B: ...., because you always copy everything I do!
5 A: Why aren't you coming to the party? ....? **(feel like going out)**
   B: ...., but I've got to babysit tonight.
6 A: You look down. ....? **(enjoy the film)**
   B: .... It was the kind of film that really depresses me.
7 A: She had her tenants evicted. ....? **(a mean thing to do)**
   B: .... She's got a reputation for being heartless.
8 A: That was a rather tactless thing to say. ....? **(realise she was Anne's sister)**
   B: .... You could have mentioned it earlier.
9 A: There was a terrible car crash. ....? **(see it on the news)**
   B: ...., I didn't get home until late last night.
10 A: It's past your bedtime. ....? **(be in bed by now)**
   B: .... I'm allowed to stay up late at the weekend.

6 Write questions to which the bold type words are the answers.

Although it is commonly assumed that **tortoises are simply small domestic pets**, a number of large species of tortoise have been living **in their natural environment** for centuries. Tortoises, **in tropical regions,** can exceed three feet in length and records show that before it became extinct, the atlas tortoise measured **almost six feet**. The turtle is very similar to the tortoise but lives **in the sea** rather than on the land. In recent years, turtles have been fished for **food and their valuable oil**. **Conservationists** are concerned about this trend, as **turtles may soon become extinct**.

1 ...*What is commonly assumed?*...
2 ....
3 ....
4 ....
5 ....
6 ....
7 ....
8 ....

Question Tags

- Question tags are short questions added to the end of a statement to ask for **confirmation** of, or **agreement** with, the statement. They are formed with an auxiliary verb and the appropriate personal pronoun. They take the same auxiliary verb as in the statement if there is one, otherwise they take **do/does** (Present S.) or **did** (Past S.). *She speaks French, **doesn't she**? He isn't rich, **is he**?*

- A positive statement is followed by a negative question tag, and a negative statement is followed by a positive question tag. *He plays well, **doesn't he**? He can't do it, **can he**?* Note that **everyone/someone/anyone/no one** form their question tags with an **auxiliary verb + they**. ***Everyone** offered to help, didn't **they**?*

- Study the following question tags.

1	"I am"	"aren't I?"	*I am older than you, **aren't I?***
2	"I used to"	"didn't I?"	*He used to go to school with you, **didn't he?***
3	Imperative	"will you/won't you?" "can you/could you?"	*Phone me later, **will you?/won't you?/ can you?/could you?***
4	"Let's"	"shall we?"	*Let's go home now, **shall we?***
5	"Let me/him" etc	"will you/won't you?"	*Let her decide for herself, **will you/won't you?***
6	"Don't" (negative imperative)	"will you?"	*Don't come round so late again, **will you?***
7	"I have" (= possess)	"haven't I?"	*She has got her own office, **hasn't she?***
8	"I have" (idiomatic use)	"don't I?"	*We had a great time, **didn't we?***
9	"There is/are"	"isn't/aren't there?"	*There is some mail for me, **isn't there?***
10	"This/That is"	"isn't it?"	*That's your car over there, **isn't it?***

- **Questions tags** can be said with a **rising intonation** when we are not sure and expect an answer, or a **falling intonation** when we are sure and don't really expect an answer. *They're moving house, **aren't they?** ↗ (not sure) He caused the accident, **didn't he?** ↘ (sure)*

---

7 Add the appropriate question tag.

1 That book is new, ...*isn't it*...?
2 Don't forget to go to the supermarket, ...?
3 Let's go out for dinner, ...?
4 They had a fight last night, ...?
5 There is a hospital near you, ...?

6 Let him finish his coffee, ...?
7 I'm due at your house at six, ...?
8 He has got a Harley Davidson, ...?
9 He used to work with Ann at Fosters, ...?
10 Pass me that pencil, ...?

- Question tags can also be **affirmative-affirmative**. If said with a rising intonation, we ask for more information. *She is seeing John, **is she**?* If said with a falling intonation, we express negative feelings such as disappointment or disapproval. We don't expect an answer. *I'll be punished, **will I**?*

- **Echo tags** are a response to an affirmative or negative sentence. They are used in everyday speech to ask for more **information** or to show **anger, concern, confirmation, interest, surprise** etc.
  Affirmative: *He quit his job. - **He did, didn't he**? (confirmation) He quit his job. - **He did**? (surprise)*
  Negative: *He hasn't called. - **He hasn't, has he**? (confirmation) He hasn't called. - **He hasn't**? (surprise)*

---

8 Add an appropriate response expressing disappointment/ disapproval, confirmation or surprise.

1 "Tulips grow in Holland." "...*They do, don't they?*..." **(confirmation)**
2 "It's ten o'clock already." ".................................." **(surprise)**
3 "I'll have to sit the exam again." ".................................." **(disappointment)**
4 "She's been to Paris." ".................................." **(surprise)**
5 "He's started smoking again." ".................................." **(disapproval)**

12 Questions / Short Answers

6 "He seems to be having a hard time." ".." **(confirmation)**
7 "She didn't accept the job offer." ".." **(surprise)**
8 "She's going out with him again," ".." **(disapproval)**
9 "They got engaged." ".." **(confirmation)**
10 "He could have been killed." ".." **(surprise)**

Short Answers

Short answers are used to avoid repetition of the question asked before. Positive short answers are formed with **Yes + personal pronoun + auxiliary verb** (do, can, have, will etc)
"Can she do it?" "Yes, she can."
Negative short answers are formed with **No + personal pronoun + negative auxiliary verb**.
"Did he mention anything?" " No, he didn't."

9 Add question tags and short answers to the statements below.

1 "There's room for me in your car, ...*isn't there*...?" "Yes, ...*there is*... ."
2 "He's got a friendly face, ...?" "Yes, ..."
3 "Leave me more space, ...?" "No, ..."
4 "You will help me with my suitcases, ...?" "Yes, ..."
5 "They are still in France, ...?" "No, ..."
6 "This is the way to Brian's house, ...?" "Yes, ..."
7 "They had a holiday in Florida last year, ...?" "Yes, ..."
8 "You won't ask for my opinion, ...?" "No, ..."
9 "He used to have a moustache, ...?" "Yes, ..."
10 "You went to Crete last month, ...?" "No, ..."

Oral Development 16

Look at the pictures, then make sentences with question tags and short answers.

S1: *He seems to be enjoying himself, doesn't he?*
S2: *Yes, he does. It takes a lot of courage to do something like that, doesn't it?* etc

190

So - Neither/Nor - But

- **So + auxiliary verb + personal pronoun/noun** (positive addition to a positive sentence).
  *She speaks Spanish. **So do we.** (We speak Spanish too.) John went to Florida. **So did Kate.** (Kate went to Florida too.)*
- **Neither/Nor + auxiliary verb + personal pronoun/noun** (negative addition to a negative sentence).
  *Sheila can't play the drums. **Neither/Nor can I.** (NOT: ~~So can I.~~)*
- **But + personal pronoun/noun + affirmative auxiliary verb** (positive contrast to negative statement)
  *Jim has never been to a pop concert, **but I have**. She hasn't done her homework, **but he has**.*
- **But + personal pronoun/noun + negative auxiliary verb** (negative contrast to positive statement)
  *John looks happy, **but Jane doesn't**. John has done his homework, **but she hasn't**.*
- When we wish to express surprise at what somebody has said, we use **so + subject + auxiliary verb**.
  *Michael: Look, that woman's got pink hair! Alison: **So she has**!*

10 Rephrase the sentences using so, neither/nor or but as in the example.

1 Both George and Mary sing really well. ...*George sings really well. So does Mary*....
2 John has passed his test. Emily hasn't passed her test. ....
3 Both Mark and Louise are English. ....
4 I have never been to Australia. David has been to Australia. ....
5 Both Sarah and Marion went to Leeds University. ....
6 Neither Cathy nor Sally saw the accident happen. ....
7 Not only Maria but also Lisa has been awarded a prize. ....
8 John and Paul don't need any help. ....

11 Add an appropriate response to the following sentences.

1 He's extremely angry. **(surprise)** ...*So he is!*...
2 I can't explain his behaviour. **(addition - I)** ....
3 She's gone on a three-month cruise. **(addition - he)**. ....
4 Betty doesn't like being kept waiting. **(addition - Jim)** ....
5 He's been voted Best Dressed Man of the Year. **(surprise)** ....
6 She's going in for a beauty contest. **(surprise)** ....

Asking for permission / Making requests	Giving/Refusing Permission / Answering requests
Can I/Could I close the window? I'm freezing. **May I/Might I** use your computer?	**Yes, you can./Yes, of course (you can)./No, you can't. Yes, you may./Yes, of course (you may)./No, you may not./I'd rather you didn't./I'm afraid not.**
Making suggestions/invitations	**Answering suggestions/invitations**
Will you/Would you/Would you like to join me for dinner? **Shall we** go out for a walk?	**I'd like to./I'd love to./Yes, all right./I'm afraid I can't./ I'd love to but I can't./I'm sorry, I can't.**
Making offers	**Answering offers**
Shall I/we, Can I/we, Would you like me to help you?	**Yes, please./No, thank you./No thanks.**

12 Fill in short answers as in the example.

1 A: Shall we spend the afternoon by the lake?
   B: ...*Yes, all right*... . The kids would love to feed the ducks.
2 A: Dad, can we go to the rodeo?
   B: .... They might even let you ride.

3 A: Would you like to meet for coffee this afternoon?

    B: .... I'm working late tonight.

4 A: Can I turn the volume down on the radio?

    B: .... I won't be able to hear it then!

5 A: Can you close the door before you go out, please?

    B: .... Shall I lock it too?

6 A: Shall I water your plants for you while you're on holiday?

    B: .... That would be very kind of you!

7 A: Would you like me to give you a lift to work tomorrow?

    B: .... I prefer to cycle.

8 A: Could I borrow some money from you, please?

    B: .... And don't worry about when to pay me back.

9 A: Will you let me know if you can't come to my party?

    B: .... I'll phone you tomorrow.

10 A: Can I have the last piece of cake?

    B: .... That piece is for your brother.

So - Not

So and **not** can be used in short answers after: think, hope, expect, suppose, I'm afraid, guess, it seems, say, tell sb, it appears, believe or imagine.

I'm afraid so - I'm afraid not	I imagine so - I don't imagine so/I imagine not
It appears so - It doesn't appear so/It appears not	He says so/He said so - He didn't say so
I believe so - I don't believe so/I believe not	It seems so - It doesn't seem so/It seems not
I expect so - I don't expect so/I expect not	I suppose so - I don't suppose so/I suppose not
I guess so - I guess not	He told me so - He didn't tell me so
I hope so - I hope not	I think so - I don't think so/I think not

"Will he pass his exams?" ***"I hope so."*** *"Could he be lying?"* ***"I don't believe so."***

---

13 Fill in the blanks with phrases using the verbs in brackets and so or not.

1 A: Is Jenny really going on safari this summer? **(say)**

    B: ...*She says so*... . She's always wanted to see a lion.

2 A: Are you going to Mary's wedding? **(afraid)**

    B: .... I'll be in Brussels that day.

3 A: Has the postman come yet? It's 11 o'clock. **(expect)**

    B: .... He usually comes at 9 o'clock.

4 A: Do you think Bill will come tonight? **(imagine)**

    B: .... He was feeling really ill earlier.

5 A: Will you be having a holiday this year? **(suppose)**

    B: .... We usually go to our villa on Crete.

6 A: You need a special visa to go to America, don't you? **(think)**

    B: .... My friend needed one last year.

7 A: Will we be paid today? **(hope)**

    B: .... I need to pay the rent.

8 A: Have the next-door neighbours moved out? **(appear)**

    B: .... The place is empty.

9 A: Is Dave going to do up the house himself? **(tell)**

    B: .... He's trying to save some money.

10 A: Do you think it's going to rain? **(appear)**

    B: .... The sky is rather cloudy.

11 A: Will you be throwing a party this year? **(think)**
   B: .... Last year's was a disaster.
12 A: Will the island be very crowded when we are there? **(imagine)**
   B: .... It's very busy all year round.
13 A: Is Janet coming to the school reunion? **(hope)**
   B: .... It wouldn't be the same without her.
14 A: Is the chairman of the company going to retire? **(seem)**
   B: .... He is suffering from poor health.
15 A: Is Susie playing badminton tonight as usual? **(guess)**
   B: .... She hasn't told me otherwise.
16 A: Has Karen lost weight? **(appear)**
   B: .... She bought herself a dress a size smaller than usual.

14 Complete the sentences using the words in bold. Use two to five words.

0 I have never met Paul's dad before.
   first   It's ...*the first time I have*... ever met Paul's dad.
1 "What a beautiful day!" my neighbour remarked.
   was   My neighbour .... a beautiful day.
2 I won't be able to go to my sister's wedding.
   possible   It won't .... go to my sister's wedding.
3 The boss cancelled the meeting because he was ill.
   off   The meeting .... the boss's illness.
4 She wouldn't go out without her umbrella because she was afraid of getting wet.
   fear   She wouldn't go out without her umbrella .... wet.
5 You should always write down what you spend each day.
   note   You should always .... what you spend each day.
6 Liz is probably going swimming tonight.
   likely   Liz is .... a swim tonight.
7 I don't often drive in the city centre.
   used   I'm .... in the city centre.
8 You don't usually see old-fashioned typewriters nowadays.
   unusual   It .... old-fashioned typewriters nowadays.

Oral Development 17

Look at the pictures below, then, working in pairs, have short dialogues. One student asks a question and the other answers using **so** or **not** and a reason of his/her own as in the example.

   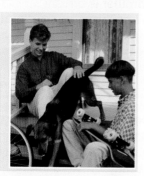

S1: Is she having a nice time?
S2: I think so. She seems to be enjoying herself.

S1: Is she at the funfair?
S2: I don't think so. She's probably in a playground. etc

193

Consolidation  12

Phrasal Verbs

turn away: 1) refuse to let in, 2) refuse to help
turn down: 1) reduce volume, power etc (opp: turn up), 2) reject
turn in: go to bed
turn into: convert into
turn off: switch off (opp: **turn on**)
turn on: switch on
turn out: 1) prove to be in the end, 2) force sb to leave, 3) produce
turn to: go to sb for help, advice etc
turn over: go to the next page
turn up: increase the volume, pressure etc (opp: **turn down**)

....

work on: be busy with
work out: 1) find by reasoning, 2) turn out successfully
work up: develop

---

15 Fill in the correct particle.

1 I'm so tired, I think I'll turn ...*in*... early tonight.
2 I always turn .... my mother for help and advice.
3 Turn the radio .... a little bit - it's too loud.
4 The club was turning people .... because it was full.
5 Turn .... the TV. It's time for the news.
6 They turned the old warehouse .... a new office block.
7 Don't forget to turn .... the TV before you leave the house.
8 I turned .... the job because the money wasn't good enough.
9 We trusted him, but he turned .... to be a thief.
10 If you turn .... the page, you'll find the answer.
11 After a day working in the fields, I had really worked .... an appetite.
12 We can't work .... this mathematical equation.
13 I wanted to become a dancer, but it didn't work ....
14 Let's work .... the best route from London to Birmingham.
15 He is working .... his new novel at the moment.

---

16 Look at Appendices 1 & 2 then fill in the correct preposition.

1 It never occurred ...*to*... me that you were right.
2 She is an attorney .... profession.
3 We mustn't dispose .... our waste in the sea.
4 He denied any knowledge .... the scandal.
5 She acts as if she were superior .... everyone.
6 The film star came accompanied .... her agent.
7 I'm tired .... commuting to work every day.
8 A car collided .... a taxi, but no one was hurt.
9 Prince Charles is the heir .... the British throne.
10 He plays squash .... his free time.
11 He was asked to leave .... short notice.
12 You're .... colour. Aren't you feeling well?
13 My brother is brilliant .... mathematics.
14 Can I pay you .... cheque?
15 My name's Elizabeth; they call me Liz .... short.
16 Watermelons are .... season now.

17 He failed .... his attempt to break the world record.
18 Ted reminds me .... an old acquaintance.
19 They left the country .... dawn.
20 Could you give me some advice .... this matter?
21 I can't cope .... this situation any longer.
22 The teacher glared .... the student who was causing trouble.
23 He was sentenced .... life imprisonment.
24 They arrived .... good time for the lecture.
25 Pollution is a threat .... the environment.
26 We entered .... a contract with the other party.
27 The students acted out the dialogue .... turn.
28 She took no notice .... the warning.
29 He invested all his money .... shares.
30 They let me have this antique chair .... nothing.

---

17 Complete the sentences using the words in bold. Use two to five words.

1 He regrets not applying for the job.
   wishes   He ...*wishes he had applied for*... the job.
2 She wants to pursue a singing career and no one can stop her.
   pursuing   No one .... a singing career.
3 The moment she left they started talking.
   sooner   No .... they started talking.
4 If he hadn't helped us, we wouldn't have finished on time.
   his   But ...., we wouldn't have finished on time.

5 This tea is so strong that I can't drink it.
   me   This tea is .... drink.
6 They gave him a gold watch as a present.
   was   He .... a gold watch as a present.
7 I think that this law should be abolished.
   do   I think they .... this law.
8 They bought very little furniture for their new flat.
   much   They .... for their new flat.
9 They are installing a new computer in our office today.
   having   We are .... in our office today.
10 You can go to the party, but be home by midnight.
   long   So .... by midnight, you can go to the party.
11 The mistake wasn't her fault.
   blame   She .... the mistake.
12 Gill sent him three letters before getting an answer.
   until   Gill didn't get an answer .... three letters.

---

18 Fill in the gaps with an appropriate form of the verb in brackets.

Laura **1)** ...*looked up*... **(look up)** her boyfriend's phone number in the telephone directory because she **2)** .... **(forget)** it. She was quite surprised when his phone **3)** .... **(answer)** by a woman. "Er, hello ... . Is John there?" "Yes, but he **4)** .... **(have)** a shower at the moment," the woman replied. So, Laura asked the woman **5)** .... **(tell)** him that his girlfriend **6)** .... **(phone)**. Half an hour passed and she **7)** .... **(begin)** to get impatient. She thought to herself, "If he **8)** .... **(not/ring)** back in two minutes, I **9)** .... **(phone)** him again." Two minutes later she phoned him back. This time a man **10)** .... **(answer)**. "John Jacobs **11)** .... **(speak)**." "You aren't my boyfriend!" exclaimed Laura. "I **12)** .... **(know)**," the man replied. "That's what I **13)** .... **(try)** to tell my wife for the past half hour!"

---

19 Think of the word which best fits each space. Write only one word in each space.

STONEHENGE

Stonehenge is a prehistoric monument **(0)** ...*on*... an area of land called Salisbury Plain which is about seven miles north of the town of Salisbury in England. Stonehenge consists **(1)** .... a series of stone settings arranged **(2)** .... a circle. It is considered one of the **(3)** .... complex stone circles in the world. Built as a religious temple, Stonehenge was first recorded by John Aubrey in the 17th century, although excavation of the site did not begin **(4)** .... 1919. Research has shown that there were three main periods of construction beginning around 1800 BC and finishing around the 15th century BC, when Stonehenge **(5)** .... completely reconstructed. The fact that the monument is **(6)** .... large implies that many people must **(7)** .... worked together in a team to help build it. There has always been controversy **(8)** .... the exact function of Stonehenge. Although **(9)** .... is no doubt that it had religious importance, it is also known to have had a special significance with regard to the sun. Records show that the site was used **(10)** .... a place of worship during the summer months and especially **(11)** .... June 21st, the longest day of the year. Stonehenge, a major tourist attraction, is believed to have a spiritual force **(12)** .... to this day.

Consolidation 12

20 For questions 1 - 12, read the text below and decide which answer (A, B, C or D) best fits each space.

Jersey

In recent years, Jersey, an island in the English Channel, has **(0)** ...*B*... a very popular holiday destination for British tourists. They are attracted by its **(1)** .... climate and magnificent scenery.

Jersey was made popular by an English television series **(2)** .... *Bergerac*, which followed a police detective on his adventures around the island. The producers of the series were **(3)** .... to show the island at its **(4)** .... Scenes were shot in all the most beautiful parts of the island so, although Bergerac was not **(5)** .... to boost the island's tourist industry, the number of visitors to the island steadily **(6)** .... as the series became more popular. Most of the tourists who come to Jersey are English. Jersey appeals to them because the ferry crossing or plane journey gives them the **(7)** .... of travelling abroad, yet the island has all the conveniences of home. For instance, English is spoken all over the island (only the older **(8)** .... still speak Jersey French), and the currency and many of the shops are familiar. Yet, because the island is so close to France, it is **(9)** .... to sense a French **(10)** .... on the food, the architecture and the **(11)** .... of life. It is this added cultural element that **(12)** .... Jersey a popular holiday destination.

0	**A** been	**B** become	**C** made	**D** changed
1	**A** easy	**B** gentle	**C** mild	**D** calm
2	**A** said	**B** pronounced	**C** told	**D** called
3	**A** careful	**B** accurate	**C** cautious	**D** exact
4	**A** best	**B** excellence	**C** prime	**D** advantage
5	**A** aimed	**B** intended	**C** determined	**D** proposed
6	**A** increased	**B** raised	**C** advanced	**D** appeared
7	**A** sense	**B** meaning	**C** perception	**D** understanding
8	**A** age	**B** group	**C** peoples	**D** generation
9	**A** easy	**B** painless	**C** obvious	**D** casual
10	**A** effect	**B** influence	**C** power	**D** pressure
11	**A** method	**B** means	**C** way	**D** type
12	**A** makes	**B** brings	**C** does	**D** gives

21 Complete the sentences using the words in bold. Use two to five words.

0 I've missed the train so it's not worth going to the station now.
point I've missed the train so ...*there's no point*... going to the station now.

1 Please allow me to pay for the meal.
let Why .... pay for the meal?

2 Mario didn't want us to help him.
turned Mario .... offer of help.

3 The actress wore dark glasses so nobody would recognise her.
as The actress wore dark glasses .... recognised.

4 The price of the armchairs includes the cost of delivery.
is The cost of delivery .... the price of the armchairs.

5 I wasn't allowed to park my car outside the building.
permission They didn't .... park my car outside the building.

6 Bill is usually on time so I'm surprised he's late.
like I'm surprised Bill hasn't arrived yet as it's .... late.

7 It was implied that the manager had stolen the money.
suggested It .... stole the money.

8 My parents don't want me to move to the city.
object My parents .... to the city.

22 For questions 1 - 10, read the text below. Use the word given in capitals at the end of each line to form a word that fits in the space in the same line.

Learning an Instrument

When most people start learning a **(0)** ...*musical*... instrument, they find it difficult to imagine ever becoming a **(1)** .... musician. This is not surprising. It takes many years of serious instruction to achieve the level of **(2)** .... required to play in an orchestra. The truth is, if you do not begin serious training in **(3)** ...., you are unlikely to play at a professional level unless you have **(4)** .... talent.

MUSIC
PROFESSION
PERFECT
CHILD
EXCEPTION

When **(5)** .... what instrument to learn, you should consider several things. Do you like the limelight or are you happier being part of a team? People who play the piano are more **(6)** .... to perform solo, whereas those who play the flute are more likely to play with an orchestra. What kind of music do you like? If it's jazz, you may want to learn a brass instrument. If it's **(7)** ...., you might want to choose the violin. It is always a good idea to speak to someone who plays the instrument. They will be able to give you some idea of the **(8)** .... involved in mastering it, and also the opportunities that will be open to you once you are able to play it.

CHOOSE

LIKE

CLASSIC

DIFFICULT

Of course not everybody learns an instrument to open the door to fame and fortune! Most people do so **(9)** .... for the sheer pleasure of it ... the pleasure of expressing the **(10)** .... side of their character through the art of music.

SIMPLE
CREATE

Part 1

For questions 1 - 12, read the text below and decide which answer (A, B, C or D) best fits each gap. There is an example at the beginning (0).

GRAFFITI

The history of writing and drawing on walls, nowadays **(0)** ...*C*... as graffiti, is much longer than most of us **(1)** .... People were painting on walls thousands of years ago. Although the paintings were probably done for religious **(2)** ...., there is also the **(3)** .... that the artists wanted to **(4)** .... their individuality at the same time. These days, graffiti can be **(5)** .... almost everywhere, from the Paris Metro to the outside walls of houses in Northern Ireland. Graffiti is often viewed as the **(6)** .... of vandals, but some people claim that it is an art form. Indeed, there have been a number of **(7)** .... of graffiti which have been shown at art exhibitions.

Most graffiti is not, however, appreciated and there are continuous **(8)** .... to have it removed which cost a great deal of money. For instance, the London Underground has to **(9)** .... £5 million a year on cleaning its stations. Unfortunately, the stations do not **(10)** .... clean for very long. Since graffiti is an art form enjoyed by a(n) **(11)** .... number of people, how about having some designated graffiti areas? This will give graffiti artists the **(12)** .... to draw without causing any trouble.

0	**A** believed	**B** said	**C** known	**D** concerned
1	**A** realise	**B** understand	**C** discover	**D** recognise
2	**A** intentions	**B** aims	**C** purposes	**D** explanations
3	**A** possibility	**B** option	**C** situation	**D** odds
4	**A** explain	**B** describe	**C** tell	**D** express
5	**A** looked	**B** inspected	**C** seen	**D** signed
6	**A** work	**B** operation	**C** job	**D** career
7	**A** copies	**B** proofs	**C** occasions	**D** examples
8	**A** tries	**B** efforts	**C** trials	**D** tests
9	**A** spend	**B** pay	**C** grant	**D** cost
10	**A** continue	**B** remain	**C** maintain	**D** hold
11	**A** developing	**B** lowering	**C** growing	**D** advancing
12	**A** chance	**B** attempt	**C** probability	**D** likelihood

Part **2**

For questions 13 - 24, read the text below and think of the word which best fits each gap. Use only one word in each gap. There is an example at the beginning (0).

Do you grab quick snacks **(0)** ...*at*... work, eat late at night and drink too **(13)** .... tea and coffee? If so, you're probably **(14)** .... stress and your eating habits are **(15)** .... the problem worse. The effects of stress can be beaten by following some simple advice. First, cut **(16)** .... on coffee, tea and cola drinks. They all contain caffeine, which **(17)** .... you feel better for a **(18)** .... minutes, but which destroy the vitamins in your body. Try not to eat sweets, biscuits and cakes. A quick burst of sugar suddenly increases blood-sugar levels, but **(19)** .... two or three minutes, you **(20)** .... left feeling tired and irritable. Don't drink alcohol to forget your worries. In the long term, alcohol **(21)** .... depression. Eat plenty **(22)** .... citrus fruits and green vegetables as they contain Vitamin C. Red meat and seafood contain iron, **(23)** .... helps fight tiredness. Remember to eat a good breakfast to start the day off well. **(24)** .... care to eat properly and avoid eating late at night. Stay away from junk food. Fresh is best!

Part **3**

For questions 25 - 34, read the text below. Use the word given in capitals at the end of some of the lines to form a word that fits in the gap in the same line. There is an example at the beginning (0).

FACTORY WORK

Factory work is often dull and **(0)** ...*repetitive*... although it **(25)** .... isn't difficult. Most people work on a **(26)** .... line, where individuals are responsible for the **(27)** .... of one stage of a process. Much of the work doesn't require training and is **(28)** ...., although it often helps if you have some knowledge.

REPEAT
GENERAL
PRODUCT
COMPLETE

SKILL

An **(29)** .... aspect of the job is that it often involves shift work, including nights. Overtime is also common, but, **(30)** ...., workers get paid extra for it. Strike **(31)** .... – when people stop work for a period of time – is not **(32)** .... in factories, and is the workers' way of asking for a pay increase.

PLEASE

NORMAL
ACT
COMMON

Some factory workers enjoy their job because it provides a **(33)** .... income. Others, because they feel they are underpaid, **(34)** .... scan the jobs column of local newspapers hoping to find something better.

RELY
FREQUENT

Part 4

For questions 35 - 42, complete the second sentence so that it has a similar meaning to the first sentence, using the word given. Do not change the word given. You must use between two and five words including the word given. There is an example at the beginning (0).

0 They worked hard on the project.
effort
They ...*put a lot of effort*... into the project.

35 "It wasn't me who broke the vase," said Tina.
admit
Tina .... the vase.

36 This music reminds me of my childhood.
brings
This music .... of my childhood.

37 If I am told in advance, I can arrange things.
let
Provided .... in advance, I can arrange things.

38 All the students did their homework except Alex.
who
Alex was .... do his homework.

39 The boss made him wait for two hours before he saw him.
kept
The boss .... hours before he saw him.

40 They just sat fishing all day.
nothing
They .... fish all day.

41 Both lawyers agreed with the judge's decision.
full
Both lawyers were .... the judge's decision.

42 We enjoyed the summer holidays very much.
fun
We .... the summer holidays.

Revision 3

A **Choose the correct item.**

1 I .... the walls painted next week.
A had
B would have
C have had
D will have

2 You won't ever say that to me again, ...?
A do you
B don't you
C will you
D won't you

3 Very .... people bought the group's last album.
A many
B much
C few
D little

4 Simon hasn't graduated yet, ... his sister has.
A and
B but
C so
D nor

5 I won't know the results for .... days.
A much
B a great deal of
C a couple of
D a little

6 No sooner .... the garden than a storm broke out.
A do we water
B had we watered
C have we watered
D will we water

7 Jane feeds the fish once .... day.
A a
B the
C —
D any

8 There were hardly ...... people at the bus stop.
A no
B some
C every
D any

9 .... Frank and Fiona are going to Ireland.
A Both
B All
C Each
D Either

10 I've never seen .... fashionable clothes before.
A so
B what
C such
D such a

11 She has .... hope of getting the job.
A little
B few
C several
D both

12 .... idea was it to visit the exhibition?
A What
B Whose
C Who
D Where

13 "I love playing tennis." ".......... do I."
A Nor
B Neither
C So
D Too

14 It was so cold, I had to spend the .... day indoors.
A whole
B every
C all
D each

15 Although Jack speaks fluent Italian, he has never .... Italy.
A gone in
B been to
C gone at
D been in

16 .... were several celebrities at the party.
A There
B They
C It
D These

17 If .... sees Sophie, can they give her a message?
A anything
B any
C anyone
D anywhere

18 "I've never been fined." ".......... have I."
A Too
B Neither
C But
D So

19 ...... of these two rings do you prefer?
A What
B Who
C Whose
D Which

20 .... said Ireland is dry!
A Whoever
B Whatever
C Whenever
D Wherever

21 New drugs .... tested at the moment.
A were being
B have been
C will be
D are being

22 Everyone has to comply with the law, ... ?
A don't you
B don't we
C don't they
D doesn't one

23 He's appearing in .... court next week.
A —
B one
C a
D the

24 We seldom .... them these days.
A see
B seen
C saw
D will see

B   Complete the sentences using the words in bold. Use two to five words.

1   In spite of appearing calm, he was really quite nervous.
    appeared   Although .... really quite nervous.

2   It's a pity I didn't invite her to the party.
    wish   I .... to the party.

3   Sarah prefers swimming to jogging.
    than   Sarah prefers .... jog.

4   "Why don't we go to the theatre?" he said.
    suggested   He .... to the theatre.

5   Jim won't apologise under any circumstance.
    will   Under .... apologise.

6   It's possible that he has already informed them.
    have   He .... them.

7   He invited twenty people, but only half of them turned up.
    whom   He invited twenty people .... turned up.

8   He bought the computer. He intended to sell it on eBay later.
    view   He bought the computer .... it on eBay later.

9   I crashed my car, so I was late for my meeting.
    crashed   If .... my car, I wouldn't have been late for my meeting.

10   Jane wants to go to the party, but her parents won't let her.
    will   If Jane's parents .... to the party.

11   Could you look after the children until I get home?
    mind   Would .... the children until I get home.

12   Ted can't read Greek. Emily can't read Greek either.
    nor   Neither .... read Greek.

13   She speaks Japanese and Chinese.
    only   Not ...., she speaks Chinese too.

14   When did you last spend Christmas with your family?
    since   How long is .... Christmas with your family?

15   Bread is sliced with a knife.
    used   A knife .... bread.

16   Mark rang them three times before getting an answer.
    until   Mark didn't get an answer .... three times.

17   Did you have a good time in America?
    yourself   Did .... in America?

18   I packed several sweaters because I was afraid I would be cold.
    case   I packed several sweaters .... cold.

19   Julie had just put the phone down when it rang again.
    sooner   No .... the phone down than it rang again.

20   Spanish and Portuguese are alike.
    similar   Spanish .... Portuguese.

21   Paul checked the tyre pressure for me.
    had   I .... pressure for me.

22   This film is so violent that I can't watch it.
    me   This film is .... watch.

23   There are only a few people who have the time to take long holidays.
    not   There .... have the time to take long holidays.

24   Experts say drinking a lot of water is good for your health.
    said   Drinking a lot of water .... for your health.

25   Skiing is more difficult than windsurfing.
    not   Windsurfing .... as skiing.

26   The woman screamed so loudly that she was heard by everyone.
    scream   The woman's ...., everybody heard it.

Revision 3

27 Susie wants to become a professional hairdresser and no one can stop her.
becoming   No one .... a professional hairdresser.

28 "I didn't exceed the speed limit," Sam said.
denied   Sam .... the speed limit.

29 Columbus was the first person to discover America.
who   It was .... discovered America.

30 I haven't very much knowledge of French history.
little   I .... of French history.

31 Mark is working; Melissa is working too.
are   Both .... working.

32 I'm sure Frank didn't see the burglar.
seen   Frank .... the burglar.

33 I'd prefer him to drive us there.
rather   I .... us there.

34 The last time we went out was three months ago.
for   We .... three months.

35 My friends have never been abroad.
have   None .... been abroad.

36 We didn't think she would be turned down for the part.
think   Little .... that she would be turned down for the part.

C   Fill in the blanks with the correct particle(s).

1 I must stand .... for Tom, who is absent.
2 The meeting has been put .... until tomorrow.
3 I've run .... coffee. Can you get me some?
4 My penfriend saw me .... at the airport.

5 He set .... his own firm last year.
6 Please turn .... the TV. I'm studying.
7 I can't work .... this equation.
8 I took .... the company when my father died.

D   Fill in the blanks with the correct preposition(s).

1 He was accompanied .... his wife.
2 He gave me advice .... how to act.
3 I'm leaving for Italy .... Sunday night.
4 He's tired .... living in the city.

5 She reminds me .... an old friend.
6 Transportation costs are included .... the price.
7 Mr Biggs is busy .... the moment.
8 Criminals are a threat .... society.

E   Use the words in capitals to form a word that fits in the space in the same line.

Bermuda's Golden Ring of Wrecks

The Bermuda Triangle is a region of the Atlantic ocean where many ships and planes have **(0)** ...*mysteriously*... disappeared. In one part of the Bermuda Triangle, there is an area **(1)** .... as the Golden Ring of Wrecks. It is a **(2)** .... area because, while the Triangle as a whole is **(3)** .... as a place where ships disappear, the Golden Ring of Wrecks is an area of *found* ships. Or, to be more **(4)** ...., shipwrecks.

Around 350 shipwrecks, **(5)** .... as far back as the 16th century, **(6)** .... the island of Bermuda. What makes the area so **(7)** ....? In summer, the seas around the island are calm and **(8)** .... However, in winter, violent storms whip up **(9)** .... rough seas. This makes the waters very **(10)** .... and difficult to navigate.

So how did the Golden Ring of Wrecks get its name? Well, many ships were carrying large cargoes of gold when they sank!

MYSTERY
KNOW
FASCINATE
FAME
SPECIFY

DATE
CIRCLE
DANGER
PEACE
EXTREME
TREACHERY

Further Practice Sections

Section A

Words Often Confused

1 Read the sentences below and decide which answer A, B, C or D best fits each blank.

1 Heavy .... prevented all planes from taking off.
- **A** fog
- **C** vapour
- **B** steam
- **D** mist

2 These days factory .... can be controlled by the use of filters.
- **A** discharges
- **C** emissions
- **B** omissions
- **D** ejections

3 She was .... that it had taken so long for the truth to be revealed.
- **A** furious
- **C** wild
- **B** savage
- **D** strong

4 The patient's condition began to .... very quickly.
- **A** fall
- **C** relieve
- **B** deteriorate
- **D** lessen

5 The children were in a state of .... after their ball broke the window.
- **A** shock
- **C** afraid
- **B** anxious
- **D** dread

6 Scientists have yet to find a .... for the common head cold.
- **A** diagnosis
- **C** solution
- **B** medicine
- **D** cure

7 Harry dreaded the thought of having a(n) .... and fainted at the sight of the needle.
- **A** infusion
- **C** prick
- **B** injection
- **D** insertion

8 It is possible for babies to .... on small objects they put in their mouths.
- **A** choke
- **C** laugh
- **B** hiccup
- **D** cough

9 There was a .... of surprise from the audience when the winner was announced.
- **A** gasp
- **C** sigh
- **B** bark
- **D** snort

10 The dog began to .... after chasing the cat round the park all morning.
- **A** cough
- **C** pant
- **B** wheeze
- **D** sniff

11 The unscrupulous .... doubled the rent of every flat, causing hardship to many families.
- **A** tenant
- **C** landlord
- **B** host
- **D** lodger

12 The teacher was extremely .... when the whole class got 100% in the exam.
- **A** suspicious
- **C** trustful
- **B** doubting
- **D** worrying

13 Each member of the group was .... a different task to complete.
- **A** determined
- **C** assigned
- **B** imposed
- **D** forced

14 When bank .... went up again, many customers closed their accounts.
- **A** charges
- **C** amounts
- **B** prices
- **D** tolls

15 Al Capone is one of the most ..... gangsters in history.
- **A** obvious
- **C** notorious
- **B** clear
- **D** evident

16 The police could find no .... between the crime and the suspect they were holding.
- **A** together
- **C** bond
- **B** connection
- **D** linkage

17 I don't believe a word he said. He's probably .... the whole story.
- **A** discovered
- **C** invented
- **B** explored
- **D** researched

18 When Carol was made captain of the school basketball ...., she was thrilled.
- **A** team
- **C** association
- **B** group
- **D** company

19 Inspector Marbles came to the .... that the bank had been robbed by one of its clerks.
- **A** outcome
- **C** conclusion
- **B** intention
- **D** result

20 The teacher asked us to collect .... for our history project.
- **A** substance
- **C** fabric
- **B** matter
- **D** material

Further Practice Sections

Open Cloze

2 Read the text below and think of the word which best fits each space. Use only one word in each space. There is an example at the beginning (0).

KOREAN DINING

Sampling the local cuisine is **(0)** ...*one*... of the great pleasures for people visiting Korea, a country famous **(1)** .... its rich array of foods. Korean cuisine is highly distinct. It is rich **(2)** .... fermented and preserved food, and full of strong, spicy flavours - no meal is complete without a selection **(3)** .... strong chilli seasonings to enhance it! Meat, seafood, vegetables and wild greens, grains **(4)** .... as rice, soups, and teas all feature heavily in the Korean diet. Korean food is hardly ever deep-fried. Instead, foods are boiled, steamed or stir-fried. It is highly nutritious, low **(5)** .... calories and fat, and very healthy. Korean's are very proud of **(6)** ....! Distinct to Korean cuisine is its way of pickling instead **(7)** .... cooking vegetables. A classic Korean dish **(8)** .... fermented vegetables, or 'kimchi'. Kimchi is highly valued because of its disease-preventing properties **(9)** .... most Koreans eat kimchi every day of the year - for breakfast, lunch, and dinner. Korean meals are almost always accompanied **(10)** .... a bowl of soup or stew and they are not served in courses. Instead, dishes are all placed on the table **(11)** .... the same time. Cooks try to create meals that harmonize five essential flavours (hot, sour, sweet, salty, bitter) and five colours (green, red, white, black and yellow). They also pay particular attention **(12)** .... the way foods are arranged on a plate and laid out on a table. Foods are meant to be arranged **(13)** .... neat circles or parallel columns. In Korea, you will never see a table with dishes laid out in a disorderly fashion!

Key-word Transformation sentences

3 Read the sentences below and complete the second sentence so that it has a similar meaning to the first one, using the word given. Do not change the word given. You must use between two and five words, including the word given. Study the example (0).

0 Do you feel like going out for some pizza?
   mood   Are ...*you in the mood*... for some pizza?

1 Sheila is expected to marry in July.
   that   It is .... in July.

2 I heard the Browns had broken up, but yesterday I saw them together.
   believed   I .... up, but yesterday I saw them together.

3 "You should apologise to Bill for breaking his mug," she said.
   had   "You .... to Bill for breaking his mug," she said.

4 I haven't heard any good news in ages.
   since   It's (been) .... any good news.

5 My son is not yet tall enough to reach the doorknob.

short My son is .... the doorknob.

6 I almost missed the last train home.

just I was .... the last train home.

7 "Who does this lovely villa belong to?"

owner "Who .... this lovely villa?"

8 It was only when I got home that I realised I had lost my mobile.

did Only when I arrived home .... I had lost my mobile.

9 "You can have a party as long as you don't invite a lot of people," said Dad.

provided Dad told me I could have a party .... invite a lot of people.

10 He could play the violin almost perfectly when he was six.

age He could play the violin almost perfectly .... six.

11 It is unusual for Cathy to have forgotten your birthday.

not It is .... Cathy to have forgotten your birthday.

12 Martin is undoubtedly the best student in his class.

no There .... Martin is the best student in his class.

13 The house the estate agent showed us was nothing like we had expected.

live The house the estate agent showed us didn't .... expectations.

14 Julie writes some really nice poems.

at Julie .... poems.

15 Despite being rather old, Mrs Radford is still extremely energetic.

although .... rather old, Mrs Radford is still extremely energetic.

16 Charles had better type those letters now.

time It's .... those letters.

17 Why don't you buy a second-hand car since you can't afford a brand new one?

were If .... buy a second-hand car, if I couldn't afford a brand new one.

18 Is the post office far from here?

way Is it .... the post office?

19 The last time I had lobster was three years ago.

had I .... three years.

20 If you see Peter, tell him to call me.

you Should ...., tell him to call me.

Multiple Choice Cloze

4 Read the text below and decide which answer A, B, C or D best fits each space. There is an example at the beginning (0).

ENDANGERED PANDAS

It can **(0)** ...*B*... be denied that the giant panda is one of the most lovable animals in the world. With its funny face and fluffy fur, its playful actions and almost human-like **(1)** .... of eating, it is easy to understand why we find the giant panda so **(2)** .... The western world has been **(3)** .... by the giant panda ever since it first learned of it from Père Armand David, who was one of the first researchers to **(4)** .... China's wildlife. Today, the giant panda is the world's **(5)** .... bear. WWF (the World Wildlife Fund) has been using it as its emblem for the past forty-six years. Each time it is reported that the giant panda is on the verge of **(6)** ...., there is **(7)** .... concern. According to scientists, only about sixteen hundred giant pandas **(8)** .... in the wild. Their numbers have been **(9)** .... rapidly due to habitat loss and poaching. Unfortunately, the mountain forests of South-West China – which is where the giant panda lives – provide local populations with wood for fuel and building houses, and land to grow food. Competition between humans and the giant panda for the forests' limited resources has **(10)** .... the panda into smaller and smaller pockets of land. Because of the numerous threats the giant panda faces in the **(11)** ...., many people now believe that breeding it in captivity is the only **(12)** .... to ensure its survival.

	A	B	C	D
0	almost	**(B)** hardly	maybe	only
1	approach	way	system	behaviour
2	appealing	happy	charmed	amused
3	enthusiastic	captivated	pleased	enjoyed
4	study	learn	experiment	find
5	loving	luckiest	favourite	darling
6	disappearance	destruction	extinction	death
7	well-known	common	publicised	widespread
8	remain	walk	active	run
9	declining	lessening	subsiding	lowering
10	affected	obliged	required	forced
11	location	environment	wild	nature
12	road	way	manner	mode

Section B

Words Often Confused

1 Read the sentences below and decide which answer A, B, C or D best fits each blank.

1 Despite her age, Mrs Park's skin was soft and
....
A smooth   **C** crude
B rugged   **D** even

2 The little boy let out a .... of pain as he fell off his bicycle onto the ground.
A roar   **C** moo
B cry   **D** squeak

3 Helen knew she would start .... if she had to speak in front of so many people.
A shimmering   **C** shining
B sparkling   **D** stuttering

4 The manager had to write a(n) .... on every employee in his department.
A examination   **C** study
B research   **D** report

5 The accused man was able to .... that he had not been at the scene of the crime.
A indicate   **C** clarify
B prove   **D** imply

6 She walked along the quiet country .... until she reached the farmhouse.
A way   **C** route
B alley   **D** lane

7 The noise made her head .... and she fell to the floor.
A twist   **C** curl
B spin   **D** turn

8 Few athletes possess the .... to set new world records.
A ability   **C** efficiency
B mass   **D** volume

9 You'll have to .... if you can't remember the answer.
A prediction   **C** forecast
B foresight   **D** guess

10 Sandy couldn't remember what her friend had told her the .... week.
A previous   **C** former
B early   **D** premature

11 The house is in an enviable .... overlooking the small harbour.
A position   **C** angle
B early   **D** mark

12 Tim knew he'd had a .... escape when he wasn't injured in the accident.
A fortune   **C** well-off
B position   **D** lucky

13 Unfortunately, Piers .... with his lessons and had to take private lessons at home.
A fell for   **C** fell behind
B fell in with   **D** fell on

14 All passengers must .... the ship at least one hour before departure.
A disembark   **C** get up
B get in   **D** board

15 Without .... technical skills, you may not find a good job.
A advanced   **C** notorious
B progressed   **D** increased

16 The seat belt .... was switched on when we entered the plane.
A signal   **C** gesture
B symbol   **D** sign

17 John continued the family .... by becoming a dentist.
A civilization   **C** habit
B culture   **D** tradition

18 I remember seeing her on one other .... when she wore a black dress.
A incident   **C** occasion
B episode   **D** celebration

19 Peter Franks was the best .... the football team ever had.
A tutor   **C** teacher
B professor   **D** trainer

20 The main tourist .... was the old castle.
A charm   **C** attraction
B appeal   **D** fascination

Further Practice Sections

Open Cloze

2 Read the text below and think of the word which best fits each space. Use only one word in each space. There is an example at the beginning (0).

Like lightning ...

From the **(0)** ...*beginning*... of time, people have been amazed and frightened **(1)** .... storms. Worldwide, about 2,000 thunderstorms and 100 lightning strikes happen **(2)** .... second. According to scientists, we all have a one in 600,000 chance of being struck by lightning. So we are **(3)** .... more likely to be struck by lightning **(4)** .... win the lottery!

There are many different types of lightning but the two most usual **(5)** .... are 'sheet' and 'ribbon' lightning. Sheet lightning is more common than ribbon lightning and is the kind that lights up the **(6)** .... sky. Ribbon lightning is the kind that zigzags to the ground.

A typical lightning bolt travels at a tenth of the **(7)** .... of light and is often more than five kilometres long. It has hundreds of millions of volts of energy – **(8)** .... to light a 100-watt light bulb for at **(9)** .... three months. **(10)** .... in a lightning bolt get as high as 50,000 °F and, because they rise so fast, there is an explosion that we **(11)** .... as thunder. If you want to calculate how near you are to a lightning flash, count the number of seconds between the lightning flash and the **(12)** .... of thunder and divide by five. The result gives you the approximate number of miles you are away from the lightning.

Key-word Transformation sentences

3 Read the sentences below and complete the second sentence so that it has a similar meaning to the first one, using the word given. Do not change the word given. You must use between two and five words, including the word given. Study the example (0).

0 Would you mind opening the window for me?
  wonder I ...*wonder if you could open*... the window for me.

1 Lisa wore a wig so that no one would recognise her at the fancy dress party.
  avoid Lisa wore a wig .... at the fancy dress party.

2 It might be better if the chapter on the legal system was not omitted.
  leave It might be better .... the chapter on the legal system.

3 I did not mean to hurt your feelings.
  intention I .... your feelings.

4 Mary never suspected that Jamie had copied her essay.
  time At .... that Jamie had copied her essay.

5 It does not matter to them which restaurant they go to.
   mind   They .... which restaurant they go to.

6 He solved the exercise in less than five minutes.
   solution   He .... the exercise in less than five minutes.

7 Jane owes her success to her family.
   indebted   Jane is .... for her success.

8 Mrs Parkinson prides herself on her award-winning roses.
   proud   Mrs Parkinson .... award-winning roses.

9 Martha does not like folk music very much.
   keen   Martha .... folk music.

10 He spent a great deal of time and effort tracing his missing father.
   trouble   He .... to trace his missing father.

11 As far as I know, it wasn't Brenda who broke the secret access code.
   knowledge   To .... the one who broke the secret access code.

12 Mrs Larson is responsible for the complaints department.
   charge   Mrs Larson .... the complaints department.

13 The cruise to the Mediterranean was not as relaxing as we had expected.
   tiring   The cruise to the Mediterranean .... we had expected.

14 My brother has been playing professional football for six years.
   started   My brother .... six years ago.

15 I threw the cheese away because it was mouldy.
   rid   The cheese was mouldy, so I decided .... it.

16 She is on the verge of bursting into tears, so be gentle with her!
   about   She is .... tears, so be gentle with her!

17 If John hadn't persuaded the little boy to come down, he would still be on the roof.
   not   Had .... to come down, the little boy would still be on the roof.

18 You should use this door only in an emergency.
   used   This door .... in an emergency.

19 The human body consists of trillions of cells.
   up   The human body .... trillions of cells.

20 I haven't heard from Vera for a very long time. I hope she's OK.
   touch   Vera .... for a very long time. I hope she's OK.

Further Practice Sections

Multiple Choice Cloze

4 Read the text below and decide which answer A, B, C or D best fits each space. There is an example at the beginning (0).

Is it worth losing sleep over?

It still remains a mystery what **(0)** ...*happens*... when we sleep, but **(1)** .... to recent research, sleep is far more significant than scientists previously thought. Studies have **(2)** .... that good-quality sleep is closely **(3)** .... to good health, both mental and physical. Some research also ties good sleep to a healthy immune system and a **(4)** .... life expectancy.

Many of us have 'sleep debt' – lack of sleep **(5)** .... up over days, weeks and months. On average, most people need about an hour's sleep for every two hours that they are awake. Research with volunteers **(6)** .... that nowadays fewer and fewer people are getting the sleep they **(7)** ....

It is easy to see how this **(8)** .... We live in a 24-hour-a-day society, with too much to do and too little **(9)** .... to do it in. We work **(10)** .... hours than ever. We sleep an hour and a half less per night than our grandparents did.

But does it **(11)** ....? Yes. Sleep debt is dangerous. Just **(12)** .... of drivers who fall asleep at the wheel, pilots who are too tired to land planes safely, doctors and surgeons who do their job badly because they are exhausted.

0 A passes	**B** goes	Ⓒ happens	**D** takes
1 A according	**B** due	**C** based	**D** following
2 A presented	**B** explained	**C** examined	**D** shown
3 A joined	**B** linked	**C** attached	**D** united
4 A extensive	**B** stretched	**C** more	**D** longer
5 A built	**B** created	**C** formed	**D** developed
6 A points	**B** refers	**C** suggests	**D** recommends
7 A ask	**B** demand	**C** have	**D** need
8 A passes	**B** happens	**C** comes	**D** works
9 A time	**B** hours	**C** instances	**D** points
10 A longer	**B** stretched	**C** extended	**D** lengthy
11 A signify	**B** matter	**C** trouble	**D** concern
12 A imagine	**B** think	**C** suppose	**D** consider

Section C

Words Often Confused

1 Read the sentences below and decide which answer A, B, C or D best fits each blank.

1 If you don't look into the matter, I'll be forced to take legal ....
A step   C move
B action   D measure

2 Adam could not .... on his work because of the noise coming from his next door neighbour's radio.
A assemble   C devote
B collect   D concentrate

3 Rosa and Miriam remained silent .... the journey so as to enjoy the spectacular scenery.
A in   C all
B at   D throughout

4 Their dream came true when they finally set off on their .... to Mount Everest.
A expedition   C travel
B sightseeing   D cruise

5 John felt .... that his mother would disapprove of his plans to work abroad.
A accurate   C definite
B guaranteed   D certain

6 You should leave early in order to .... the heavy traffic.
A pass   C keep
B avoid   D prevent

7 She was so angry that she could barely .... her voice.
A manage   C check
B rule   D control

8 She has been .... day and night for the piano recital next month.
A practising   C exercising
B applying   D learning

9 The university has ten professors, each .... in their particular field.
A high   C central
B eminent   D deep

10 I have perfect .... I don't need glasses.
A seeing   C picture
B view   D vision

11 The results of the .... were published in a medical journal.
A try   C effort
B experiment   D attempt

12 The play was a huge success. Over three thousand people .... the opening night.
A observed   C attended
B heard   D listened

13 Dave said something .... going for dinner tonight but I don't remember what.
A about   C along
B in   D on

14 What did I like the ....? The wonderful scenery.
A great   C much
B more   D most

15 Could you please .... on the light? It's getting dark in here.
A press   C touch
B switch   D push

16 Mary was thrilled when she found out that she had been .... a place at Harvard University.
A told   C proposed
B offered   D said

17 The teacher .... the student's attention to the blackboard.
A directed   C focused
B aimed   D looked

18 If they .... the prisoners early, the public will be outraged.
A release   C leave
B loose   D open

19 The captain managed to .... the boat between the narrow rocks.
A drive   C tour
B lead   D steer

20 Jenny was ...... with both her teachers and classmates.
A popular   C well-known
B famous   D well-off

213

Further Practice Sections

Open Cloze

2 Read the text below and think of the word which best fits each space. Use only one word in each space. There is an example at the beginning (0).

What to wear?

Where we live **(0)** ...*has*... a lot to do with the kinds of clothes we wear. Different people around the world wear **(1)** .... clothes and we can often guess where a person might be from simply from what they are wearing. People **(2)** .... live in cold climates need to keep warm. Inuits from Greenland and Northern Canada for example, wear clothes **(3)** .... from animal skins. They need to wear fur trousers, mittens and jackets to protect themselves from the cold. People from hot countries **(4)** .... the other hand, wear clothes to keep cool. Africans and Arabs **(5)** .... in the Sahara wear long, light-weight, loose robes to stay cool in the hot sun.

(6) .... addition to the weather, there are many other factors that influence what we wear. For example, people decorate **(7)** .... in brightly coloured clothes and with different objects to celebrate special occasions, to tell other people what group or tribe they belong to, or simply to **(8)** .... good. Also, people in certain **(9)** .... wear clothes that will identify them to others. Police officers, soldiers, firefighters and nurses the world over wear uniforms so **(10)** .... everyone can recognise them, and many children wear a uniform to school.

So, all around the world, clothes seem to be an important part of our lives no matter where we live. They **(11)** .... us warm or cool, and whether we like it or **(12)** ...., they reveal a lot about who we are.

Key-word Transformation sentences

3 Read the sentences below and complete the second sentence so that it has a similar meaning to the first one, using the word given. Do not change the word given. You must use between two and five words, including the word given. Study the example (0).

0 Was it necessary for you to buy a new car?
  need　　　　Did ...*you need to buy*... a new car?

1 It's the first time he has ever used a computer.
  never　　　He .... a computer before.

2 Despite earning a large salary, he's dissatisfied with his job.
  earns　　　He's dissatisfied with his job, ... a large salary.

3 It was obvious that someone had been looking at her diary.
  through　　It was obvious that someone .... her diary.

4 You need to have a visa or you won't be allowed to enter the country.
  unless　　　You won't be allowed to enter the country .... a visa.

5 I truly understood the importance of studying only when I had failed all my exams.
did   Only when I had failed all my exams .... the importance of studying.

6 I am sure he has been exercising lately.
doubt   I have .... been exercising lately.

7 When they lived in New York, they used to spend Sunday afternoons in Central Park.
would   When they lived in New York, ... Sunday afternoons in Central Park.

8 I wanted to bake some chocolate chip cookies, but I couldn't find the recipe.
going   I .... some chocolate chip cookies, but I couldn't find the recipe.

9 Mr Swanson is unaccustomed to walking to work.
used   Mr Swanson .... to work.

10 He didn't open his birthday gifts until after all the guests had left.
before   He waited until all the guests .... his birthday gifts.

11 How long is it since you graduated from high school?
ago   How .... from high school?

12 I've never heard such a funny story!
ever   That's the .... heard!

13 I don't believe he took so long to fix the roof!
him   Fancy .... to fix the roof!

14 The children found the story of Robinson Crusoe fascinating.
were   The children .... the story of Robinson Crusoe.

15 The soup is so spicy, that I can't eat it.
me   The soup is .... eat.

16 She paid £50 for the silk scarf.
her   The silk scarf .... £50.

17 Shall we take the children to the funfair on Saturday?
about   How .... to the funfair on Saturday?

18 Rex hasn't had a proper meal for a week.
last   It's a week .... a proper meal.

19 I'm sure she's been to Budapest before.
have   She .... to Budapest before.

20 The office needs a fax machine.
need   The office .... a fax machine.

Multiple Choice Cloze

4 Read the text below and decide which answer A, B, C or D best fits each space. There is an example at the beginning (0).

A Guardian of History

At first **(0)** *...glance...*, the city centre of Cardiff seems an unlikely place to find a castle. Situated in the South of Wales, this capital is a **(1)** .... city, busy with traffic and bustling with people. Yet, in the middle of all this, stands a monument to Welsh history: Cardiff Castle. Some people **(2)** .... that the castle is not a true castle – that it has been constructed too recently to be taken seriously. It is true that in the 19th century, the Marquess of Bute and his architect **(3)** .... significant alterations to the castle which **(4)** .... dramatically with the earlier stonework. But Cardiff Castle is indeed a(n) **(5)** .... castle. If one looks **(6)** ...., one can still see the **(7)** .... of the original castle. And, as one approaches the **(8)** .... entrance, remains of the Roman period are still **(9)** .... visible.

You can also still see the moat — the water-filled ditch surrounding and **(10)** .... the castle — which is of 13th century Norman **(11)** ....

All in all, Cardiff Castle is an impressive relic to Wales's past. Despite the changes made to it, it is a remarkable tribute to all those who **(12)** .... and dreamed inside the castle walls.

0	**A** sight	**B** glance	**C** eye	**D** look
1	**A** typical	**B** distinguishing	**C** character	**D** featured
2	**A** demand	**B** claim	**C** ask	**D** request
3	**A** built	**B** did	**C** made	**D** caused
4	**A** contrasted	**B** distinctive	**C** compared	**D** opposed
5	**A** valid	**B** reliable	**C** authentic	**D** accurate
6	**A** slowly	**B** heavily	**C** closely	**D** nearly
7	**A** crumbs	**B** remains	**C** leftovers	**D** scraps
8	**A** special	**B** direct	**C** particular	**D** main
9	**A** openly	**B** brightly	**C** clearly	**D** surely
10	**A** supporting	**B** keeping	**C** caring	**D** protecting
11	**A** origin	**B** beginning	**C** creation	**D** start
12	**A** occupied	**B** survived	**C** lived	**D** were

Section D

Words Often Confused

1 Read the sentences below and decide which answer A, B, C or D best fits each blank.

1 Jim was .... into the army with promises of a life full of action.
A hired   C employed
B engaged   D recruited

2 He .... as if he were the boss of the company.
A performs   C executes
B acts   D plays

3 Your trousers won't .... if you have them dry-cleaned
A reduce   C shrink
B lessen   D shorten

4 The secretary .... important files from the computer by mistake.
A wiped out   C deleted
B took out   D cancelled

5 Children, if you don't .... yourselves, I'll give you extra homework!
A work   C act
B perform   D behave

6 She finds it very .... to stick to a diet.
A stiff   C difficult
B bad   D uneasy

7 My brother earns a .... as a cartoon artist.
A job   C career
B living   D profession

8 Elvis Presley was one of the .... singers of the 20th century.
A grandest   C hardest
B largest   D greatest

9 She has only one .... in life and that is to be a successful writer.
A aim   C strive
B seek   D sight

10 On the flight to Zurich, I sat .... two elderly women who wouldn't stop chatting.
A along   C between
B connecting   D linking

11 Could you tell me what this word .... in French?
A defines   C represents
B means   D terms

12 They often .... to hot countries such as Tahiti and Australia during the winter.
A tour   C travel
B journey   D wander

13 The contract for my flat .... in four months, so I'll have to find a new place.
A expires   C concludes
B cancels   D closes

14 I .... to know exactly where he hid the money.
A pass   C occur
B happen   D find

15 Parking in this area is against the ...., so please drive on.
A guideline   C order
B law   D guide

16 The hotel manager .... that we try the new Japanese restaurant.
A meant   C suggested
B pointed   D offered

17 She was .... of flour, so she couldn't make any bread.
A short   C poor
B small   D tiny

18 He decided to .... out of medical school in his last year.
A abandon   C drop
B leave   D cut

19 When old Mr Evans opened his mouth, his .... teeth fell out.
A artificial   C fake
B counterfeit   D false

20 The burglar broke in without .... the people who were sleeping upstairs.
A annoying   C interrupting
B disturbing   D bothering

Further Practice Sections

Open Cloze

2 Read the text below and think of the word which best fits each space. Use only one word in each space. There is an example at the beginning (0).

SOS: Orang-utans

Orang-utans are among the **(0)** ...*most*... endangered species on our planet. **(1)** .... we do more to protect them, some scientists predict they will disappear within 50 years. There are **(2)** .... about 55,000 orang-utans left in the world and this number is falling. Hunters kill the adults and sell the babies **(3)** .... circuses and zoos. Natural disasters have also taken a toll on orang-utan numbers. Indonesia, for example, one of the **(4)** .... orang-utans come from, was devasted by severe forest fires in 1997. Hundreds of orangutans **(5)** .... killed and thousands left **(6)** .... food and a place to live. Luckily, however, many were rescued and taken to Tanjung National Park where they received medical care and food.

The Indonesian government has now **(7)** .... permission for a new centre to be built which will protect and care for any orang-utans that need help. The Orang-utans Foundation in London is helping to raise **(8)** .... for the construction of the centre. If you would like to help raise funds, we would love to hear from you. An organisation **(9)** .... Care For The Wild is running an Orang-utan adoption scheme if you are **(10)** .... in contributing to the care and upkeep of one particular animal. There are many ways you can help to **(11)** .... sure that these lovely animals don't **(12)** .... extinct. So, why don't you help make a difference!

Key-word Transformation sentences

3 Read the sentences below and complete the second sentence so that it has a similar meaning to the first one, using the word given. Do not change the word given. You must use between two and five words, including the word given. Study the example (0).

0 Little Tommy looks a lot like his father.
   takes   Little Tommy ...*takes after*... his father.

1 They promised me they would deliver the fridge by the end of the week.
   word   They .... they would deliver the fridge by the end of the week.

2 Today, I feel more relaxed than I ever have.
   as   I've never .... I do today.

3 I'm really sorry, but this is the best I can do.
   any   I'm really sorry, but I .... than this.

4 Why didn't you buy a cheaper sofa?
   cheapest   Was this .... buy?

5 We have got the same number of students as you.
many   We have got .... you.

6 Would you know how old she is?
happen   Do .... how old she is?

7 They are going to demolish the old building tomorrow.
pulled   The old building is going .... tomorrow.

8 Someone must have added curry to the sauce.
if   The sauce tastes .... curry to it.

9 He painted the kitchen like you told him to.
way   He painted .... told him to.

10 The museum was so crowded that we left immediately.
a   It was .... we left immediately.

11 The concert was cancelled due to the soprano's illness.
of   The concert was cancelled .... soprano's illness.

12 I lost my umbrella, so I had to buy another one.
result   I lost my umbrella and .... to buy another one.

13 John couldn't take his eyes off Mary the moment he saw her.
for   John .... the moment he saw her.

14 The child thought he wouldn't be punished for breaking the vase.
get   The child thought he .... breaking the vase.

15 Whenever I go to Ireland, I always stay with friends.
up   Friends always .... whenever I am in Ireland.

16 The students had difficulty finding a solution to the problem.
work   The students found it difficult .... the problem.

17 The lecture proved to be really interesting.
out   It .... a really interesting lecture.

18 Everybody tells me I should stop eating so much chocolate.
down   Everybody tells me I should .... chocolate.

19 By the end of January, the soldiers' supplies had come to an end.
run   By the end of January, the soldiers .... supplies.

20 I didn't have a chance to explain to her what had really happened.
opportunity   I .... explain to her what had really happened.

Further Practice Sections

Multiple Choice Cloze

4 Read the text below and decide which answer A, B, C or D best fits each space. There is an example at the beginning (0).

Waterless planet?

Water is the world's **(0)** ...*most*... precious resource. People can **(1)** .... for quite a long time without food but can only live for a few days without water. It is very important then that we take care of our rivers, lakes, and streams.

The problem is that while populations keep **(2)** ...., the amount of fresh water in the world stays the same. Since 1950, water use has tripled. **(3)** .... predict that by the year 2025, two thirds of the world's population will suffer water **(4)** ....

There is also the problem of keeping our water **(5)** .... to drink. Many of our rivers and lakes are polluted with chemicals and industrial waste from factories. In fact, in the year 1995, 20% of people in the world did not have **(6)** .... to safe water.

Luckily, we can all take steps to protect our water supply. First of all, we should try not to waste water at home. Turning the tap off when we brush our teeth, fixing leaky pipes and taking showers instead of baths are all **(7)** .... we can do to help. Factories can stop dumping their waste in rivers and take steps to **(8)** .... their water use by recycling it. Farmers could **(9)** .... 25% less water if they used new technology for watering their fields.

Everyone needs **(10)** .... water for a healthy life. This is why we all need to protect our rivers, oceans, lakes, and streams. It's time we all took **(11)** .... and did our part to reduce pollution and preserve the environment. After all, our lives **(12)** .... on it.

0 **(A)** most   **B** best   **C** more   **D** very

1 **A** continue   **B** stay   **C** survive   **D** remain

2 **A** rising   **B** extending   **C** developing   **D** progressing

3 **A** Professionals   **B** Experts   **C** Masters   **D** Specialists

4 **A** shortages   **B** losses   **C** famines   **D** deficits

5 **A** certain   **B** safe   **C** secure   **D** right

6 **A** way   **B** access   **C** approach   **D** availability

7 **A** answers   **B** keys   **C** things   **D** results

8 **A** slow down   **B** reduce   **C** restrain   **D** measure

9 **A** waste   **B** ruin   **C** destroy   **D** spoil

10 **A** purified   **B** clear   **C** clean   **D** spotless

11 **A** responsibility   **B** duty   **C** reliability   **D** safekeeping

12 **A** build   **B** determine   **C** depend   **D** base

A

abide by (v)
absent from (adj)
abstain from (v)
accompanied by (adj)
according to (prep)
account for (v)
accuse sb of (v)
accustomed to (adj)
acquainted with (adj)
addicted to (adj)
adequate for (adj)
adjacent to (adj)
advantage of (n) (but: there's an **advantage in** – (have) an **advantage over** sb)
advice on/against (n)
afraid of (adj)
agree to/on sth (v)
agree with sb (v)
ahead of (prep)
aim at (v)
allergic to (adj)
amazed at/by (adj)
amount to (v)
amused at/with (adj)
angry at what sb does (adj)
angry with sb about sth (adj)
angry with sb for doing sth (adj)
annoyed with sb about sth (adj)
(in) answer to (n)
anxious about sth (adj)
(be) anxious for sth to happen (adj)
apologise to sb for sth (v)
(make an) appeal to sb for sth (n)
appeal to/against (v)
apply in writing (v)
apply to sb for sth (v)
approve of (v)
argue with sb about sth (v)
arrange for sb to do sth (v)
arrest sb for sth (v)
arrive at (a small place) (v)
arrive in (a town) (v)
ashamed of (adj)
ask about/for (v) (but: **ask sb a question**)
assure (sb) of (v)
astonished at/by (adj)
attached to (adj)
attack on (n)
attack sb for sth (v)
attend to (v)
(un)aware of (adj)

B

bad at (adj) (but: He was very bad to me.)
ban sb from sth (v)
base on (v)
basis for (n)
beg for (v)
begin by/with (v)
believe in (v)
belong to (v)
benefit from (v)
bet on (v)
beware of (v)
(put the) blame on sb (n)
blame sb for sth (v)
blame sth on sb (v)
boast about/of (v)
bored with/of (adj)
borrow sth from sb (v)
brilliant at (adj)
bump into (v)
busy with (adj)

C

call at/on (phr v)
campaign against/for (v)
capable of (adj)
care about (v)
care for sb (v) (= like)
(take) care of (n)
care for sth (v) (= like to do sth)
careful about/of/with (adj)
careless about/with (adj)
cause of (n)
certain of (adj)
change into (v)
characteristic of (n/adj)
charge for (v)
charge sb with (v)
check for (v)
choice between/of (n)
clever at (adj) (but: It was very **clever of** you to buy it.)
close to (adj)
coax sb into (v)
coincide with (v)
collaborate with (v)
collide with (v)
comment on (v)
communicate with (v)
compare with (v) (how people and things are alike and how they are different)
compare to (v) (show the likeness between sb/sth and sb/sth else)
comparison between (n)
compete against/for/with (v)
complain of (v) (= suffer from)
complain to sb about sth (v) (= be annoyed at)
compliment sb on (v)
comply with (v)
conceal sth from sb (v)
concentrate on (v)
(have) confidence in sb (n)
confine to (v)
confused about/by (adj)
confusion over (n)
congratulate sb on sth (v)
connection between (n) (but: in connection with)
conscious of (adj)
connect to/with (v)
consider sb for sth (v)
consist of (v)
contact between (n) (but: in contact with)
content with (adj)
contrary to (adj)
contrast with (v)
contribute to (v)
convert to/into (v)
cope with (v)
correspond to/with (v)
count against (v)
count on sb (phr v)
cover in/with (v)

covered in/with (adj)
crash into (v)
(have) a craving for sth (n)
crazy about (adj)
crowded with (adj)
cruel to (adj)
cruelty towards/to (n)
cure for (n)
curious about (adj)

D

damage to (n)
date back to (v)
date from (v)
deal with (v)
dear to (adj)
decide on/against (v)
decrease in (n)
dedicate to (v)
deficient in (adj)
definition of (n)
delay in (n)
delight in (v)
delighted with (adj)
demand for (n)
demand from (v)
depart from (v)
departure from (n)
depend on/upon (v)
dependent on (adj)
deputise for (v)
descended from (adj)
describe as (v)
describe sb/sth to sb else (v)
description of (n)
die of/from (v)
die in an accident (v)
differ from (v)
(have) difference between/of (n)
different from (adj)
difficulty in/with (n)
disadvantage of (n) (but: there's a **disadvantage in** doing sth)
disagree with (v)
disappointed with/about/by (adj)
disapprove of (v)
discharge sb from (v)
discouraged from (adj)
discussion about/on (n)
disgusted by/at (adj)
dismiss from (v)
dispose of (v)
disqualified from (adj)
dissatisfied with (adj)
distinguish between (v)
divide between/among (v)
divide into/by (v)
do sth about (v)
doubtful about (adj)
dream about (v)
dream of (v) (= imagine)
dressed in (adj)

E

eager for (adj)
economise on (v)
efficient at (adj)
(put) effort into sth (n)

emphasis on (n)
engaged to sb/in sth (adj)
engagement to sb (n)
enthusiastic about (adj)
envious of (adj)
equal to (adj)
escape from/to (v)
example of (n)
excellent at (adj)
exception to (n) (**make an exception of
  sth/sb** = treat sth/sb as a special case –
  take exception to sth = object to sth)
exchange sth for sth else (v)
excited about (adj)
exclaim at (v)
excuse for (n)
excuse sb for (v)
exempt from (adj)
expel from (v)
experienced in/at (adj)
experiment on/with (v)
expert at/in (sth/doing sth) (n) (= person
  good at)
expert at/in/on (sth/doing sth) (adj) (= done
  with skill or involving great knowledge)
expert with sth (n) (= good at using sth)
expert on (n) (= person knowledgeable about
  a subject)

F

face up to (phr v)
fail in an attempt (v)
fail to do sth (v)
failure in (an exam) (n)
failure to (do sth) (n)
faithful to (adj)
fall in (n)
familiar to sb (adj) (= known to sb)
familiar with (adj) (= have knowledge of)
famous for (adj)
fed up with (adj)
fill sth with sth else (v)
finish with (v)
fire at (v)
flee from (v)
fond of (adj)
forget about (v)
forgive sb for (v)
fortunate in (adj)
free from/of/for (adj)
friendly with/to (adj)
frightened of (adj)
full of (adj)
furious with sb about/at sth (adj)

G

generosity to/towards (n)
genius at (n)
glance at (v)
glare at (v)
good at (adj) (but: He was very good to me.)
grateful to sb for sth (adj)
grudge against (n)
guess at (v)
guilty of (adj) (but: he felt guilty about his
  crime)

H

happen to (v)
happy about/with/for (adj)
harmful to (adj)
hear about (v) (= be told)
hear from (v) (= receive a letter)
hear of (v) (= learn that sth or sb exists)
heir to (n)
hinder from (v)
hint to sb about sth (v) (but: hint at sth)
hope for (v)
hope to do sth (v)
(no) hope of (n)
hopeless at (adj)

I

idea of (n)
identical to (adj)
ignorant of/about (adj)
ill with (adj)
impact on (n)
impressed by/with (adj)
(make an) impression on sb (n)
improvement in/on (n)
incapable of (adj)
include in (v)
increase in (n)
independent of/from (adj)
indifferent to (adj)
indulge in (v)
inferior to (adj)
information about/on (n)
(be) informed about (adj)
inject sth into sb/sth (v)
inoculate against (v)
insist on (v)
instead of (prep)
insure against (v)
intelligent at (adj)
intent on (adj)
(have no) intention of (n)
interest in (n)
interested in (adj)
interfere with/in (v)
invasion of (n)
invest in (v)
invitation to (n)
invite sb to (v)
involve in (v)
irritated by (adj)

J

jealous of (adj)
join in (v)
joke about (v)

K

knock at/on (v)
know about/of (v)
keen on sth (adj)
keen to do sth (adj)
kind to (adj)
key to (n)
knowledge of (n)

L

lack in (v)
lack of (n)
laugh at (v)
lead to (v)
lean on/against (v)
learn about/by (v)
leave for (v) (= head for)
lend sth to sb (v)
listen to (v)
live on (v)
long for (v)
look at (v)
look for (v) (= search for)

M

married to (adj)
marvel at (v)
mean to (adj)
mention to (v)
mistake sb for (v)
mix with (v)

N

name after (v)
necessary for (adj)
need for (n)
neglect of (n)
nervous about (adj)
new to (adj)
nice to (adj)
nominate sb (for/as sth) (v)
(take) (no) notice of (n)
notorious for doing sth (adj)

O

obedient to (adj)
object to (v)
objection to (n)
obliged to sb for sth (adj)
obvious to (adj)
occur to (v)
offence against (n)
operate on (v)
opinion of/on (n)
opposite of/to (n)

P

part with (v)
patient with (adj)
pay by (cheque) (v)
pay for (v) (but: **pay a bill**)
pay in (cash) (v)
peculiar to (adj)
persist in (v) (but: **insist on**)
(take a) photograph of (n)
picture of (n)
pity for (n)
take pity on sb (exp)
pleasant to (adj)
pleased with (adj)
(take) pleasure in (n)
(have the) pleasure of (n)
point at/to (v)

(im)polite to (adj)
popular with (adj)
praise sb for (v)
pray for sth/sb (v)
prefer sth to sth else (v)
(have a) preference for (n)
prepare for (v)
present sb with (v)
prevent sb/sth from (v)
(take) pride in (n)
pride oneself on sth/on doing (v)
profit from (v)
prohibit sb from doing sth (v)
prone to (adj)
protect against/from (v)
protection from (n)
protest about/at (v)
proud of (adj)
provide sb with (v)
punish sb for (v)
puzzled about/by (adj)

Q

quarrel about sth/with sb (v/n)
qualify as/in (v)
qualified for (adj)
quick at (adj)
quotation from (n)

R

rave about (v)
react to (v)
reaction to (n)
ready for (adj)
reason for (n)
reason with (v)
rebel against (v)
receive from (v)
(keep) a record of (n)
recover from (v)
reduction in (n)
refer to (v)
(in/with) reference to (n)
refrain from (v)
regard as (v)
regardless of (prep)
related to (adj)
relationship between (n) (but: a **relationship with** sb)
relevant to (adj)
rely on (v)
remind sb of/about (v)
remove from (v)
replace sth with sth else (v)
reply to (n/v)
report on (n/v)
reputation for/of (n)
research on/into (n)
respect for (n)
respected for (adj)
respond to (v)
responsibility for (n)
responsible for (adj)
result from/in (v) (= be the consequence of)
result in (v) (= cause)
result of (n)
resulting from (adj)

rhyme with (v)
rich in (adj)
(get) rid of (phr)
rise in (n)
(make) room for (n)
rude to (adj)

S

safe from (adj)
same as (adj)
satisfied with/by (adj)
save sb from (v)
save sth for sb (v)
scared of (adj)
search for (v/n)
(be) in search of (n)
sensible of sth (adj) (= aware of sth)
sensitive to (adj)
sentence sb to (v)
separate from (v)
serious about (adj)
settle for/on (v)
share in/of sth (n)
shelter from (v)
shocked at/by (adj)
shoot at (v)
short of/on (adj)
shout at (v)
shy of (adj)
sick of (adj)
silly to do sth (adj) (but: it was **silly of** him)
similar to (adj)
skillful/skilled at (adj)
slow in/about doing sth/to sth (adj)
smell of (n/v)
smile at (v)
solution to (n)
sorry about (adj) (= feel sorry for sb) (but: I'm **sorry for** doing sth)
speak to/with sb about (v)
specialise in (v)
specialist in (n)
spend money on sth (v)
spend time in/doing sth (v)
split into/in (v)
spy on (v)
stare at (v)
strain on (n)
study for (v)
subject to (adj/v)
submit to (v) (but: **submit sth for** publication)
subscribe to (v)
succeed in (v)
suffer from (v)
sufficient for sth/sb (adj)
suitable for (adj)
superior to (adj)
sure of/about (adj)
surprised at/by (adj)
surrender to (v)
surrounded by (adj)
suspect sb of (v)
suspicious of (adj)
sympathetic to/towards (adj)
sympathise with (v)

T

take sth to sb/sth (v)
talent for sth (n)
talk to sb about sth (v)
(have) taste in (n)
taste of (v)
terrible at (adj)
terrified of (adj)
thank sb for (v)
thankful for (adj)
think about/of (v)
threat to sb/sth/of sth (n)
threaten sb with sth (v)
throw at (v) (in order to hit)
throw to (v) (in order to catch)
tire of (v)
tired of (adj) (= fed up with)
translate from ... into (v)
tread on (v)
trip over (v)
trouble with (n)
typical of (adj)

U

unaware of (adj)
understanding of (n)
uneasy about (adj)
upset about/over sth (adj)
(make) use of (n)
used to (adj)
useful for/to (adj)

V

valid for (length of time) (adj)
valid in (places) (adj)
value sth at (v)
vote against/for (v)
vouch for (v)

W

wait for (v)
warn sb against/about/of (v)
waste (time/money) on (v)
weak in/at (adj)
wink at (v)
wonder about (v)
work as/in/at sth (v)
worry about (v)
worthy of (adj)
write about (v)
write to sb (v)
wrong about (adj)

Appendix – Prepositional Phrases

Against

against the law

At

at an advantage
at the age of
at the airport
at an auction
at the beginning of (when sth started) (but: **in the beginning** = originally)
at one's best
at breakfast/lunch etc
at the bottom of
at the bus stop
at church
at college
at the corner/on the corner
at all costs
at the crossroads
at dawn
at one's desk
at the door
at ease
at the end (= when sth is finished) (but: **in the end** = finally)
at your expense
at fault
at first
at first hand
at first sight
at a glance
at hand
at heart
at home
at/in a hotel
at ... miles per hour
at large
at last
at the latest
at least
at the very least
at length
at liberty
at a loss
at the match
at midnight
at the moment
at most
at night
at noon
at once
at peace/war
at a place
at present
at a profit
at the prospect
at random
at any rate
at one's request
at the same time
at school
at sea
at short notice
at (high/full) speed
at/in the station

at sunset
at the table
at the time
at times
at the top of (but: **on top of**)
at work
at 230 Mills St.

Before

before long

By

by accident
by all accounts
by appointment
by the arm/hand
by auction
by birth
by bus/train/plane/
    helicopter/taxi/ship/
    boat/sea/air/car etc
    (but: **on a/the** bus/
    plane/train/ship/ boat
    – **in a** taxi/car/
    helicopter/plane)
by chance
by cheque
by correspondence
by day/night
by degrees
by the dozen
by eye
by far
by force
by hand
by heart
by invitation
by land/sea/air
by law
by marriage
by means of
by mistake
by nature
by now
by one's watch
by oneself
by order of
by phone
by mail
by profession
by request
by (the/one's) side
by surprise
by the time
by the way

For

for ages
for breakfast/lunch/dinner
for certain
for a change
for ever
for fear (of)
for fun (= for amusement)
for good
for granted
for hire

for a holiday
for keeps
for instance
for luck
for life
for love
for nothing
for once
for the rest of
for safe keeping
for one's sake
for the sake of
for sale (= to be sold)
for short
for the time being
for a walk
for a while

From

from now on
from scratch

In

in action
in addition to (+ -ing form)
in advance (of)
in agreement (with/on/ about)
in aid of
in all (= all in all)
in an attempt
in answer to
in an armchair
in bed
in the beginning (= originally)
in blossom
in a book
in brief
in business
in any case
in cash
in the centre of
in charge (of)
in cities
in code
in colour
in comfort
in common
in comparison with
in conclusion (to)
in (good/bad) condition
in confidence
in control (of)
in the corner
in the country
in danger
in the dark
in debt
in demand
in detail
(be) in difficulty
in the direction of
in doubt
in dollars
in a ... dress
in due course
in the end (= finally)

in exchange for
in existence
in fact
in fashion
in favour of
in flames
in the flesh
in focus
in one's free time
in full swing
in fun
in the future
in gear
in general
in good time
in half
in hand
in haste
in good/bad health
in hiding
in honour of
in hopes of
in the hospital
in a hotel
in a hurry
in ink/pencil/pen
in sb's interest
in length/width etc
in all sb's life
in the limelight
in a line
in the long run
in love (with)
in luxury
in the meantime
in a mess
in the middle of
in a mirror
in moderation
in a moment
in a good/bad mood
in the mood
in the morning
in mourning
in name only (= not in reality)
in need of
in the news
in a newspaper
in the name of (= on behalf of)
in the nick of time
in the north/south
in a nutshell
in the open
in one's opinion
in orbit
in order of/to
in other words
in pain
in pairs
in the park
in particular
in the past
in person
in pieces
in place of
in politics
in practice/theory
in principle

in prison
in private/public
in all probability
in progress
in question
in reality
in return
in the right/wrong
in a row/rows
in ruins
in safety
in season
in secret
in self-defense
in the shape of
in short
in sight (of)
in the sky
in silence
in some respects
in stock
in style
in the streets
in succession
in the suburbs
in the sun/shade
in good/bad taste
in tears
in theory
in time
in no time
in touch
in town
in tune (with)
in turn
in two/half
in uniform
in use
in vain
in view of
in a loud/low voice
in a way (= in a manner)
in the way
in writing
in a word
in the world

On

on account of
on a ... afternoon/ evening
on the agenda
on the air
on approval
on arrival
on average
on bail
on balance
on the beach
on behalf of
on one's birthday
on board
on the border
on the bottom
on business
on call
on a campsite (**at a campsite**)
on the coast
on condition
on the contrary

on credit
on a cruise/excursion/
   trip/tour
on (a ...) day
on demand
on a diet
on duty
on earth
on edge
on an expedition
on a farm (but: **in a field**)
on fire
on the (4th) floor (of)
on the floor
on foot
on the ground
on the one hand
on the other hand
on the weekend
on vacation
on horseback
on impulse
on the Internet
on an island (but: **in the
   mountains**)
on a journey
on one's knees

on leave
on the left
on loan
on the market (= available
   to the public)
on one's mind
on that morning
on the move
on New Year's Day
on the news
on this/that occasion
on order
on the outskirts
on one's own
on page ...
on parade
on the pavement
on the phone
on a platform
on principle
on purpose
on the radio/TV
on the right
on the Missouri River
on sale (= sold at reduced
   price) (but: **for sale** =
   to be sold)

on schedule
on the screen
on second thought(s)
on the side
on sight
on the sofa
on this street/on the
   street(s)
on strike
on good/bad terms
on time
on top of
on the trail of
on a trip
on the way (to) (= as I
   was going)
on the whole

Out of

out of breath
out of character
out of condition
out of control
out of danger
out of date
out of debt

out of fashion
out of focus
out of hand
out of luck
out of order
out of the ordinary
out of place
out of practice
out of print
out of the question
out of reach
out of season
out of sight
out of step
out of stock
out of tune
out of turn
out of use
out of work

Off

off the air
off colour
off duty
off limits
off the map

off the point
off the record
off the road
off school/work
off the top of your head

To

to some extent

Under

under arrest
under one's breath
under control
under the control of
under discussion
under the impression
under orders
under pressure
under repair
under the weather

Without

without fail

Spelling Rules

1 **-(e)s ending**	
a. words ending in -s, -ss, -ch, -x, -sh, -z, -o add -es	*bus - buses, mass - masses, pitch - pitches, mix - mixes,* *topaz - topazes, tomato - tomatoes, zoo - zoos*
b. nouns ending in vowel + o, double o, short forms/ musical instruments/proper nouns ending in -o add -s	*rodeo - rodeos, igloo - igloos, radio - radios, piano - pianos,* *Filipino - Filipinos*
2 **-f/-fe ending** **nouns ending in -f/-fe drop -f/-fe and add -ves**	*wife - wives, leaf - leaves*
3 **-y ending**	
a. words ending in consonant + y drop -y and add -ies, -ied, -ier, -iest, -ily	*hurry - hurries - hurried, funny - funnier - funniest,* *worry - worrying*
b. words ending in consonant + y add -ing	*employ - employs - employed - employing*
c. words ending in vowel + y add -s, -ed, -ing, -er, -est	*coy - coyer - coyest*
4 **-ie ending** **words ending in -ie change -ie to -y before -ing**	*die - dying*
5 **dropping -e**	
a. words ending in -e drop -e and add -ing, -ed, -er, -est	*save - saving - saved (but: be - being)* *tame - tamer - tamest*
b. adjectives ending in -e add -ly to form their adverbs	*rare - rarely, nice - nicely (but: true - truly)*
c. adjectives ending in -le change -le to -ly to form their adverbs	*incredible - incredibly (but: whole - wholly)*
d. verbs ending in -ee add -ing	*see - seeing*

Pronunciation

Pronunciation of -(e)s ending (noun plurals and the 3rd person singular of verbs in the Present Simple)		
/s/ after /f/, /t/, /p/, /k/	**/ɪz/ after /z/, /dʒ/, /tʃ/, /s/, /ʃ/**	**/z/ after /b/, /g/, /m/, /d/, /l/, /n/, /v/ or any vowel sound**
laughs, spots, drips, racks	*houses, dodges, ditches, passes, lashes*	*dabs, rigs, beams, thrills, pains, leaves, toys*
Pronunciation of -ed ending		
/ɪd/ after /t/, /d/	**/t/ after /k/, /tʃ/, /f/, /s/, /ʃ/, /p/**	**/d/ after /b/, /dʒ/, /m/, /v/, /g/, /l/, /n/, /z/, vowel + /r/**
lifted, branded	*baked, matched, laughed, lanced, dashed, trapped*	*snubbed, nudged, dimmed, craved, drugged, spilled, opened, cruised, cared*

Nouns (people)	Concrete/Abstract nouns	Verbs	Adjectives
	(in/dis)ability	disable, enable	(un)able, disabled
	acceptance, acceptability	accept	(un)acceptable, accepted
	accident		accidental
(under)achiever	(under/over)achievement	(under/over)achieve	achievable
actor, actress	(inter/re/in)action, act, (in)activity, acting, activation	activate, (re/over/inter)act	(re/in/over)active
admirer	admiration	admire	admiring, admirable, admired
	admittance, admission, admissibility	admit	(in)admissible
adventurer	adventure		adventurous
adviser, advisor	advice, advisability	advise	(in)advisable, advisory
	alarm	alarm	alarming, alarmed
analyst	analysis	analyse	analytic(al)
	anxiety		anxious
applicant	applicator, application, applicability	apply	(in)applicable, applied
artist	art, artistry		artistic, arty
	assumption	assume	
attendant	attendance, (in)attention, (in)attentiveness	attend	attendant, (in)attentive
beginner	beginning	begin	beginning
behaviourist	(mis)behaviour, behaviourism	(mis)behave	behavioural
benefactor, beneficiary	benefit	benefit	beneficial
	breath, breathing	breathe	breathless, breathy, breathtaking, (un)breathable
	calculator, calculation	calculate	calculated, calculating, (in)calculable
celebrity	celebration	celebrate	celebrated, celebratory
	centre, centralisation	centralise, centre	central, centralised
	characteristic, character, characterisation	characterise	(un)characteristic, characterless
child, (childminder)	childhood, childbirth, childcare		childless, childish, childlike
	choice	choose	choos(e)y
	classification	classify	classified, classifiable
collector	collection	collect	collected, collective, collectable
comforter	(dis)comfort	comfort	(un)comfortable, comfortless, comforting
	commitment, (non)committal	commit	(un)committed
communicator	communication	communicate	communicable, (un)communicative
competitor	competition, competitiveness	compete	(un)competitive, competing
	complaint	complain	
	(in)completeness, completion	complete	(in)complete
confidant(e)	confidence, confidentiality	confide	confident, confidential, confiding
	consciousness		(sub/un)conscious
	(conserve), conservation	conserve	conservative
	(re/in)consideration	consider	considerable, considerate, considered

Nouns (people)	Concrete/Abstract nouns	Verbs	Adjectives
constructor	(re)construction	(re)construct	(re)constructive
	(in)correctness, correction	correct	(in)correct, corrective
correspondent	correspondence	correspond	corresponding
creator, creature	(re)creation, creativeness, creativity	(re)create	creative, recreational
	cure	cure	curable, curative
	curiosity		curious
	danger	endanger	dangerous, endangered
	(mid)day, daylight, daily		daily
	decision, (in)decisiveness	decide	decided, (in)decisive
demonstrator	demonstration	demonstrate	demonstrative
depressant	depression	depress	depressed, depressing, depressive
	depth	deepen	deep
	description	describe	(in)describable, descriptive
	despair, desperation	despair	despairing, desperate
destroyer	destruction, destructiveness	destroy	destructible, destructive
	determination	determine	determined
discoverer	discovery	discover	discoverable
dramatist	drama, dramatisation	dramatise	dramatic
	ease, easiness	ease	easy
economist	economy, economics	economise	economic, economical
educator, educationalist	education	educate	(un)educated, educational, educative
elector, electorate	election	elect	elective, electoral
electrician	electricity, electrocution, electrification	electrify, electrocute	electric, electrical, electrifying, electrified
employer, employee	(un)employment	employ	(un)employed, (un)employable
	encouragement, discouragement	encourage, discourage	encouraging, discouraging, encouraged, discouraged
	end, ending	end	endless
	energy	energise	energetic, energising
	enjoyment	enjoy	enjoyable
enthusiast	enthusiasm	enthuse	enthusiastic
	envy	envy	envious, enviable
escapee, escapist, escapologist	escape, escapism	escape	
	exactness, exactitude	exact	exact, exacting
examiner, examinee	exam(ination)	examine	
	excitement	excite	(un)exciting, (un)excited, excitable
	exhaustion, exhaust	exhaust	exhausted, exhausting, exhaustive
	existence	exist	existent, existing
	expectation, expectancy	expect	(un)expected, expectant
	expense(s), expenditure	expend	(in)expensive, expendable
	explanation	explain	explanatory
	fame		famed, famous, infamous
	fascination	fascinate	fascinating, fascinated
	fashion	fashion	fashionable

Appendix – Word Formation 3

Nouns (people)	Concrete/Abstract nouns	Verbs	Adjectives
	fault	fault	faulty, faultless
financier	finance	finance	financial
	fluency		fluent
	(mis)fortune		(un)fortunate
	(in)frequency	frequent	(in)frequent
general, generalist	generalisation, generality	generalise	general, generalised
	globalisation, globe	globalise	global
government, governor, (governess)	government, governance, governorship	govern	governing, governmental, ungovernable
sguide	guidance	guide	(mis)guided, guiding
	happiness		(un)happy
	health, healthiness		(un)healthy
	(dis)honesty		(dis)honest
host, hostess	hospitality	host	(in)hospitable
human, humanist	humanism, (in)humanity		human, humanly, humane, humanitarian
	idiom		idiomatic
	illness, ill		ill
	imagination, image, imagery	imagine	imaginary, (un)imaginable, (un)imaginative
	importance		(un)important
	impression, impressiveness	impress	(un)impressive, impressionable
	inspiration	inspire	inspirational, (un)inspired, (un)inspiring
insurer	insurance	insure	(un)insured
	intelligence		(un)intelligent
	(dis)interest	interest	(un/dis)interested, interesting
interpreter	(mis)interpretation	(mis)interpret	interpretive, interpretative
	introduction	introduce	introductory
intruder	intrusion	intrude	intrusive
investigator	investigation	investigate	investigative, investigatory
	invitation, invite	invite	(un)inviting, (un)invited
	isolation	isolate	isolated, isolating
jeweller	jewel, jewellery		jewelled
learner	learning	(un)learn	learned
	likelihood		(un)likely
	likeness	liken	like, alike, unlike
	loudness		loud
luxuriance	luxury	luxuriate	luxurious, luxuriant
	madness	madden	mad
	majority		major
medic	medicine, medication		medical, medicated, medicinal
(im)mortal	(im)mortality	immortalise	mortal
(re)mover	movement, (re)move, motion, removal	(re)move	moving, (re)movable, motionless, unmoved
musician	music, musical		musical
	(de)mystification, mystery, mysteriousness	(de)mystify	mysterious, mystery

Nouns (people)	Concrete/Abstract nouns	Verbs	Adjectives
(im)mortal	(im)mortality	immortalise	mortal
(re)mover	movement, (re)move, motion, removal	(re)move	moving, (re)movable, motionless, unmoved
musician	music, musical		musical
	(de)mystification, mystery, mysteriousness	(de)mystify	mysterious, mystery
natural	nature, naturalisation	naturalise	(un/super)natural
	necessity, necessaries	necessitate	(un)necessary
	nerve, nervousness	(un)nerve	nervous, nerveless, nervy, unnerving
	norm, normal, (ab)normality, normalisation	normalise	(ab)normal
operator, operative	operation	operate	(in)operable, (non-)operational, operative
opportunist	opportunity, opportunism		(in)opportune, opportunistic
	option	opt	optional
organiser	(dis/re)organisation	(dis/re)organise	(dis)organised, organisational
patient	(im)patience		(im)patient
	peace, peacefulness		peaceful, peaceable
	percent, percentage		
perfectionist	(im)perfection, perfectionism, perfectibility	perfect	(im)perfect, perfectible
performer	performance	perform	
person, personnel	personality, personification	personalise, personify	(im)personal, personable
pessimist	pessimism		pessimistic
	pleasure, pleasantness	please	(un)pleasant, (un)pleasurable, (dis)pleased, pleasing
politician	policy, politics	politicise	political
pollutant, polluter	pollution	pollute	polluted, polluting
	population, (un)popularity, popularisation	populate, popularise	(un)popular
	possibility		(im)possible
	(super)power, powerlessness, empowerment	(over/em)power	powerful, powered, powerless, overpowering
practitioner	(im)practicality, practice, (im)practicability	practise	(im)practical, (im)practicable
	prevention	prevent	preventable, preventive, preventative
	privacy, privatisation	privatise	private
	probability		(im)probable
producer	product, produce, (re)production, productivity	(re)produce	(un/re)productive, reproducible
professional	profession, professionalism		(un)professional
promoter	promotion	promote	promotional
proposer	proposal, proposition	propose	proposed, propositional
protector	protection, protectiveness	protect	(over)protective, (un)protected
psychologist	psychology, psyche, psychosis	psych(e)	psychological, psychic, psychotic
public, publicist	publicity, publication	publicise	public
pursuer	pursuit	pursue	
qualifier	(dis)qualification	(dis)qualify	(dis/un)qualified
realist	(un)reality, realism, realisation	realise	(un)real, (un)realistic
	recognition	recognise	(un)recognisable

Nouns (people)	Concrete/Abstract nouns	Verbs	Adjectives
referee	reference	refer	referable
reject	rejection	reject	reject, rejecting
relation, relative	relation, relationship, relativity	relate	(un)related, relative
	relaxation	relax	relaxing, relaxed
	reliability, reliance	rely	(un)reliable, (self-)reliant
repeater	repetition, repeat	repeat	(un)repeatable, repetitive, repetitious
	replacement	replace	(ir)replaceable
	requirement	require	
respondent	response, responsiveness, (ir)responsibility	respond	(un)responsive, (ir)responsible
	restriction	restrict	(un)restricted, restrictive
saver, saviour	safety, safe, savings	save	(un)safe
	(dis)satisfaction	(dis)satisfy	(dis)satisfied, (un)satisfactory, (un)satisfying
	scene, scenery		scenic
scientist	science		(un)scientific
	(in)security	secure	(in)secure
	(non)sense, sensation, (in)sensitivity, (in)sensibility, sensor	sense	(in)sensible, (in)sensitive, sensory, sensational, senseless
	skill	(de)skill	(un)skilled, skillful
spectator	spectacle(s), spectacular	spectate	spectacular
	starvation	starve	starving, starved
stranger	strangeness, estrangement		strange, estranged
	stress	stress	stressful, (un)stressed
	success	succeed	(un)successful
	suit, suitability	suit	(un)suitable, (un)suited
	suggestion	suggest	suggestive, suggestible
	summary	summarise	summary
	surprise	surprise	(un)surprising, surprised
	surroundings, surround	surround	surrounding
sympathiser	sympathy	sympathise	(un)sympathetic
tempter	temptation	tempt	tempting, tempted
	tendency	tend	
	threat	threaten	(non-)threatening
trainer, trainee	training	train	(un)trained, training
	trend, trendiness	trend	trendy
	(un)truth, truthfulness		(un)true, (un)truthful
	type		(a/un)typical
	(mis)understanding	(mis)understand	understandable, understanding, misunderstood
valuer	value, (over/under/de)valuation	(over/under/de)value	(in)valuable, valueless, (over/under)valued
	variety, variation, variability	vary	various, varied, (in)variable
warmer	warmth, warm	warm	warm, warming
westerner	west	westernise	western, west, westernised, westerly, westward
watcher	watch	watch	watchful, watchable
worker	work	(re)work	(un)workable, working, overworked

Infinitive	Past	Past Participle	Infinitive	Past	Past Participle
be	was	been	lie	lay	lain
bear	bore	born(e)	light	lit	lit
beat	beat	beaten	lose	lost	lost
become	became	become	make	made	made
begin	began	begun	mean	meant	meant
bite	bit	bitten	meet	met	met
blow	blew	blown	pay	paid	paid
break	broke	broken	put	put	put
bring	brought	brought	read	read	read
build	built	built	ride	rode	ridden
burn	burnt	burnt	ring	rang	rung
burst	burst	burst	rise	rose	risen
buy	bought	bought	run	ran	run
can	could	(been able to)	say	said	said
catch	caught	caught	see	saw	seen
choose	chose	chosen	seek	sought	sought
come	came	come	sell	sold	sold
cost	cost	cost	send	sent	sent
cut	cut	cut	set	set	set
deal	dealt	dealt	sew	sewed	sewn
dig	dug	dug	shake	shook	shaken
do	did	done	shine	shone	shone
draw	drew	drawn	shoot	shot	shot
dream	dreamt	dreamt	show	showed	shown
drink	drank	drunk	shut	shut	shut
drive	drove	driven	sing	sang	sung
eat	ate	eaten	sit	sat	sat
fall	fell	fallen	sleep	slept	slept
feed	fed	fed	smell	smelt	smelt
feel	felt	felt	speak	spoke	spoken
fight	fought	fought	spell	spelt	spelt
find	found	found	spend	spent	spent
fly	flew	flown	spill	spilt	spilt
forbid	forbade	forbidden	split	split	split
forget	forgot	forgotten	spoil	spoilt/spoiled	spoilt/spoiled
forgive	forgave	forgiven	spread	spread	spread
freeze	froze	frozen	spring	sprang	sprung
get	got	got	stand	stood	stood
give	gave	given	steal	stole	stolen
go	went	gone	stick	stuck	stuck
grow	grew	grown	sting	stung	stung
hang	hung	hung	strike	struck	struck/stricken
have	had	had	swear	swore	sworn
hear	heard	heard	sweep	swept	swept
hide	hid	hidden	swim	swam	swum
hit	hit	hit	take	took	taken
hold	held	held	teach	taught	taught
hurt	hurt	hurt	tear	tore	torn
keep	kept	kept	tell	told	told
know	knew	known	think	thought	thought
lay	laid	laid	throw	threw	thrown
lead	led	led	understand	understood	understood
learn	learnt	learnt	wake	woke	woken
leave	left	left	wear	wore	worn
lend	lent	lent	win	won	won
let	let	let	write	wrote	written